D0387584

Advance Praise for *Companies on a Mission*

"True innovation comes from the fringes—from smaller players running rings around incumbents. After focusing for decades on corporate Goliaths, we need to investigate and support entrepreneurial Davids. Russo shows how mission-driven companies think, act, and cluster—and, critically, explains how we can help them jump to the next level."

—**John Elkington**, co-founder and Executive Chairman of Volans Ventures, co-founder of Environmental Data Services and SustainAbility, and co-author of *The Power of Unreasonable People*

"Mission-driven companies continue to grow in number and are moving from a small niche into the mainstream. The time is right for an analysis of these firms and their approaches to business. In *Companies on a Mission*, Michael Russo documents both the direct economic benefits of taking a mission-driven approach and the intangible benefits of brand value, product positioning, customer satisfaction, and more. Full of stories about well- and lesser-known companies, this book will give any business reader—from entrepreneurs to managers in big corporations—take-away points to transform their businesses into profitable, mission-driven enterprises."

—**Andrew Winston**, author of *Green Recovery*
and co-author of *Green to Gold*

"The stories in this lively, well-researched book have much to teach all of us. Michael Russo has done a great service to the field by writing this important work."

—**Marjorie Kelly**, co-founder of *Business Ethics* magazine
and author of *The Divine Right of Capital*

"What a fresh approach to green marketing! This book contains information on the subject not available anywhere else."

—**Jacquelyn Ottman**, Eco-innovation expert
and author of *Green Marketing*

Companies on a Mission

Entrepreneurial Strategies for Growing
Sustainably, Responsibly, and Profitably

Michael V. Russo

With a Foreword by
L. Hunter Lovins

STANFORD BUSINESS BOOKS
An Imprint of Stanford University Press
Stanford, California

Stanford University Press
Stanford, California

Special discounts for bulk quantities of Stanford Business Books are available to corporations, professional associations, and other organizations. For details and discount information, contact the special sales department of Stanford University Press. Tel: (650) 736-1782, Fax: (650) 736-1784

Printed in the United States of America
❀

Text and cover printed on 80% recycled stock, post-consumer waste.
The physical characteristics of the stock are as follows:
Text: 50# Eagle PC Offset, guaranteed 80% recycled, 30% post-consumer waste
Jacket: 88# New Leaf Primavera Gloss, 80% Recycled, 60% post-consumer waste

Library of Congress Cataloging-in-Publication Data

Russo, Michael V.
  Companies on a mission : entrepreneurial strategies for growing
sustainably, responsibly, and profitably / Michael V. Russo ; with a
foreword by L. Hunter Lovins.
     p. cm.
  Includes bibliographical references and index.
  ISBN 978-0-8047-6162-8 (cloth : alk. paper)
  1. Social responsibility of business--United States. 2. Small business--
United States--Management. 3. Business planning--United States. 4.
Business ethics--United States. I. Title.
  HD60.5.U5R87 2010
  658.4'08--dc22
                                          2009049643

Typeset by Bruce Lundquist in 10/15 Sabon

To Doris and Vince,
with love, admiration, and gratitude

CONTENTS

Companies on a Mission is a long-awaited book, badly needed and destined to become a classic in shaping how people think of the role of business in meeting the challenges of this new century. It will be required reading for all of my business students.

All who dabble in big ideas owe debts to prior thinkers. As one who is credited with putting forth some of the principles for the field of sustainable management, for arguing that behaving in ways that are more responsible to people and to the planet is actually a better way to do business, I owe many.[1] Dr. Donella Meadows, lead author on the book *Limits to Growth*, was the first to use the word *sustainability*. Partnerships created my various books. The team with whom I continue to cocreate Natural Capitalism Solutions brings joy to my professional life.

All of us in this field are immensely enriched by colleagues around the world. One of the first, however, to suggest to me that doing business honorably in a time of planetary crisis could actually be more profitable was Mike Russo, the author of the volume you now hold.

Several decades ago, Mike suggested that the anecdotal examples we'd found of companies that prospered by using resources more productively and of companies that attracted the best talent because they treated their workers fairly were not anomalies but the first signs of a profound shift in business logic.

This bordered on heresy in the unfettered era of greed that characterized the late twentieth century. But Mike was right. In the past several years a solid business case has emerged in dozens of studies showing that the companies that are the leaders in environmental responsibility and in ethical behavior to people are outperforming their peers as measured by all traditional business standards. Not only is there a moral imperative for business to change its course to deal with the increasingly sobering challenges facing us, but it also makes sense regardless of what you think about climate, environmental destruction, or human fulfillment.

Companies around the world are recognizing what I've called the sustainability imperative. Large and small businesses have found that actions taken to make their operations more sustainable also make them more money. Companies that focus on and implement sustainability programs are demonstrating greater profitability, and faster stock growth, than their industry peers. They are less exposed to value erosion and strengthen every aspect of shareholder value.[2] Even one of the world's largest companies, Wal-Mart, has announced such goals as zero waste, 100% use of renewable energy, and its aspiration to sell only sustainable products, in part to enable it to better manage its supply chains and stakeholders. These and about a dozen other elements of enhanced shareholder value make up what we call the integrated bottom line.[3]

Mike was one of the first to notice the underlying causes that have driven the trend toward building value through sustainability. Now, in this book, he presents yet another shift that businesses will ignore at their peril. It is the rise of small and medium-size companies that are as committed to social and environmental stewardship as they are to strong financial performance. These enterprising upstarts have an impact far in excess of their collective size.

The idea that smaller companies form a cornerstone of our economy is not new. The 27 million small and medium-size companies in the United States and Canada are responsible for roughly half of all North American economic activity (and 90% of the nongovernmental jobs). The engines of job creation, small businesses have been ignored as a critical part of the global recovery we all now seek. Instead, government support has targeted the giants of Wall Street and the dinosaurs of the last century in a futile effort to prop up the failing ideology that big companies are the strength of America—or the rest of the world for that matter.

Mike rightly directs our attention to mission-driven smaller companies. In this book he becomes the first leading academic to apply strategic analysis to the role of entrepreneurs in crafting a future that works for everyone. It's well past time.

In the realm of green business, essentially all the books profile companies that are making a billion dollars a year or more. Yet almost unnoticed, it has been the little mission-driven companies, created by the entrepreneurs profiled in this book, members of such organizations as the Social Venture Network, Green America, and now the Business Alliance for Local Living Economies, that have done the heavy lifting of creating a value proposition that is as much about the way they do business as it is about their products. The real proof of their pioneering efforts is that this evolving and growing trend has now influenced such large companies as Wal-Mart. Its ongoing transformation would have been unthinkable without the example set by the leaders profiled in this book.

Few books give guidance to ordinary businesspeople about how to profit from this inevitable shift to more responsible and sustainable ways of doing business. This one does just that. Welcome to the thinking of a truly prescient man, who like his subjects is on a mission. This book combines analytical rigor with a passion that delivers an easy reading style. In the pages to follow you'll find stories of business heroes from across the globe, the wellspring of the amazing responsible business revolution now sweeping the planet. This book shows that being in business to make money *and* to serve humanity and the planet is the sweet spot in the twenty-first century.

L. Hunter Lovins

It's a July morning of biblical perfection in the Oregon Cascades. Having rescued my 1970s-era Kelty backpack from a series of garage sales, I have gotten on the trail with it and my oldest son, Andy. It's the day after we scaled South Sister Mountain from our campsite above Moraine Lake, a technically undemanding but steep and lengthy trudge. We've got a free morning before hiking out to civilization, enough time to trek over to Green Lakes and back before breaking camp. We are in great spirits, surrounded by beauty and bearing the lightest of loads—just the bare essentials for the few hours that we'll be away.

As we walk above Fall Creek, we witness magic: Clouds forming overhead. One after another, feathery wisps appear literally out of thin air just above us. Bounding along the air current, each evolves into a stringy cotton ball of mist before rising and growing into a recognizable cloud. As it turns out, we're lucky. Just the right atmospheric conditions predicate cloud formation, including a threshold level of moisture in the air.

The companies I write about in this book have much in common with these cloudlets. Starting from imperceptible origins, this group of small and medium-size companies has cohered into something genuine and noteworthy—a movement. A threshold level of social, environmental, and economic conditions has opened up a space in the marketplace for entrepreneurs who blend together exciting new products and services with cutting-edge social and environmental practices. And even through a difficult economy, the movement is holding its own.

As clouds gather and their collective potential materializes, they can influence weather across a landscape. Will the collective impact of mission-driven companies change the landscape of enterprise? It's still early, but like those clouds we saw, it is captivating to study them and try to peer into their future. In this book, we'll study a variety of these companies, piecing together theories about the strategies they use and analyzing what separates success from failure. We'll learn that the mission-driven companies that have emerged as leaders exhibit common traits, distinct from those that struggle and distinct from mainstream businesses too. And we'll breathe life into academic theories by developing ideas through extensive contacts with entrepreneurs who are captivated by more than money—pathfinders who offer up stories of inspiration, perseverance, and (often) high achievement.

This book is intended to speak to a number of audiences. If you are interested in how entrepreneurs can escape the ethical drought that sometimes characterizes mainstream business, read on. If you are considering starting a mission-driven business, there's plenty of advice for you. And if you are looking to take stock of the mission-driven movement, this is the book for you. In any case, my own mission in crafting this book is to conduct a careful analysis of the topics but also to use a style that is accessible and engaging. I do hope that you will enjoy reading this book as much as I did writing it.

Let's get started. The weather is about to change.

Companies on a Mission

1

CAPITALIZING ON AN UNDERGROUND CONSUMER MOVEMENT

A REVOLUTION IN SCHOOL LUNCHES

The second time through, it's easier to find Revolution Foods. You simply drive west on Atlantic Avenue in Alameda, California, and make a right at the A-7 Corsair fighter jet. Odd, until you realize you're in the section of town that used to be the Alameda Naval Air Station. So you might say that Revolution Foods is beating swords into plowshares. Founders Kristen Richmond and Kirsten Tobey have converted a couple of commercial buildings that used to serve the military into a base camp from which they are transforming school lunch programs. They are introducing nutritious organic food to schools with disproportionate numbers of disadvantaged kids and creating jobs for low and moderately skilled workers. And they've created a profitable, growing concern with a full plate of opportunities before them.

Revolution Foods is just one example of a movement of for-profit enterprises that are meeting financial goals, promoting social equity, and exercising environmental stewardship. Its story is the story of thousands of small and medium-size companies that have quietly begun demonstrating that business can be about more than money. But don't think for a minute that there's a foolproof recipe for success. Companies on a mission, which I call mission-driven, face all the challenges that their mainstream counterparts do. In addition to financial goals, they confront an additional class of issues stemming from their social and environmental commitments. Indeed, it is a balancing act for companies managing this "triple bottom line," one that requires thoughtful planning, skillful execution, and perhaps most important, an intuitive feel for where and when financial goals and social and environmental initiatives reinforce each other.

The story of Revolution Foods begins with the personal histories of its two founders, who met while graduate students at Berkeley's Haas School of Business. Both Richmond and Tobey had experience in the food service industry, but their passion for serving society and the planet intensified at Haas.[1] The school's leadership in those areas had made it a magnet for enlightened entrepreneurs, and its faculty featured a number of practitioners, such as Will Rosenzweig, founder of the Republic of Tea and a longtime entrepreneur who worked closely with students to develop new businesses.[2] Eventually, Richmond and Tobey decided to create a business that brought healthy school lunches to kids, delivered by an organization that provided its employees with benefits and wages that exceeded industry norms.

But how does a company enter a $7 billion market dominated by such giant food producers as Tyson and Archer Daniels Midland and such large food service providers as Sodexo and Aramark?[3] Not by competing directly with those companies for supersized contracts with San Francisco or Oakland Unified School Districts, that's for sure.

But there was another point of entry.

Charter schools—public schools that receive a per-student allotment from their funding districts and that are allowed considerable autonomy in determining their governance structures, educational missions, and staffing and procurement procedures. A prime example of a new approach to purchasing was when charter schools activated their autonomy to break out of the nutritional null set that represented most school lunches. When parent committees and not administrators made decisions on food, they took the Revolution Foods value proposition seriously. It didn't hurt that charter schools are free to make decisions that aren't bound solely by price and are open to a company that, quite literally, caters to their wishes for better school lunch nutrition.

Still, it wasn't easy. Food procurement at publicly funded schools is bound by federal laws that mandate caloric and vitamin content in lunches and limit fat calories and saturated fat calories to 30% and 10% of the meals, respectively. With reimbursement rates that top out at about $3.00 for the poorest students, it's a tall order to serve a balanced meal. So providers often start with inexpensive fatty foods and then hunt for cheap high-calorie, low-fat ingredients to round them out. The usual choice: sugar, which crowds out healthier but also more expensive vegetables. When bids are based strictly on cost, truly nutritious foods lose out.

To get started, Richmond and Tobey spoke with educators, parents, school administrators . . . and children. That last group was forthright. Collectively, students were saying, "People don't care about us. We can tell by the food they serve us."[4] Tobey recalled one physical education teacher who routinely devoted class time to nutrition, only to feel like a hypocrite when he strolled through the cafeteria and met students who wanted answers about why their lunches violated his principles.[5]

The partners found a school willing to pilot their program and started assembling a client base of schools. One of the first schools they approached was Monarch Academy, located in a depressed section of Oakland, California, where 95% of students were on free or reduced lunch programs. This and other initial efforts were a huge success, and Revolution Foods quickly found itself receiving so many inquiries and referrals that it no longer needed to seek out business.

The easy part was creating better meals, of course. The hard part was making them on a budget, because even when a school's administrators agreed to go above the $3.00 federal limit, it was by only a few pennies. Keeping overhead to a minimum was a start. Think entrepreneurship: cheap rent, a meeting room with six unmatched chairs, a thermostat set at a brisk level in February. When it came to food operations, the proper depth of analysis and careful cost and waste control were absolutely critical.

The ingredients for meals, though, presented the company with classic trade-offs with which mission-driven companies invariably wrestle. Executive chef Amy Klein makes all meals from scratch, bypassing high-fructose corn syrup and trans fats and including fresh fruits and vegetables with every meal. But she has to keep an eye on costs, so although being

100% organic is a worthy goal, Revolution Foods is not there yet. Instead, the company must balance the environmental and social value of going organic with the need to be cost competitive. The company also has made progress on biodegradable packaging and composting, but there is still room to grow in this area.

The social mission, however, is paramount at Revolution Foods, whose central core value is "to create healthier schools" specifically "for the kids that have the least amount of access."[6] As of early 2009, 80% of the students that Revolution Foods served had free and reduced lunch status. Hand in hand with this value was one of creating good stable jobs for lower and moderate-income individuals, who now number more than 100 at the Revolution Foods facilities. They are paid above prevailing wages, enjoy full benefits, and are extended access to ownership positions in the company.[7] A further fringe benefit is shared with the entire organization: the educational value of learning about nutrition and the importance of using fresh ingredients and balancing meals.

Hiring the right employees is essential to the Revolution Foods mission, as is their fit into the team concept that drives operations at the company. Diversity in culture, educational opportunity, and work experience is evident at the company, and an important duty for Richmond and Tobey is to keep everyone on the same page (both speak Spanish, a plus in that regard). As they grow from a current staff of 100 by expanding in Los Angeles and entering new markets in other American cities, retaining their company's culture of fluid communication and teamwork will be a challenge.

The company has grown quickly, though, doubling sales in 2007 and then again in 2008, with prospects for another doubling to about $10 million in fiscal 2009.[8] Revolution Foods was serving 14,000 lunches a day by spring 2009, and Richmond and Tobey were choosing between Denver and Washington, D.C., for their next beachhead. The company's long-term goal: nothing less than becoming a "transformative catalyst" for school nutrition nationwide.[9] So although its meals are already touching the lives of thousands of schoolchildren each day, Revolution Foods has ambitions that match the size of the problem it sees. And indeed, it is part of a movement that is changing the nature of social innovation as citizens recognize that many of society's needs can be recast as opportunities for private enterprise.

A DEFINITION

What is a mission-driven company? The term can be used in a variety of ways, but within the pages of this book, a mission-driven company refers to a for-profit enterprise that seeks to simultaneously meet profit goals and social and environmental goals that reflect the values of its owners. Values are abstract principles about what is right or proper, such as social justice.[10] In practice, these values are reflected in the goals of mission-driven firms to, for instance, purchase locally wherever possible, improve working conditions in the developing world, and reduce the carbon footprint of their operations.[11] My focus on small and medium-size firms is not meant to suggest that larger firms can't be mission-driven, but as we'll see, most of the creative ideas and new approaches to management come from this less noticed corner of industry.

EMBRACING MISSION-DRIVEN OPPORTUNITIES

A New Marketplace

Pick up yogurt for tomorrow's lunch, and you'll find organic Stonyfield Farm products on your grocer's shelf. Invest in mutual funds, and you might sock away a few dollars in one of the Pax World Funds, screened to exclude firms that are deemed to be social or environmental laggards. Shop for a sweater to warm up the winter, and you might consult the website of Fair Indigo, a seller of fair trade clothing. In fact, seemingly everywhere you look in the marketplace, there are examples of companies that are offering products and services that represent an important way of creating value for customers—by selling products and services that reflect explicit attention to social and environmental values. And the movement is growing.

Sellers of fair trade clothing—produced by fairly compensated workers under humane conditions—project that sales will grow from virtually nothing to 15% of all clothing sold by 2016.[12] In 1995 there were 55 socially screened funds in the United States with assets of $12 billion, but by 2007 (the last year for which totals were reported by the Social

Investment Forum) the number of funds was 260, with assets of $202 billion.[13] Socially responsible investing (SRI) is also a worldwide trend: In 2007, OWW Consulting Research reported 163 SRI funds in Asia, with assets of $24 billion.[14] Even South Africa is home to twenty-one SRI funds and a $1.6 billion investment.[15] Organic product sales still grew 17% in the rough economy of 2008 before entering 2009, where they were projected to slip 1%.[16] But after years of 20–30% gains, the global organic food and beverage industry, which hit $23 billion in 2007, has firmly established itself.[17]

Just who is purchasing the products of mission-driven companies? The Natural Marketing Institute, which for years has been tracking how consumers convert values into purchasing decisions, released new figures in 2009 for the size of the LOHAS (lifestyles of health and sustainability) market segment. Even in the midst of a serious economic downturn, this segment still includes 43 million Americans (77 million counting the not-quite-ready-for-LOHAS segment, the Naturalites).[18] It's been awhile since the overall market for goods and services that specifically target the LOHAS segment was estimated, but in early 2007 it was placed at $209 billion.[19]

Fad or long-term trend? The latter, despite what economic turbulence may bring.

Although many mission-driven companies have roots in social and environmental activism, they have outgrown these beginnings to become an influential commercial presence. The drivers behind this movement provide clear notice that mission-driven companies will become even more important in local and national economies.

The first driver creating opportunities for mission-driven companies is conscious consumerism. For an increasing number of consumers, buying decisions don't simply reflect personal needs and aspirations. For these individuals, purchases also reflect the attributes of the selling company in ways that may have nothing to do with the product or its performance. Products from Equal Exchange, a company that guarantees good wages and working conditions in coffee-growing areas where it buys beans,[20] may be indistinguishable from conventional coffees in flavor. But consumers see their purchases from Equal Exchange as a way to improve conditions in developing countries.

Opportunities also flow from the transparency movement. Consumers have never had access to as much information about companies as they do today. A wealth of information appears in the news media, spotlighting companies' social and environmental behavior when it is praiseworthy—or blameworthy. More specifics are on the packages, where certification marks reassure consumers about the ingredients and supply chain of many products. And company details are on the Internet, where sites such as Green America's (formerly Co-Op America's) Responsible Shopper program and Good Guide provide details on hundreds of well-known companies and products.[21] Transparency creates opportunities for mission-driven companies by drawing attention to issues where they benefit from comparisons with their conventional counterparts.

The final driver is the consumption economy. Many consumers worry about their consumption patterns, which are reflected in trends running from increased obesity to the use of shopping carts in department stores. Consumers' sense that they do not have control over their own consumption habits may be one reason that levels of happiness have not increased along with the GDP in most countries. And the social and environmental fallout from this economy is severe, especially in the developing world. Many consumers prefer to purchase from companies that do not compound these problems or that make a proven contribution to their solution.

All these factors direct consumer attention to mission-driven companies. And when consumers care about the broader attributes of companies, social and environmental performance becomes a vital competitive asset.

Different by Design: Social and Environmental Differentiation

In the marketplace for enlightened consumers, innovative social and environmental practices that confer authenticity on the company and supply chain practices that break new ground in reducing social and environmental footprints are the keys to success. And this distinctiveness goes above and beyond the types of goods and services sold. That is, the differentiation pursued by mission-driven companies depends less on the product or service itself than on the social and environmental practices and policies of the company. And this form of differentiation erects a barrier to imitation by larger companies, where entrenched constituencies can view social and environmental initiatives as an additional burden or costly distraction.

As with traditional product differentiation,[22] social and environmental differentiation can generate a price premium that outweighs higher costs that the strategy normally embodies. You won't find the lowest prices on produce at the Portland, Oregon, New Seasons Market. But you will find the freshest, often organic and locally grown fruits and vegetables. And they're sold by a company that won many awards in 2008 for charitable donations, community activism, and environmental leadership, and for being Oregon's top recycler in 2009.[23] The result is that New Seasons attracts customers as much with its social and environmental leadership as it does with its groceries. It turns out that the many products from mission-driven companies are woven with common threads, in terms of which product categories yield higher price premiums. I'll demonstrate how this framework predicts price premiums in practice in Chapter 3.

Mission-driven companies build customer value through brand-building strategies as well. Success in marketing depends on two key variables: the performance of the product and the emotional bond that a company can forge with customers. Using the example of green products, we'll see the importance of breaking through perceived trade-offs as a route to success in Chapter 4. For example, environmentally sensitive products that also meet product performance standards of conventional products can attract consumers and elicit marketplace following. But beyond simple product attributes, if a company can bond with customers on an emotional level, this connection also will drive sales. Mission-driven companies use a unique assortment of programs to bond with customers, and the best of these integrate social and environmental advancement into their products and marketing strategies. The mission of TOMS Shoes, to give away a pair of shoes for every one it sells, is skillfully fused into its business model and communications strategy in a way that draws consumers to its footwear. But none of this works without a careful selection of sales channels and a well-considered communications strategy to back up the products and democratize company values.

Growing a Mission-Driven Organization

As with any small or medium-size company, hiring decisions are crucial for mission-driven enterprise, and a bad hire can cause problems that reverberate throughout the organization. What is unique about managing mission-driven companies is that the recruitment process needs to recognize that prospective employees have not only the business skills necessary to succeed in a more generic sense but also values consistent with those of the company. Sometimes, the selection process creates trade-offs. Should a company hire the Ivy League MBA holder with a social and environmental commitment that is lukewarm or a less well prepared prospect with the "right stuff"? Choosing the latter candidate may necessitate some training costs, but that can also be viewed as an investment in the culture of the mission-driven company. And this culture is absolutely essential to meeting the long-term aspirations of the company, in terms of both profits and its social and environmental goals.

To manage a mission-driven company is to be pushed by employees—sometimes to uncomfortable levels. Companies that excel recognize the practical limits that bound their goals, but they also understand that by listening to employees, they can stretch out and reach even loftier goals. Fashioning a mission-driven organization that can facilitate and accommodate such growth requires a high-performance workplace. A model of capability building for mission-driven companies presented in Chapter 5 will illustrate how to develop a responsible *and* responsive organization while avoiding common hazards that have tripped up unprepared companies.

The Bottom Line on the Triple Bottom Line

What all this adds up to is a strategic niche that resists incursions by conventional companies. Figure 1.1 shows this conceptually. The top diagram is often used to illustrate the different domains of social and environmental improvement and economic improvement.[24] When it comes to social and environmental activities, companies are generally advised to engage in those that lie in the win-win zone, lest they waste financial resources.[25] As shown in the bottom diagram, compared to mainstream companies, today mission-driven companies enjoy a *greater* win-win zone, thanks to company effects such as authenticity. For example, because customers

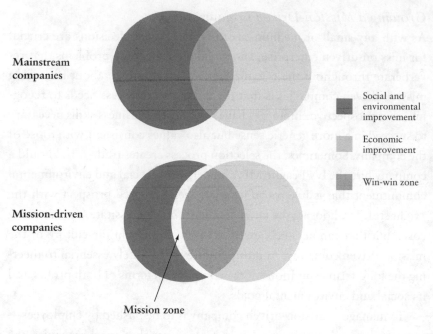

Mainstream
companies

Social and
environmental
improvement

Economic
improvement

Win-win zone

Mission-driven
companies

Mission zone

FIGURE I.I
The win-win zone and the mission zone.

trust them, policies and practices that would not pay off for mainstream companies do yield profits for their mission-driven counterparts because they receive their due credit for them.

Notice that there is a slice to the left of the win-win zone, which I've labeled the mission zone. This zone represents the activities pursued by mission-driven companies that are *not* subject to an economic test. Rather, companies undertake these activities to recognize and celebrate their values and the type of moral imperatives to which they hold themselves. This slice is necessarily slender, though, because all companies must meet their minimum economic return to stay viable.[26] Most of New Seasons Market's social and environmental programs and policies are perfectly consistent with boosting its profits, putting them in the win-win zone. But New Seasons president Lisa Sedlar is also proud of the bioswales in store parking lots, which remove pollutants from rainfall before releasing water to drains.[27]

The swales are a classic mission zone investment, done without regard to return on investment. These and some other initiatives most likely will never produce economic returns—even if we widen our lens to appreciate how they bolster the organization's brand, culture, and productivity. Instead, they are moral actions that affirm a company's mission.

But let's be clear. In this book I do *not* focus on the highbrow question of whether it pays to be responsible; rather, I focus on a more hardheaded assignment: how to make being responsible pay. And that is a daunting task, if for no other reason than the need it creates to focus simultaneously on different performance outcomes.

The Challenging Task of Balancing Social, Environmental, and Economic Goals

Pursuing social, environmental, and financial goals simultaneously surely is more complex and perilous than embracing only the traditional single (financial) bottom line approach. Difficulties confront mission-driven companies when they face trade-offs between the three goals, and it is dangerously easy to compromise values in the pursuit of profits. What do you do, for example, when a retailer of your products experiences a strike and your company values support union rights? For traditional businesses, a labor action is no issue—it's someone else's problem, unless your company's profitability is threatened. But for mission-driven companies, it's not that simple—and the dilemma is real. Every single entrepreneur interviewed for this book recounted facing a situation in which their social and environmental values were in tension with profits.

And managing through these episodes can be like crossing a minefield. No company is perfect, and stakeholder revolts over responsibility outcomes can be acutely damaging to mission-driven companies. Lose your authenticity or mismanage your supply chain and you'll soon lose customers. For one thing, the same press that beatifies managers and their companies is constantly vigilant for duplicity and doublespeak.[28] Yet managers who address crises with integrity and aplomb can bolster their company's image and galvanize commitment to its brand. I devote considerable space in this book to identifying how to build and bolster credibility, beginning in Chapter 6.

TAKEAWAYS FOR MAINSTREAM
COMPANIES AND POLICY MAKERS

This book has implications for several important groups beyond entrepreneurs. Mainstream companies will be interested in the lessons that mission-driven companies offer to them. Not the least of these is the importance of moral reflection to the core values of companies. I'll review these in Chapter 7. Mission-driven companies leverage their values to help guide decisions and avoid controversy. They also use core values to get ahead of societal expectations for business. As such, their policies provide an early warning system that informs mainstream companies of coming issues. For example, in many cases, mission-driven companies have been the first to remove unhealthy food ingredients and toxic product additives, well ahead of the societal demands for policies banning those substances.

Policy makers will be interested in a provocative finding: that mission-driven companies congregate in identifiable geographic areas. Geographic clustering strategies have been studied a great deal.[29] All the applications of clustering frameworks, however, are to industries: movie-making, electronics, leather goods, and other discrete, well-defined sectors. The twist for mission-driven companies is that they agglomerate where coherence forms not from industry membership but rather from shared values. Across the United States, we see hotbeds of socially and environmentally oriented companies emerging in tightly networked towns and cities such as Portland, Oregon, Burlington, Vermont, and Austin, Texas. The emergence of these groupings is not an accident. Instead, as I'll argue in Chapter 8, local factors can predict the presence and absence of such clusters of companies.

ASKING TOUGH QUESTIONS

Despite its great promise, the movement of mission-driven companies must first confront uncomfortable issues. Mission-driven companies and their community of practice can display tendencies toward political correctness and groupthink when discussions of social and environmental policies take place. Is nuclear power development really an environmentally irresponsible source of energy in a world where fossil fuels generate dangerous greenhouse gases? Another question considers means and ends. What if the goal of reducing world poverty is accomplished by companies using completely traditional methods of operation, with no social or environmental mission beyond being profitable? Such questions, several of which have not been addressed by those in the mission-driven community, are taken up in Chapter 9.

Questions about governance also apply to mission-driven companies. One question is whether or not public ownership is healthy for them—or their higher order goals. How about being purchased by a company that may appreciate the market niche created by the company but not its mission-driven nature? Ben & Jerry's struggled to preserve its social mission after its sale to Unilever. This and other episodes suggest that the freedom of privately held companies to determine and pursue goals beyond simple profitability is uniquely valuable for mission-driven companies.[30]

DEFINING BOUNDARIES

It is worth noting the topic areas that lie outside this book's focus.

The late Milton Friedman identified one and only one performance criterion for companies: to maximize their profits.[31] Other activities that did not contribute directly to this purpose were dangerous diversions that must be avoided. But innumerable debates from lecture halls to boardrooms have underscored an important aspect of Friedman's argument: It can be perfectly consistent with profitability to engage in these activities. What if philanthropy bolsters the brand image? What if liberal maternity policies draw better employees for a given wage? Hundreds of academics have poured time and effort into the study of whether corporate social responsibility pays off.[32] To reiterate, this question is not addressed here. The debate over whether it pays to be responsible cannot be resolved because it depends on the circumstances under which the responsible behavior takes place.[33] Writing in generalities only clouds the issue further.

This book is also not about the normative element of executive behavior—that is, determining the proper level of responsibility for companies. These questions, which have been pondered by ethicists, CEOs, and politicians, are fascinating in their own right.[34] But here again, the issues are quite impossible to resolve. It may be that the growing markets for responsibly produced goods and services reflect government failings in one or more regard. For example, attempts to purchase goods made without sweatshop labor reflect the relative disinterest by governments (in both developed and developing countries) in adopting and enforcing laws that could protect laborers. I can offer one observation: Markets alone will never deliver optimal social and environmental performance. The more interesting issue is which social and environmental problems *can* be attacked using markets and which are better left to regulatory means. Any market solution, however, should recognize that unlike the policy process, the "votes" in a market are not allocated equally among all individuals but rather according to their disposable incomes.[35]

Nonprofit organizations are outside the boundaries of my discussion. The enormously valuable work conducted by these organizations, whose founders are resourceful, charismatic, and driven to succeed, is worthy of in-depth treatment on its own.[36] Those interested in the unique issues facing nonprofits can find an excellent source in Daniel Bornstein's moving account of Bill Drayton, his Ashoka Foundation, and its fellows: *How to Change the World*.[37] This focus also makes it difficult to integrate the pioneering work of Jed Emerson and Greg Dees, whose schema spans nonprofit and for-profit organizations.[38]

Finally, the focus of the book is on the developed world, although some examples occasionally are taken from emerging economies. The fascinating and far-reaching efforts of companies working at the "base of the pyramid"—countries with a per capita income below $1,500—have been chronicled elsewhere.[39] The strategic challenges of those doing business at this level are elemental, and overcoming them is transformative to business and inspiring on many levels. But the issues facing businesses in this context are so different from those facing companies in more developed countries that it is impossible to do justice to both worlds in one volume.

GETTING A START

In the pages that follow I review choices made by managers to create defensible market space, bring popular products to that space, and build organizations that can deliver results in financial, social, and environmental terms. Clear managerial rights and wrongs apply to these pursuits, and I aim to identify how mission-driven companies succeed. This book's focus is on small and medium-size companies, although the implications of my analysis have clear takeaways for larger companies.

I apply principles of strategic analysis to mission-driven companies. In many respects, these companies operate in ways that conform to well-known strategic axioms. But in other ways, they exhibit unique twists that are interesting to observe and elicit further questions about the long-run influence of these companies on human enterprise in the twenty-first century. As the story unfolds, readers will gain an appreciation of the opportunities for companies that can blend great products with social and environmental leadership, enhancing the value proposition for an increasing number of enlightened customers.

2

THE OPPORTUNITY
Social Movements Meet the Marketplace

What's behind the thriving market for goods and services produced by mission-driven companies? In this chapter, I survey three intertwining elements that together are producing an unprecedented marketplace opportunity: (1) the empowerment of conscious consumers, (2) information availability and transparency, and (3) fallout from the consumption economy. We'll see how responding to these drivers is not, in general, easy for established companies. In turn, the description of these three important elements will sketch the strategic case for mission-driven companies that I develop in succeeding chapters.

CONSCIOUS CONSUMERS

It's a beautiful fall day in Rogers, Arkansas. Inside the John Q. Hammons Convention Center, Wal-Mart's Lee Scott has assembled hundreds of CEOs, top managers, and their Wal-Mart buyers for the company's "Live Better Sustainability Summit." Leveraging his disarming humor and gentle Southern drawl, Scott subtly but firmly brings the hammer down on suppliers. Ninety-two percent of the environmental impact of Wal-Mart is due to suppliers, according to Scott, and it's time for them to get serious about implementing change.[1] He brushes aside a front-page *Wall Street Journal* article published seven days earlier that declared that as a result of changing patterns of shopping and consumer tastes, the "Wal-Mart Era" was over.[2] But Scott nonetheless notes that a good number of shoppers will no longer set foot in a Wal-Mart store, owing to their perceptions of its social and environmental practices.[3] There isn't a hint of altruism in the room; it's about the bottom line and everyone knows it.

That Wal-Mart has begun to emerge from its historically reactive, defensive posture toward social and environmental issues[4] is worth noting on its own. But the company's recent change-oriented mood ratifies the importance of what could be called conscious consumers. The rise of this poorly defined and evolving group can be traced back at least to the consumer rights movement of the 1960s. But for my purposes, I'll define this group as those consumers who, in making purchasing decisions, consider not just product attributes but also the companies from which they buy and the social and environmental impacts of their production, distribution, and sales. Who are these consumers?

NEW POWER FOR A NEW CONSCIOUSNESS

There is no shortage of polls that focus on socially and environmentally conscious consumers and their marketplace behavior. A mid-2007 posting by journalist Joel Makower on his Greenbiz.com Web site listed no less than six segmentation studies.[5] The studies ask different questions and use different methodologies. Two of the more authoritative surveys are conducted by the Roper Organization and the Natural Marketing Institute (NMI). Each relies on a segmentation model that places consumers into one of several categories, based on its data and methodology. The Roper studies focus more on green issues, whereas the NMI studies use a broader lens that adds a social emphasis. For this reason, I discuss the NMI results.[6]

The Natural Marketing Institute, established in 1990, conducts market analyses for its clients, primarily in the area of healthy products that have lessened social and environmental impacts.[7] For a number of years the institute has conducted surveys to determine how consumers react to issues such as social responsibility and sustainability as they relate to consumer goods. The current methodology places consumers into one of five segments. The 2009 results are shown in Table 2.1.[8] At its peak are LOHAS (lifestyles of health and sustainability) consumers.

TABLE 2.1
Natural Marketing Institute consumer segments

Segment	Description	Percentage of market
LOHAS (lifestyles of health and sustainability)	"Dedicated to personal and planetary health. Not only do they make environmentally friendly purchases, but they also take action—they buy green products, support advocacy programs, and are active stewards of the environment."	19
Naturalites	"Focused on natural/organic consumer packaged goods with a strong health focus when it comes to foods/beverages. They are not politically committed to the environmental movement."	15
Drifters	"This segment has good intentions," but "when it comes to behavior, other factors influence their decision more than the environment."	25
Conventionals	"This very practical segment does not have green *attitudes*" but does exhibit some pro-environment behaviors, such as "recycling, energy conservation, and other more mainstream behaviors."	24
Unconcerned	"Environment and society are *not* priorities to this segment. They are not concerned and show no environmentally-responsible behavior."	17

SOURCE: Natural Marketing Institute, "NMI's 2009 Consumer Segmentation Model" (2009), http://www.nmisolutions.com/lohasd_segment.html, accessed November 7, 2009.

Let's take a closer look at those LOHAS consumers because their purchasing habits provide clues about how they are driving marketplace behavior. A 2004 survey by the Natural Marketing Institute found some provocative tendencies that together define the market opening for small and medium-size companies using a differentiation strategy.[9] First, LOHAS consumers are not persuaded solely by low prices. They are 14% less likely than the general population to purchase whatever is lowest priced. Second, brands are influential in their purchases: LOHAS consumers are 35% more likely than the general population to agree completely or somewhat that brand image is important to product purchases. Third, they play an important role as product evangelists; 90% agree or agree somewhat that they attempt to influence and teach others about the benefits of LOHAS-related goods. Here, their behavior doubles the prevalence of influence behavior of the general population. The punch line: LOHAS consumers are more than twice as likely as the general public to pay 20% more for goods that they view as connected to their lifestyle.

During the sharp downturn that began in late 2008, a number of researchers suggested surprising conviction on the part of consumers when it came to responsible shopping. When specifically asked by the Opinion Research Corporation (ORC) about how the current economy had affected their shopping habits, only 8% of 1,087 adults responded in January 2009 that they were "less likely to buy environmentally responsible products today."[10] This finding was echoed in a second ORC study conducted at that time of 1,000 consumers, which set the number who were "buying fewer environmental products" at 14%.[11] By contrast, the two studies found that 34% and 19% of customers, respectively, were "more likely to buy more" or were "buying more" environmentally responsible products.

Journalist Makower points out that these and other studies were funded by entities that have direct business interests in green marketing.[12] The first ORC study was funded by Cone, a marketing consultancy based in Boston; the second was co-funded by EnviroMedia, a social marketing firm, and Green Seal, a product certifier. But the Opinion Research Corporation is a credible third party, and the posed questions appear reasonable. In one study, the Opinion Research Corporation asked consumers if they were "less likely to buy environmentally responsible products today," and critics might view this wording as reflecting an implicit value judgment.[13] On the other hand, the question could have been worded to ask whether or not the respondent was "more likely to buy environmentally irresponsible products," clearly a more leading phrase.

Nonetheless, can we trust these or any other surveys on spending? Reporting virtuous behavior on surveys is easy when no one's checking the sales receipts. Even worse, such surveys suffer from "social desirability bias," when respondents deliver answers that they believe will please the survey provider.[14] Many would feel social pressure to respond positively when asked if they care about global warming and its effect on polar bears, or if they agree with the imperative to abolish hard labor by preteens.[15]

Fortunately, academics have developed methods that can be used to reduce these biases. One method uses a technique called conjoint analysis to parse the value of environmental or social attributes of a product from the rest of its constituent elements, such as quality, design, and of course, price.[16] Essentially, respondents are asked to rank the desirability of a number of similar goods, each of which contains a different combination of product attributes. One might be asked to rank the desirability of wooden tables, for example, with different combinations of style, price, type of wood, and whether or not the wood was environmentally certified (sourced from a sustainably harvested forest). In such a study, because the environmental certification is bundled with other product attributes, it is possible, using sophisticated analysis, to obtain a value for the certification itself. Most studies of this type indicate that a sizable slice of consumers will pay for environmental and social attributes of products.[17]

Even these studies, however, do not use actual purchasing behavior. However, the few studies that do use purchasing data from tracked consumers show some willingness to pay for goods with improved environmental product credentials.[18] And by using Neilsen data that tie records of actual checkout stand purchases to characteristics of the buyer, the Natural Marketing Institute reports that of all their segments, the LOHAS segment is most apt to practice what they preach.[19]

Thus there is reasonably persuasive evidence that the surveys are matched with actual behavior: LOHAS consumers *are* backing up their attitudes with marketplace purchases. They are far more likely to recognize and purchase specific brands that populate what might be called the LOHAS space. And their behavior is not limited to consumer products: LOHAS consumers are two and half times as likely to engage in socially responsible investing by contributing to mutual funds that purchase shares in companies that pass social and environmental screening. It all adds up to an informed, engaged consumer. And the depth of information available to consumers about social and environmental records of companies will only increase in coming years.

INFORMATION AVAILABILITY AND TRANSPARENCY
Not all clichés have lost their relevance. Information *is* power. And to the extent that it is no longer controlled within companies but rather

communicated to a broad, inquisitive, and empowered populace, information can influence the marketplace. The anticipation that information will be available in the public sphere can preempt one course of action by companies and bend decisions toward a different path. Perhaps more important, wider provision of information provides a powerful basis on which mission-driven entrepreneurs can support their brand and differentiate themselves from larger, more conventional competitors. Primarily (although not exclusively) because of the Internet, the availability of information to consumers has exploded. And this information has provided consumers with the means to make more informed marketplace judgments.

Just a Click Away

Have a look at www.scorecard.org, a Web site developed by the Environmental Defense Fund that leverages the power of the Internet with the federally mandated availability of toxic releases by companies. Plug in your zip code, and you will receive an online report—down to the pound—of the amount of toxic releases in your neighborhood, organized source by source. A few more clicks and if you are sufficiently outraged about a facility, you can send a fax to its management, email the EPA, or network with other like-minded citizens. A new Web site assembled by the Commission for Environmental Cooperation, a joint body of the three countries, combines the toxic release databases of Canada, Mexico, and the United States with Google Earth so that viewers can surf across satellite-shot landscapes and pinpoint facilities to learn about.[20] Then, in a couple of clicks, the tabulated emissions data for the facility pop up.

If you are particularly interested in labor practices, several Web sites provide reports on the behavior of companies. Depending on which source you consult, you can find a range of information on companies and their factories.[21] Some Web sites provide actual reports, whereas others tabulate companies whose factories have passed their standards. Unfortunately, it's hard to find an objective source. One survey reviewed seven separate codes of conduct for overseas labor standards and found significant differences among them.[22] But there is no doubting that the provision of labor information is expanding.

Of course, few consumers have bookmarked the Web sites described here. That doesn't stop the information from getting to them for two important reasons. First, the information is aggregated and simplified by a number of sources that are available to consumers. For example, Green America provides summaries of company performance on social and environmental dimensions on its Responsible Shopper Web site.[23] Several popular magazines, including *Business Ethics* and the United Kingdom's *New Consumer* and *Ethical Consumer*, regularly report on and sometimes rank companies. Furthermore, for citizens with investments in socially responsible mutual funds, periodic quarterly reports list the companies whose stock they own, another simplified source of information. Increasingly, you don't even need books or a computer to learn about products. The Web site GoodGuide[24] has an iPhone application that will send information about tens of thousands of products directly to shoppers who type names or barcodes into their phones (can a scanner function be far behind?).[25] Daniel Goleman, in his book *Ecological Intelligence*, sees the blending of values and purchasing as creating a radical awakening among citizens.[26]

The Transparency Movement

Working hand in hand with the dissemination of information is the provision of information by companies. "Sunshine is said to be the best of disinfectants," opined Supreme Court justice Louis D. Brandeis.[27] But information has to come to light first, and the transparency movement is pushing companies to open themselves up as never before. In *The Naked Corporation*, Don Tapscott and David Ticoll describe five drivers of the transparency movement: (1) the success of market economies and globalization, (2) the rise of knowledge work and business webs, (3) the spread of communications technology, (4) demographics and the rise of the Net Generation, and (5) the rising global civil foundation.[28] One important commonality across these drivers is that they have staying power and are likely to increase in importance in future years. Even in 2009, amid difficult economic times, the public relations firm Edelman reported that honest, frequent reports about the state of its business were the third most prominent contributor to corporate reputations.[29] This movement dovetails with the previous set of observations about LOHAS consumers, who connect social and environmental records of companies with purchasing decisions.

A measure of the rise of transparency among larger companies has been the emergence of so-called nonfinancial reporting, wherein firms issue reports on their social and environmental performance.[30] From a standing start in 1990, these reports have become increasingly prevalent. The Global Reporting Initiative (GRI) listed 957 reports for 2006 that were consistent with its guidelines, up from 380 in 2003.[31] The total number of reports created annually, including non-GRI formatted ones, is now in the neighborhood of 2,000.[32]

The broadening of the adoption of GRI standards has been matched by a requirement for increasingly specific data. Companies can adopt several levels of reporting, but a core of data must be contained in each report. For example, in the section on human rights, the following data must be provided:

- Total number of incidents of discrimination and actions taken.
- Identification of operations in which the right to exercise freedom of association and collective bargaining may be at significant risk and the actions taken to support these rights.
- Identification of operations that have significant risk for incidents of child labor and the measures taken to contribute to the elimination of child labor.

In the environmental section, the following data are considered core to the report:

- Percentage of materials used that are recycled input materials.
- Direct energy consumption by primary energy source.
- Total direct and indirect greenhouse gas emissions by weight.

Although considerable guidance is provided on how to calculate these factors, some judgment is generally necessary. And although some companies use consultants to help them prepare reports, the data are self-provided. Just as financial reporting revolutionized corporate governance when it was introduced in the 1930s, the rapid spread of nonfinancial reporting is well on its way to having a similar effect. Although it is voluntary, nonfinancial reporting is a de facto requirement for companies seeking legitimacy in the eyes of socially and environmentally attuned observers.

Naturally, the transparency movement has created some serious angst for corporations that would rather keep information to themselves. Especially for privately held companies, the provision of information to outside parties frequently is not part of their organizational DNA. Take the long campaign by Fidelity against disclosing how it votes its shares in proxy fights.[33] Or consider the efforts by Bechtel Corporation in 2007 to shield from public scrutiny the details of its construction contract for a subway extension to Dulles International Airport.[34] Scandals surrounding secrecy simply serve to underscore a sense among the populace that silence means guilt.

Even without an accusation, silence can imply guilt. For example, a 2008 article in *Fast Company* ranked the world's ten largest oil companies on their social and environmental impacts.[35] The first nine companies ranked between 35 and 54 on a 100-point proprietary rating system developed by HIP Investor Inc. and Social Venture Technology Group. In last place was Valero Energy Corp., at a lowly 19 points. Valero's main sin: lack of transparency. Despite being ranked as one of the best companies to work for, never experiencing layoffs, and having a prestigious record of safety at its refineries, its penchant for secrecy and refusal to participate in industry transparency initiatives were repeatedly cited for its poor score. Indeed, what you don't say *can* hurt you.

THE CONSUMPTION ECONOMY

Mission-driven companies also fill a need for individuals to feel connected to organizations that they come in contact with and to feel more in control of their lives. We face many societal issues that trace back to feeling a lack of control. Some of the rather alarming statistics suggest an explosion of consumption and acquisition in an effort to gain a sense of control. A survey of the state of consumption before the onset of the serious recession in 2008 is instructive.

The acquisitive nature of Americans is well documented. In 2004 the Worldwatch Institute devoted its annual *State of the World* volume to

"The Consumer Society," documenting the global rise of consumption.[36] The typical American woman owns nineteen pairs of shoes; the average woman has worn a quarter of her shoes only once.[37] One study of Australian consumers showed that the typical household spent $1,026 annually on goods that went to waste.[38] While also the result of higher incomes and housing construction innovation, American homes are getting larger. In 1970 the median home measured 1,385 square feet; in 2007 it grew nearly 80% to 2,479 square feet.[39]

Even put literally, rampant consumption is a reality. The instance of obesity is vastly greater than it was even as recently as the 1980s. The Centers for Disease Control and Prevention (CDC) provides an especially instructive online slide show that shows a color-coded state-by-state progression toward expanding girth. The CDC began the march in 1986 with an upper category of 10–14% of a state's population being obese. Since then, the CDC has had to introduce four new categories of obesity, as states have entered the 15–19% range, the 20–24% range, the 25–29% range, and finally in 2005 the "more than 30% obese" range.[40] Movie seats and even caskets are now several inches wider than they were in the 1970s.[41] Even the *International Journal of Obesity* is in a growth mode. The journal printed 509 pages in 1993, when it was launched; by 2006 it spanned 2,322 pages.[42]

Sadly, all this consumption does not seem to be making people happier. Although in real terms the average income of Americans doubled between 1957 and 2002, the percentage of "very happy people" identified in surveys bounced around within about a 25–35% range, never returning to its peak in the early 1960s.[43] Results for the United Kingdom are strikingly similar.[44] This unease has given energy to the so-called voluntary simplicity movement, wherein individuals seek to reduce the breadth of their consumption and divert their attention from work to family, volunteerism, and other prosocial pursuits.[45] The examination of one's consumption patterns that is implied by voluntary simplicity is consistent with a shift not only toward less consumption but also toward a pattern of consumption that is more cognizant of the impacts of purchases on society and the environment.

Fallout from the Consumption Economy

At least three by-products of the consumption society weigh on the minds of consumers. The first, most prevalent in the United States, is the explosion of debt, which is necessary to support constant consumption. In 2005, for the first time since the Great Depression, the Federal Reserve Board reported that the nation's personal savings rate was negative.[46] Household debt service ratios compiled by the Fed reached historic highs at the same time.[47] Whether for the need to replace something more meaningful in life with material possessions or simply the onslaught of increasingly clever advertising, the impact of the consumption economy is evident in the bottom lines of our households.

The long-standing concerns over the treatment of manufacturing workers overseas represents the second by-product of the consumption economy. The issue goes back at least to the early 1990s, when Nike became the poster child for worker exploitation in locations spanning the developing world. From Indonesia to Pakistan, the shoe, apparel, and sporting goods giant was vilified for the activities of its subcontractors.[48] Its difficulties were undoubtedly compounded by Nike's clumsy handling of the problem, but the many scandals that followed validated the notion that an increase in globalization, driven by consumption in richer countries, was creating significant social and environmental impacts overseas.

Although the effect of the publicity surrounding these episodes has forced corporations to take more responsibility for their suppliers' actions, the scandals persist.[49] One of the more recent involves manufacturing facilities in Saipan, part of the Commonwealth of the Northern Mariana Islands, a U.S. territory. There have been persistent allegations that workers are enticed to the islands from China, the Philippines, and elsewhere in the region with false promises of American-style conditions and pay. Once in Saipan, they experience horrific conditions and wages so low that the workers can never pay the recruiter the $5,000–$7,000 charged to bring them there.[50] This creates indentured servitude, forcing many to turn to the sex trade to create the income necessary to survive.[51]

The scandals surrounding Saipan are especially provocative because the island is a U.S. territory, and therefore goods manufactured there can be marked "Made in the U.S.A." Thus consumers cannot even be certain that this label guarantees U.S. standards of pay and labor conditions for goods they purchase from The Gap, Ralph Lauren, Ann Taylor, and other well-known fashion brands.[52] The notion that even the most reliable indications of product sourcing are not what they appear to be heightens buyers' frustrations when they are trying to make purchases that are not associated with environmental and social damage.[53]

The third by-product of the consumption economy is the waste that this economy creates, which by any account is staggering. Although higher recycling rates have slowed the rise in solid waste, each American still produces nearly a ton of waste each year.[54] The problem is not just the waste created at the end of the product stream. We've become profligate in the use of products while we own them. For example, 60% of personal computers are left on overnight, creating an equivalent contribution to greenhouse gases of 2.5 million automobiles.[55] Overall, the Union of Concerned Scientists estimates that each American's activities release 20 tons of carbon dioxide annually.[56] Another concern is the release of toxic emissions by manufacturers in the United States, now at 14.6 pounds per American.[57] Astute consumers are also aware that this last figure does not include the toxins associated with products that are manufactured offshore and imported into the country—surely adding to the impact of the consumptive lifestyles of the developed world.

But it is not just the domestic level of the waste that is of concern. It is also that consumers are increasingly likely to have heard about and been otherwise sensitized to the offshoring of waste products. The global disposition of electrical waste provides a powerful example. Portrayals of the toxic job of drawing usable materials from e-waste have now been brought to mainstream audiences. For example, a 2008 *National Geographic* feature story, "High Tech Trash," spotlighted this issue using color and drama.[58] Among the photos was one of an open fire in Accra, Ghana, used to melt off insulation and other undesirable materials from a few strands of prized copper wire; this process released fumes laden with dioxins and heavy metals. Graphic photos from India and China portrayed the activities of other scavengers that carry equally wretched implications, such as using the family wok to melt away lead from circuit boards. With a circulation of 8 million—more than *Time* and *Newsweek* combined—*National Geographic* brought this story to a broad audience.[59]

The disposition of electronic waste is just one case where consumers of goods are beginning to understand how their buying behavior is connected to unregulated and unprotected behavior in production of those same goods. When stories such as these appear in *National Geographic*—as opposed to muckraking magazines such as *Mother Jones*, whose readership is well attuned to social and environmental impacts of business—they bring unsettling realities to the living room. Newly aware consumers are more likely to reassess their buying, use, and disposal habits.

The Search for Responsible Purchasing

The financial calamity that began in 2008 had a sobering effect on consumption. As households increasingly came down to earth under this pressure, savings rates rebounded to a point where in early 2009 households were saving 5% of their disposable personal income.[60] It is entirely possible that hand in hand with this reassessment of the need to save will be a reassessment of how to spend, which in turn will direct consumption toward products and services that can create a better sense of long-term happiness. If economist Robert Frank is correct and our consumption patterns are socially determined, then as others reduce their purchasing, so should we.[61]

But there's more going on than simply reducing consumption. All the drivers that I have identified lead to the search for what might be called responsible purchasing. In many cases, a solution has been to simply consume less. When a product isn't demanded, production decreases, as do the social and environmental footprints that accompany production. (For many economists, this isn't as clear as it may seem; our purchases can provide the jobs that provide a step up for many in the developing world, and this can be a prosocial outcome under the right conditions.)[62] But for much of our consumption, from dish soap to retirement investments to the occasional granola bar, nonconsumption isn't viable. And so the need for various goods, coupled with the drive for responsible purchasing, opens up a sizable market opportunity for mission-driven firms.

As noted in the introduction, a number of these segments have been growing robustly. In succeeding chapters, we'll work to understand variations in market acceptance for the offerings of mission-driven firms. A number of dimensions that are important in many markets are present here. For LOHAS consumers and many others, quality is more important than price in most purchases. Quality comes in many flavors, including a number that relate to our purposes here. For mission-driven companies, the market opportunity involves selling products that are provably long-lasting, healthy in production and use, and unique in ways that relate to the company's mission. Without product quality, the success of any mission-driven venture is at risk.

But a number of product and service attributes that respond to these drivers are specific to the mission-driven opportunity. To appreciate this point, consider two simple cotton T-shirts, identical in price and quality, both sourced offshore. One may be produced in a plant where workers enjoy a good measure of job security and where environmental practices are the industry's best. The other may be produced where underage workers toil for long hours and little pay in the presence of toxic fumes and safety hazards. Thus seemingly identical products can have dramatically different responsibility profiles, solely as a result of their production processes. In the absence of such detailed information, careful consumers will purchase T-shirts from the company that they associate with responsible behavior. The takeaway: For a significant slice of the consuming public, the social and environmental profile of the *company* making a product can be a decisive selling point, sometimes even more important than the product sold.

Two company-related sets of attributes are pivotal: authenticity and responsible supply chain practices. As consumers, we search for products that are the real thing. Naturally, authenticity is in the eye of the beholder. Recently, James Gilmore and Joseph Pine II have argued in their book *Authenticity* that we yearn for products that are what they promise to be and that perform as expected.[63] For my purposes, the first of these is critical. The recent allegation that organic milk sold by Costco, Target, and other large chains was produced using conventional means shows that there is considerable risk even in the perception that a company is not delivering goods that match its commitments. The flip side is that products that carry authenticity resonate with consumer desires that reflect each of the drivers I've described.

Increasingly, consumers throughout the world don't see a supply chain—they see a responsibility chain.[64] This revelation will drive all managers to seek more responsible behavior in their supply chains. The key takeaway in terms of the market opportunity for mission-driven companies is that if they can make credible and verifiable claims about stewardship of their goods, from raw materials to use and reuse or recycling, they are in a position to create powerful brand equity. But excelling in this regard requires investments in areas that run from supplier education to careful tracking of valid measures across time.

Of course, the types of products sold by a company matter too. As I'll show in Chapter 4, product categories have an important relationship to the price premiums that a company can charge. What is unique and provocative about mission-driven companies is how their social and environmental attributes can stimulate sales.

A FINAL NOTE

It is worth closing with a note about the effects of company attributes on success. Small and medium-size mission-driven companies have a major advantage in this area because they can build social and environmental authenticity and responsible supply chain practices into their organization from the first day that their founders begin to envision their company. It is important to note how difficult it is for large companies to change their stripes in this regard. For example, from General Electric's Ecomagination initiative to Wal-Mart's Sustainable Value Networks program, large companies are launching new efforts aimed at reducing their environmental impacts and capitalizing on emerging markets for green goods and services. But that's little comfort to consumers still peeved by GE's role in fouling the Hudson River and its involvement in dozens of Superfund sites, or Wal-Mart's role in forcing suppliers to drive down costs in ways that have significant social implications. For large companies, past behavior and policies often serve as a reputational lead ball weighing down their efforts to stride toward the opportunities created by the market drivers identified in this chapter. This creates a barrier to imitating the innovative behavior of mission-driven companies.

The market opportunity for mission-driven companies is real and it is growing. In the next several chapters, I apply strategic principles to the establishment and development of mission-driven organizations and to the pursuit of marketplace opportunities through focused differentiations. I begin by spotlighting the creation of socially and environmentally responsible organizations—the foundation for building a brand that carries authenticity to the marketplace.

3   TURNING DISTINCTIVENESS
INTO MARKET ACCEPTANCE
The Mission-Driven Difference

A SURVIVAL STORY

Gone. Everything, save a little off-site inventory and thankfully, a computer backup. On August 11, 2004, a devastating fire ripped through the warehouse, showroom, and offices of Ecohaus, a Seattle seller of sustainable building supplies. Tim Taylor, who was the CEO of the company at the time (then known as Environmental Home Center) shakes his head when he recalls the event. "When you strip away even physical assets," you are left with only two things, "your people and your brand."[1] The strength of these assets was to carry Ecohaus not just through rebuilding but to a position of still growing strength in its retail niche.

Taylor is a savvy pro with experience in all facets of building, from design to construction to renovation. Nursing one of those endless winter colds that seem indigenous to the clammy Northwest, he recounts how his years working on 250–300-year-old houses in New England gave him an appreciation for sustainability in the built environment. In the early 1990s, he was also busy forging links to the nascent social investing community, engaging in weighty discussions about the fundamentals of sustainability. Then, while running the Laird Norton Company, parent of one of the country's largest building materials retailers, Lanoga, he was approached by Ecohaus owner Matt Freeman-Gleason. It took years of persuasion, but in June 2000 Taylor signed on as CEO. His timing was spot on, coinciding with the emergence of the Forest Stewardship Council, the U.S. Green Building Council, and awakening consumer demand. Together, Freeman-Gleason and Taylor would animate and institutionalize the green building movement.

At Ecohaus, Taylor moved aggressively to fill out a product line that was quirky and incomplete, although he was careful to put in writing negative and positive screens that guided what the company would and would not carry. Some materials coated with dangerous solvents and tropical woods of uncertain origin were rejected, whereas leading-edge materials, such as new forms of insulation and environmentally sensitive paints, were welcomed to its shelves.[2] Over time, Taylor has had some success educating and encouraging suppliers to green up, yielding new items to offer for sale. Under Taylor's guidance, sales climbed steadily until the housing slowdown in 2008 arrived. Then, like all retailers, Ecohaus waited for better times.

But there's no doubting that the model has resonated with customers, and Taylor has taken advantage of this goodwill to form customer councils. He went well beyond simple questions about products and service to probe customers about how they viewed the company. He would push them to articulate why his products were better. "They're healthier. They're better for the environment. They save energy," customers would say. Then Taylor would ask them about the source of their confidence. Was it the labeling of the products? Not really. Recalls Taylor, "Fundamentally, when you peeled the onion to the core, it was remarkably consistent. Our customers on these councils said, 'We trust you as a business'—that's what it came down to."[3] Furthermore, "There seemed to be a connection between our customers and our products and the customer's belief that our products would help create balance in their life." When you hear this story, you begin to understand what happened after the fire.

The same day of the fire, Ecohaus was already making sales through its Web sites and taking calls from local customers. According to Taylor, there was no question that many sales were from customers who treated Ecohaus like a friend in need. One customer with whom Taylor had a long-term dispute over a $5,000 charge called after the fire to set aside the disagreement, asking only where to send the check.[4] Ecohaus rebuilt and less than six months later reopened its showroom, with sales exceeding prefire levels.[5]

The story of Ecohaus and its resurrection from an ash heap is a story about the power of a brand and the company standing behind it. In this chapter I'll review how mission-driven companies build their brands through differentiation. The central organizing idea is that this differentiation forms the essence of the value proposition offered by mission-driven companies. My goal in this chapter is to analyze the link between social and environmental differentiation and the price premium. In so doing, we can begin to understand the unique value proposition presented by mission-driven companies and their products.

In this chapter, I'll separate two key sources of social and environmental differentiation. The first is *company effects*, which stem from authenticity and responsible supply chain practices. The second is *product category effects*, which apply to products in a given category regardless of the company selling them. We'll see that these two sources of differentiation intertwine to produce different opportunities for value propositions that can draw customers—and different prospects for capturing price premiums. As I'll describe in the following pages, although a price premium is not a sufficient condition, generally it is a necessary condition for profitability for mission-driven companies. This is because many of the products and services I describe entail higher costs. Let's begin by briefly reviewing just what constitutes differentiation of goods and services.

DIFFERENT BY DESIGN
Conventional Differentiation Strategy

Strategist Michael Porter defined a differentiation strategy as one in which "a firm seeks to be unique in its industry along some dimensions that are widely valued by buyers."[6] Products can be differentiated from one another in an unlimited number of ways. For marketing experts Philip Kotler and Kevin Keller, these many dimensions of differentiation can be categorized as follows:[7]

- Product (as in John Deere's reliability)
- Service (as in Nordstrom's customer attentiveness)

- Personnel (as in Bain & Company's relationship consulting)
- Image (as in Harley-Davidson's maverick aura)
- Channels (as in Trek bicycles selling through dedicated bike shops)

As a general rule, differentiation adds costs.[8] Chart House restaurants are differentiated by the beautiful views they afford, which increases the cost of real estate acquisition. Apple's electronic gadgets are differentiated by their hip image and slick styling, which necessitates greater advertising and design costs. All-Clad is differentiated by the quality of its cookware, which requires premium materials and finishing processes. For these companies, or any other differentiators, the trick is to command a price premium that more than outweighs the additional costs associated with that strategy.

The Concept of Social and Environmental Differentiation

In precisely the same way that mainstream companies use differentiation as a vehicle to drive conventional products to profitability, so too can mission-driven companies leverage differentiation.[9] In fact, all mission-driven companies—by definition—can boast at least some form of differentiation. The problem, however, is that conventional differentiation schemas don't map very well onto the areas emphasized by mission-driven companies. For a more useful framework, let's go back to two critical dimensions that I introduced in Chapter 2: company authenticity and company supply chain practices.

COMPANY EFFECTS: AUTHENTICITY

Figure 3.1 shows the social and environmental differentiation map. Company authenticity is pivotal for mission-driven companies because it breathes personality and equity into brands. Without doubt, the black eye that results from a crisis of confidence when a company strays from its mission can be costly to the brand. But a solid reputation based on authenticity in various areas is, in fact, a sine qua non for mission-driven companies. It lays the foundation for a trusting relationship with customers. To the extent that companies push the envelope in this regard, they can establish important sources of differentiation. Let's consider methods that companies use to differentiate themselves on social and environmental dimensions.

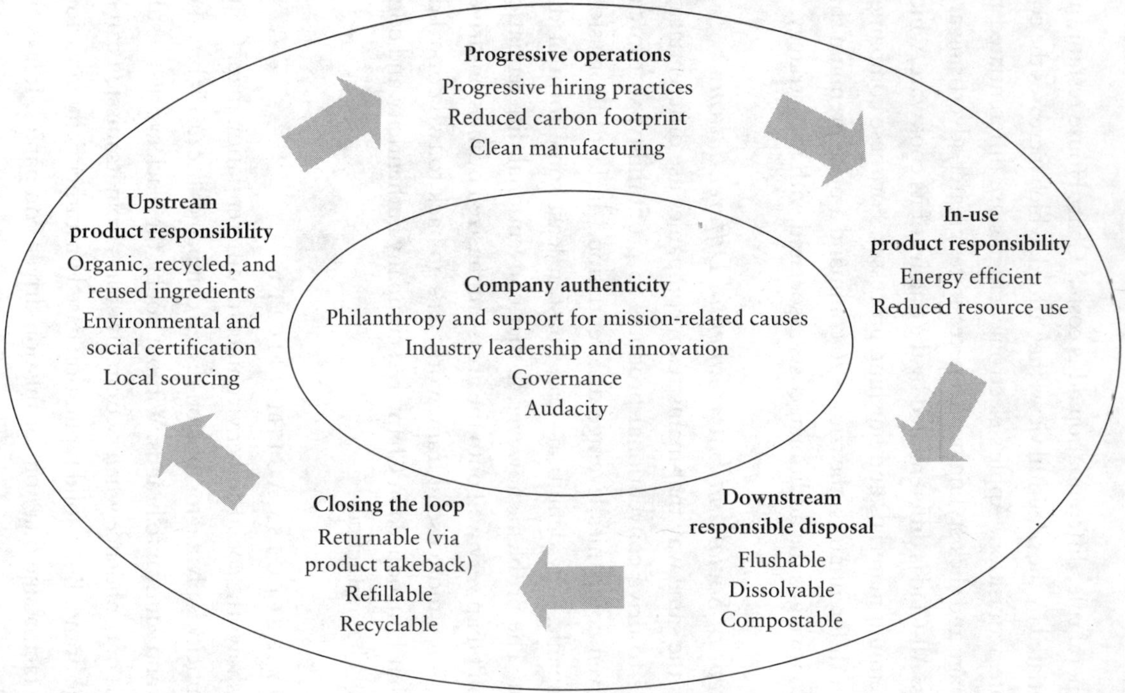

FIGURE 3.1 Social and environmental differentiation map.

Philanthropy and Support for Mission-Related Causes

Some companies are marked not only by the size of their philanthropic program but also by whom they target for support and the company's willingness to take chances. Since 1985, Patagonia's support for environmental causes has totaled more than $29 million. Each year, the company provides the greater of either 10% of pretax profits or 1% of sales to grassroots environmental groups.[10] What marks Patagonia's program and sets it apart from many other companies' giving programs is the tight relationship between this giving and the company's mission statement: "Build the best product, cause no unnecessary harm, use business to inspire and implement solutions to the environmental crisis."[11]

Started in 1991, the Oakland, California, company Give Something Back Business Products donates nearly all its profits to charity. Not all profits, because it needs to retain earnings, just like conventional companies, so that it can grow in a financially healthy way. It may sound eccentric, but as founder Mike Hannigan explains, given his experience and skill set, running a company was simply the best way he knew of to generate money to give away.[12] Four million dollars of philanthropy later, the company continues to be profitable, and Hannigan and partner Sean Marx's initial investment of $40,000 to start the company has increased to nearly $2 million. They've also grown at a measured pace so as to never need outside investors who would have a claim on profits that now go to charity. The strategy of philanthropy differentiates Give Something Back in the marketplace, as when it asks customers to cast ballots for which organizations should receive donations each year. It also doesn't hurt customer awareness that the company's philanthropy programs have won wide acclaim.[13] As much a cost-fixated manager as he is a social visionary, Hannigan is most proud of his company's ability to be a rare animal: at once differentiated by its social mission and fully price-competitive.

Industry Leadership and Innovation

A real boost to differentiation can come from industry leadership and innovation. Leadership can come from many sources. Often, mission-driven companies and enterprises have the advantage of being the nationally known voices of social and environmental stewardship. For more than thirty-five years, Amory Lovins, founder of the Rocky Mountain Institute, has held forth on topics relating to the energy, environment, and technology fields. His intellectual bandwidth, creative reflexes, and voluminous writings have brought him wide acclaim. A reverent 2007 *New Yorker* profile dubbed him "Mr. Green" and spoke of his focus on solutions to problems that others consider insoluble.[14] Rocky Mountain's phone was one of the first to ring when Wal-Mart decided to dramatically improve the efficiency of its transportation infrastructure.[15]

Bill McDonough, of McDonough Braungart Design Chemistry (MBDC), provides support for design of greener products and services. Along with Michael Braungart, McDonough has written a wide number of well-read articles and a book, *Cradle to Cradle*, that challenges design and operations professionals to create a world of zero waste.[16] His well-attended and widely delivered speaking engagements provide an audience and buzz for his work that draw clients to MBDC.

Being the first with an important innovation can serve as a valuable and long-lived asset. The nonprofit Bainbridge Graduate Institute was the first to offer an MBA degree that was truly (to use a bit of MBA jargon) "out of the box." The Bainbridge program offers such classes as "Finance, Accounting, and the Triple Bottom Line," "Systems Thinking in Action," and "Creativity and Right Livelihood." This is not your father's MBA. Further, the institute's faculty leans heavily on practitioners, favoring professional experience over theoretical depth.

Kettle Foods, known for it natural potato chips, built the first LEED gold-certified food plant in the United States, in Beloit, Wisconsin (LEED—Leadership in Energy and Environmental Design—is a green building rating and certification system). This milestone, which attracted the attention of MSNBC and industry media outlets, clearly established an authentic commitment to green building.[17] Kettle Foods believes that if many of the building's innovations had been subjected to a strict cost-benefit analysis, they would have been screened out of consideration.[18] In a conventional company, that most likely is just what would have happened.

Governance

A company's structure of ownership and control can now be a differentiator. As we'll learn, it's difficult to maintain social and environmental purpose through changes in governance, such as selling the company to a larger corporate parent or taking the company public. One way that a company can gain authenticity is by convincing customers that regardless of governance changes, its mission will emerge intact. Enter B Corporation—B Corp. for short—which offers to certify companies that meet performance and transparency standards but that also change their articles of incorporation to recognize the rights of employees, communities, and the environment.[19] The idea is that these articles of incorporation ensure that the mission of the company will continue indefinitely. We'll learn more about B Corp. in Chapter 9, but for now it is important to note that a major thrust for the organization is creating brand awareness for companies that are B corporations. As co-founder Bart Houlahan says, "We will be defined most importantly by the company we keep."[20] The flip side of this is that companies that are B corporations can differentiate themselves by placing the B Corp. logo on their business cards, in store windows, and on products.

Audacity

Mission-driven companies can display a degree of audacity that goes beyond what might be expected from a Fortune 500 company. For example, in 1990, Patagonia paid to bail out a number of its workers who were arrested at protests of Pacific Lumber Company's clear-cutting of ancient redwoods.[21] Although building the brand name was likely far from the minds of Patagonia's managers when they sprung part of their workforce, the action was rooted in the company's mission statement. Yet for mission-driven companies, brand names and the mission are interwoven, one reason Patagonia founder Yvon Chouinard found himself on the cover of *Fortune* in 2007. The tag line: "The Coolest Company on Earth."[22]

Authenticity is a powerful force in connecting companies to customers, and social and environmental authenticity is often difficult for larger mainstream companies to replicate. Authenticity also can lead to the type of trust that Ecohaus enjoyed with its customers.

COMPANY EFFECTS: SUPPLY CHAIN PRACTICES

A second, equally powerful differentiator is a company's supply chain practices. Here, too, mission-driven companies can create unique strategic positions by viewing the product stream not solely as a target for economizing but as an opportunity for social and environmental differentiation.

Upstream Product Responsibility

Social and environmental differentiation in the upstream portion of the supply chain can be created in a variety of ways. First, there are ingredients. Differentiation can be created by the use of organic ingredients in food products ranging from frozen pizzas to bran muffins. When Clif Bar decided to get serious about its environmental commitment and include organic ingredients in its line of energy bars, it was shocked at the power of the marketplace reception.[23] Use of recycled ingredients also can bolster marketplace perceptions that a company is working to minimize its environmental footprint. Sometimes standards actually drive the market entirely: In August 2006, Green Seal announced standards for recycled latex paint, adding credibility and validation to the market for that product.[24]

Environmental and social certification applies a stamp of propriety to a company's upstream activities. Increasingly, relying on just any certification won't do. Consider standards for the workplace, which are especially important for overseas sourcing. As mentioned previously, by one count, there are seven separate codes of conduct for labor, all with a unique set of characteristics.[25] Which of the standards are unduly influenced by industry or unions is debatable, but a company can be differentiated by choosing a standard that is perceived as having teeth. For example, a certification system that requires unannounced plant visits by independent monitors will be viewed as more effective than a certification system in which company officials receive prior notification of visits.

Fair trade certification, associated primarily with food products, also signifies that a product was purchased at a price that is generally higher than prevailing commodity prices and ensures that more of the upstream value of a particular product is captured by the farmers and growers at its origin. Fair trade certification, primarily through the international agent

FLO-CERT, requires a rigorous independent inspection process and considers not only pricing but also several other dimensions, including working conditions, wages, child labor, and environmental sustainability.[26]

Upstream responsibility can also be signaled by the use of recycled content. Some recycled content is the norm for paper and cardboard products at this point. But the creative reuse of products and ingredients is gathering steam. This is particularly true in fields such as building products, where reused tiles, flooring, and beams are currently rising in popularity. The presence of such Web sites as the California Integrated Waste Management Board now provide detailed contact information that brings together sellers and buyers in what was previously a thin market.[27]

Local purchasing has recently become an important issue for many consumers, not least of them members of the LOHAS community. Partly this is a reflection of national media stories that have focused attention on the sometimes difficult trade-off between organic and local production of food. When the cover of *Time* exhorted readers to "forget organic, eat local," it was only the latest reflection of several trends that had been percolating for some time.[28] The so-called 100-mile diet, which uses only food purchased within a 100-mile radius, sensitized consumers to localism. The localism movement now extends well beyond food. The Web site of the Business Alliance for Local Living Economies (BALLE), links to local businesses described as "independent retail" and "community capital."[29]

Progressive Operations

A company's own operations can help to differentiate it in the social and environmental domain. A number of mission-driven companies have reached out to their communities to hire nontraditional and difficult-to-hire individuals. Greyston Bakery of Yonkers, New York, has a motto: "We don't hire people to bake brownies. We bake brownies to hire people." Its mission pervades its policies and processes. This means, for example, that apprenticeship involves teaching individuals how to work rather than how to bake, focusing on "punctuality, attendance, and productivity."[30] But president and CEO Julius Walls Jr. has made the recipe work. Greyston has enjoyed profitable growth for some time, expanding its facilities and sharing that success in the form of profit sharing with employees.

The company, which got a major break when Ben & Jerry's agreed to use its products in its ice cream, funnels all its profits into a foundation for its community.[31]

Companies also can bring responsibility into operations by reducing environmental impacts. Either by on-site energy generation or use of carbon offsets, a number of companies are now claiming that their products are created using alternative energy. New Leaf Paper, which focuses on developing beautiful, environmentally responsible paper goods, aims to offset all the carbon emissions associated with its electricity usage. The commitment to alternative energy is another factor that helps to create a market image of innovation and commitment to its mission.

Carbon reductions don't always necessitate offset purchases. DKV Seguros, a Barcelona-based health care and insurance company, assigned the job of reducing its footprint to a young associate, Carlos Martinez Gantes. He quickly focused on the key areas of energy, employee transportation, and paper use. One of the outcomes of a careful study was a companywide mandate against using the "sky shuttle" for its frequent trips to Madrid. The reason: With the new high-speed rail link, door-to-door travel was competitive in price and time with air travel and less prone to delays. Add to this that the carbon impact of the train was less than 10% of that of the airlines (Martinez calculated air travel at 600 kilograms of carbon to less than 60 kilograms for the train), and it's a no-brainer. By coincidence, the day we spoke in Barcelona, July 1, 2009, marked the institution of new rules that further liberalized Spain's electricity market. A new task for Martinez: using new abilities to contract for energy to secure for DKV Seguros clean sources of electricity for its offices.[32] The company keeps a low profile about its programs (including a highly successful program to hire disabled people at its call centers). But its reputation among customers and workers has trended upward in measurements it routinely keeps on variables such as credibility and responsibility.[33]

In-Use Product Responsibility

Some products are differentiated by their lessened social and environmental impact during their use. Here again, companies primarily differentiate with respect to environmental issues. Products that are especially energy efficient or reduce the usage of other resources, such as water, can be branded as creating less impact across the product life cycle. In this category, true differentiation is somewhat more difficult, because decreasing energy usage can work on purely economic terms. Thus consumers may not value a more mission-driven tie to the product. It is best seen as part of a holistic package, in which environmental or social differentiation is pursued.

Downstream Responsible Product Disposition

Garbage and therefore the landfill is where most products wind up after the consumer is finished with them. A product can be differentiated by its disposition in a number of ways, however. By now, we've all seen packing peanuts that have been made from cornstarch and can be dissolved in the kitchen sink and run down the drain. But not every product should be dissolved and disposed in this way. An example of an entirely new approach to baby diapers is promoted by gDiapers. These diapers, because of their patented formula, can be flushed down the toilet after changing the baby (a video on the company's Web site demonstrates the simple process). The first of its kind, the product is a revelation for those parents worried about the impact of either disposable or reusable cloth diapers.

A dramatic example of products that have no postuse impact are those that are naturally compostable. These products include some of the fabrics produced by Switzerland's Rohner Textil in its Climatex line. Based on a cradle-to-cradle design created by William McDonough and Michael Braungart, the fabric can be returned to nature as compost. Given the dyes used in furniture cloths and the difficult design specifications (e.g., for long-term sitting and durability), this cloth is a repository of significant research and development efforts. But it is highly differentiated and has been a marketplace success.

Closing the Loop

Many products cannot simply become part of the ecosystem or otherwise dissolve into the waste stream. For those, the final step in the product supply chain can be the return of the good—or most of it—to the original seller. For years now, consumers have refilled printer cartridges, saving a hefty percentage of the cost of new ones. A number of companies have sprung up to fill this need. Note that closing the loop begins with product design itself. Designing products for disassembly, for example, necessitates simple steps—as trivial as using a common screw head—that must be part of the design phase.[34]

For other companies, closing the loop means taking the product back in its entirety. Consider Hartmann & Forbes, a seller of handwoven window coverings. The products are made of jute, bamboo, and other fast-growing plants. The dyes are made from traditional vegetable bases. The fasteners that hold the coverings are steel. All together, the entire product can be either returned to nature (the fabric) or recycled (the steel fasteners). Armed with this information, Hartmann & Forbes was the first in its industry to take back its window coverings in 2005. Its timing was perfect, coinciding with a surge in interest in green home design. Its customers, less so the homeowners than their interior decorators and architects, found its differentiation attractive. And the array of free advertising that the company received is impressive, with articles in outlets running from *This Old House* to *Inc. Magazine* to the *Harvard Post* to Treehugger.com.[35]

Indeed, the best supply chain is a supply cycle.

The company effect is one key way to infuse a brand name with meaning and value that resonate with enlightened consumers. To leverage this company effect to its fullest effect, however, mission-driven companies must invest in actions and programs that may seem far from the conventional business model but that actually support their marketplace positioning. Differentiation that involves the company rather than the product stream can also be more difficult for competitors to imitate, because it is based on a set of values that is often in conflict with traditional business.

To summarize, creating value for customers can be done in many ways that are linked less to products than to the companies that make and sell them. All these different paths meet up to form avenues to price premiums, although as I'll discuss further, in all cases, market structure and the nature of competition are important influences as well. The product itself also matters, of course, and an important determinant of prospects for a price premium element is the extent to which a product creates private benefits that the purchaser enjoys.

PRODUCT CATEGORY EFFECTS:
THE IMPORTANCE OF PRIVATE BENEFITS

As anyone who has brought home a head of pesticide-free romaine lettuce or a free-range cut-up fryer can attest, compared to their conventional counterparts, organic or natural food items are expensive. Organic produce and dairy products and natural meats command impressive price premiums.

The experience with certified wood products, however, has been completely different. The leading certifier of wood, the Germany-based Forest Stewardship Council, lists a number of requirements for certification, and this list reflects activities that may frequently take place in developing countries. One requirement is compliance with all applicable laws and international treaties, clear rights to use the lands being logged, a long-term management plan for the forest, and contributions to the long-term social and economic welfare of work and communities.[36] Markets for certified wood have existed for well over a decade in developed countries. Unfortunately, no entity collects consistent, broadly valid pricing data on sales certified by the Forest Stewardship Council.[37] But from studies conducted on consumer preferences, experiments using actual behavior, and anecdotal reports, it is likely that any price premium will be small, if it exists at all.[38]

Both organic and natural foods and certified wood are authentic and externally validated. Both products are widely available. And both products meet consumer desires for goods with lessened social and environmental impacts. Why is the price premium for organic foods many times that of certified wood?

I've already provided some of the story by identifying ways that the two differ on company effects. Organic produce sometimes carries a brand name, and of course it is free of pesticides and artificial additives. It is also more likely to be produced locally from absolutely authentic sources. In many small communities, the individuals involved in the production of these goods are known personally or through a degree or two of separation, further bolstering their reputation in the eyes of local consumers. But these differences between organic produce and certified lumber, although important, do not justify such a high price premium. To get the whole story, we must consider the private benefits of organic produce compared with certified lumber. To do that, we have to analyze product category effects, the second determinant of social and environmental differentiation.

In a nutshell, the product category effect turns on the extent to which the point of differentiation creates private benefits for individuals.[39] Private benefits are those that accrue directly to the buyer of a product and service. They don't necessarily have to be tangible, as in the avoidance of potential health risks from eating food with fewer pesticides. The private benefit may be psychological and may derive from the warm glow of altruism. Also, the private benefit is not the whole story, as I'll develop later. But, it is an element that must be weighed and appreciated.

One company whose experience validates the importance of stressing private benefits is Seventh Generation. Just after taking the company private in 1999, former president Jeffrey Hollender had a revelation about the natural products industry as a whole. Viewing the success of natural foods, he noted that "people don't buy organic apples because they are worried about the pollution of a stream; for the most part they are worrying about consuming pesticides."[40] Hollender repositioned Seventh Generation as a purveyor of healthy, safe, and effective products, switching its tagline from "Products for a Healthy Planet" to "Healthier for You and the Environment."[41] Academic research supported this repositioning.[42] Seventh Generation then promoted its products by spotlighting their health benefits, especially with regard to asthma, allergies, and chemical sensitivities. Consistent double-digit growth followed.[43]

For Golden Temple, a $100 million maker of natural cereals and teas, the tie-in to personal welfare stems from the company's core values of health and healing. Rooted in the ancient Indian healing philosophy of Ayurveda, Golden Temple's products seek to balance body and mind through a food-based approach to wellness. It communicates healing through consistent messaging—all the way down to a bit of wisdom printed on each tea bag's tag.[44]

Let's think more rigorously about private benefits by considering them as lying on a continuum. Organic produce is an example of a product that commands a sizable price premium, but it is widely viewed by consumers as possessing considerable private benefits to their own health. At the other end of the spectrum we find products such as certified wood. Here, the end product is precisely the same as the conventional one. Shown two lengths of lumber, you would not be able to tell the difference or be able to identify which was from a certified forest without considerable analysis. Here, if there is a private benefit, it relates to that warm glow of altruism.

But the extent of private benefits is a continuum, and indeed there are intermediate positions. A good example is nontoxic cleaners. These products still have price premiums, but those premiums do not rise to the level of organic produce. And the private benefits, although still a strong selling point, are less substantial. In addition, nontoxic cleaners may be valuable for consumers who have chemical sensitivities or must avoid some of the ingredients of conventional cleaners for other reasons. Let's collect some data on selling prices to see whether this framework holds in the marketplace.

The Product Category–Private Benefit Connection in the Marketplace

I obtained data for products in each of three categories: (1) products with perceived direct health benefits, such as organic food items; (2) other items with more indirect health benefits, such as nontoxic cleaners; and (3) products with little or no direct or only indirect health benefits, such as certified wood. In all cases, data for the conventional and alternative products were taken from the same source at the same time, to ensure comparability.[45]

I found that the highest premiums were for organically produced poultry, at a lofty 208%, and for broccoli, at 152%.[46] The premium for organic produce and dairy was uniformly high, with carrots averaging a 147% premium, milk 93%, and eggs 271%.[47] Products in the intermediate area—household cleaners and toothpaste—were those for which the private benefits were tangible but were not as direct as for food items. Even though these products had the advantage of being able to leverage a brand name in the marketplace, the price premium still did not rise to the level of products that are eaten.

I considered both the household cleaners and toothpaste on a price per ounce basis. For household cleaners I averaged national prices for Formula 409 and Pine-Sol and compared them to Simple Green, a nationally known nontoxic cleaner.[48] For toothpaste I compared Tom's of Maine to the average of five national brands: Aim, Crest, Gleem, Arm & Hammer, and Pepsodent.[49] The nontoxic cleaners' price premium was 46%, and the natural toothpaste premium was 98%. So although significant, in both these cases, the premiums did not rise to the levels associated with most of the food items. I'll comment on the size of that premium for toothpaste shortly.

My final comparison considered products with little or no private benefits: electricity and lumber. For data on nationwide price premiums for green electricity, I relied on information from federal agencies.[50] For lumber prices, because there is no national source of data, I obtained pricing information from Collins Pine Company, a well-regarded environmental leader and a major source of lumber certified by the Forest Stewardship Council.[51] I considered prices for certified and noncertified White Fir 2 × 4 lumber.[52] The results again conformed to expectations: The price premium for green electricity was 20%, and for the certified lumber it was 5%.

There are a number of takeaways from studying price premiums. First, this survey of actual products validates, in a raw sense, the hypothesis that the greater the extent of the private benefits derived from a natural product, the greater the price premium it can command in the marketplace. Second, and relatedly, the comparisons suggest that significant challenges await entrepreneurs who are organizing to sell products and services for which clear private benefits can't be communicated to customers. And finally, the private benefit contribution to the price premium is easier to make when health is involved, and this is more typically tied to environmental rather than social missions of companies.

Products and Altruism

For both green electricity and certified wood, there is evidence that altruism is at work. First, let's consider green power. A kilowatt-hour is a kilowatt-hour, one might surmise. Yet green power has significantly diffused throughout developed countries, and this market has grown steadily. Of interest is the asymmetric pattern of growth across the United States. In a recent study, Magali Delmas and Maria Montes-Sancho of the University of California, Santa Barbara, and I found that the greater the percentage of pro-environmental citizenry in a state, the more green power was sold there.[53] We also found that this effect strengthened in states where deregulation was under way, which could mean that when deregulation gives electricity consumers a choice, many will use that prerogative to purchase renewables. In either case, the presence of LOHAS-type customers promotes the use of renewable energy. This is connected not to direct private benefits but to a sense of altruism toward the environmental commons.

I believe that this altruistic effect can be observed for a range of products that do not embody clear private benefits, from fair trade clothing to "cruelty-free" products (those made without animal testing). Although not as powerful as the private benefit effect, the effect of altruism can create value.

PUTTING IT ALL TOGETHER

Figure 3.2 provides an illustration of company effects and product category effects. In both cases the effects change gradually and without clear break points, but I have placed them in a typology for ease of exposition. The highest possible price premiums are for goods sold by authentic companies with responsible supply chain practices. These products are the most likely to be purchased by LOHAS consumers, and they enjoy strong customer

Authentic and responsibly sourced	Low but stable	Significant	Highest possible
Company effects			
Inauthentic and irresponsibly sourced	Very low and unstable	Moderate but temporary	Significant but temporary
	Pure altruism	Indirect private benefits	Direct private benefits

Product category effects

FIGURE 3.2
Company and product category effects on price premiums.

loyalty. When the private benefits are more indirect, the price premiums are moderate, but the same customer loyalty effects are possible. The final category in the upper half of the chart is for product categories in which private benefits are minimal and pure altruism is in force. (This is not to say that an element of altruism is not evident in the categories with higher private benefits, where it also frequently is a factor.) So in the upper left-hand box, price premiums are lower, but they are stable when the products in question are sold by companies with strong social and environmental records that are respected and sought out by consumers.

The lower half of Figure 3.2 shows the situation for products sold by companies that lack authenticity and source irresponsibly. At worst, this situation describes greenwashing, in which companies misrepresent or fabricate social and environmental records. Here, all price premiums for these companies' products are subject to erosion, perhaps rapid erosion, as the transparency movement pushes their true records into the public eye. Customers purchase these goods because they may not have other choices and are not aware of the companies' records. These particular customers are less likely to be LOHAS consumers and so lack the LOHAS characteristics of brand loyalty and willingness to pay for desired products. Therefore, in all cases, the price premium will be lower than for products sold by more responsible companies. Where there are private benefits, there will be a price premium, but it is likely to be temporary and subject to loss if a company's true record is publicized. For product categories in which the price premium is due to pure altruism, the premium is very low and transitory. In fact, it may be unstable because customers for whom altruism influences purchasing decisions will be especially affronted by revelations about poor company practices. These companies may be one scandal away from abandonment.

One observation that can be made is that, to the extent that greenwashing can go on without detection by the broader class of consumers, it can pay in the short term. This regrettable outcome occurs because, although the price premium is lower for the products sold by irresponsible companies, so are their costs. By cutting corners on social and environmental policies and programs, irresponsible companies can reduce costs to levels at which a lower price premium keeps them profitable.

PRICE PREMIUMS AND PROFITABILITY

I can only provide part of the story here. All things being equal, a price premium that is supported by the purchasing public can lead to profits, but there is no guarantee that this will be so. What if the underlying costs of a product are so high that even with a price premium, the company loses money? Having a social and environmental mission is a viable business strategy for a company only if its customers are willing to pay a price high enough to not only cover its costs but also ensure a profit.

The ability to command a price premium is undoubtedly affected by factors other than company and product effects. The size of the premium for Tom's of Maine may reflect a number of elements, including the fact that the product is sometimes available as the only unconventional toothpaste in mainstream outlets. Another product that has some private health benefits, as anyone who has lived in a house during renovation will attest, is zero-VOC paint (VOCs are volatile organic compounds, which are responsible for the powerful paint odor). But low-VOC paint and even zero-VOC paint command limited price premiums. One reason is the vast number of sellers of these products in the national market. Another is that often decisions are made not by the consumer but by a contractor who is likely to scrutinize higher prices with a good degree of skepticism.

The upshot is that it may be true that "another business world is possible,"[54] led by mission-driven companies, but principles of profit, loss, and business continuation remain acutely relevant. The point here, however, is that differentiation is the key to creating the type of value proposition that can lead to profits by boosting the price that a good or service can command to a level that will exceed costs. For many if not most products sold by mission-driven firms, this premium is essential to the viability of the organization and therefore to its mission.[55]

MAINTAINING THE DIFFERENTIATION EDGE

One element of the unique forms of differentiation that I've discussed here is completely consistent with conventional types of differentiation: For the strategy to be successful, it must be difficult to imitate. The strategic twist for mission-driven companies is how their mission-driven nature creates deterrents to imitation by their conventional counterparts.

The Bainbridge Graduate Institute may attract competitors from de novo entry (such as the newer Presidio School of Management), but it would be difficult for a traditional university MBA program to replicate Bainbridge's approach. This is because traditional MBA programs have an enormous strategic commitment to theory-based research, the tenure system, and faculty governance. All these factors will act to deter their infringement on the strategic space that Bainbridge has carved out.

This example from the nonprofit sector is matched by countless ones from the for-profit sector. The massive commitments to conventional products and sourcing used by most companies erect a formidable barrier to shifting to modes that reflect cutting-edge levels of responsibility. For companies that are used to a network of offshore sources with relationships that are made and broken depending solely on costs, developing a more socially and environmentally responsible supply chain is an enormous challenge. Also, institutional rules within the private sector restrict imitation of mission-driven strategies, especially when the mission-driven company is privately held and the conventional company is publicly held. For example, it is difficult for publicly owned companies to engage in levels of philanthropy that some privately owned mission-driven companies can maintain, because their managements must observe conventional norms of fiduciary responsibility.

As with all differentiators, a mission-driven company must be a moving target. In the eye of the consumer, what constitutes leading-edge social and environmental performance is evolving rapidly. It is just as important for Fair Indigo to determine and employ the latest social and environmental policies and practices as it is for Tommy Hilfiger to determine and employ the latest colors and styles in its fashions.

FINAL WORD: THE PARAMOUNT IMPORTANCE OF BUILDING THE BRAND

Social and environmental differentiation can follow many routes, and individual entrepreneurs can develop and position their products in a way that maximizes that strategic advantage. I've noted throughout this chapter that this differentiation, in and of itself, can build brand equity through company effects that create reputational capital. But company effects may elicit price premiums on their own. Many products from great companies don't generate meaningful private benefits beyond the warm glow of altruism. Are such products doomed to be the cellar dwellers of profitability, relegated to a world of subsistence capitalism?

The answer is a resounding no.

We all can name mission-driven companies and products that do not display private benefits but yet are popular and, we assume, profitable. The reason for this success is that these entrepreneurs have created powerful *brands* that command marketplace presence and support higher prices. In fact, common to *all* mission-driven companies, regardless of where their products lie on the horizontal scale of Figure 3.2, is the potential to build brand equity in the marketplace by creating value that customers associate with their products and services.

In the next chapter I'll outline how a well-conceived and skillfully executed marketing strategy can boost brand equity and expand opportunities for mission-driven companies.

CREATING AND COMMUNICATING THE BRAND
From Customers' Values to Customer Value

Peering out of the kitchen window of his cramped apartment in Zurich one morning, Markus Freitag found inspiration. A graphic designer by training, he was searching, along with his brother Daniel, for a way to make a durable messenger bag for carrying documents. Nothing seemed to capture his imagination in a radically different way until he considered the trucks rumbling by on the autobahn outside his room. Instead of just rattling the cupboard, maybe they could do him some good. In fact, they would change his life.[1]

Tarps. Colorful, durable, and at the end of their industrial life, free and with an unlimited set of designs and color combinations from which to choose. Sure, they were a little *stinkend* at first, but a trip to a washing machine, piece by piece, took care of most of that. Along with some recycled seat belts for straps and after some cutting and stitching, the original Freitag Top Cat bag was born.[2]

Julie Lewis had her own vision. A high-energy activist with a long history in recycling, she was frustrated by a lack of markets and alternative uses for recycled goods.[3] Harkening back to a pair of huaraches made out of old tires that she had once worn in Mexico, she began to piece together a supply chain to turn recycled goods into shoes.

It wasn't easy. But Lewis was determined and sought out the advice of a great many industry professionals in and around her Portland, Oregon, base. Aided by their counsel and several grants, she was able to acquire raw material, locate manufacturers, and create a prototype. After a number of supply-related misadventures, the shoes were ready for rollout.

Five years after its founding, Freitag was expanding its product line and sales outlets. In 2008, sales reached about $30 million.[4] Five years after its founding, Lewis's Deja Shoe voluntarily liquidated its assets to pay off its creditors.[5]

Freitag and Deja Shoe are similar in many ways, beginning with their rough launch dates in the early 1990s. Both were based on the use of re-cycled goods, and both aimed at the higher end of the price spectrum. In both cases, innumerable glowing accounts in the media lavished free advertising on the start-ups.[6] Several factors, such as involvement of top industry professionals, actually weighed in Deja Shoe's favor.

What can explain the differing outcomes of the two companies? They operated in different markets and used different financial structures. But their marketing decisions played a key, perhaps determining role in their fates. To examine marketing with a broader lens, in this chapter I focus on three critical marketing issues, any of which can make or break products sold by mission-driven companies: (1) product positioning, (2) distribu-tion choices, and (3) communication strategies.

CUSTOMER VALUE FOR RESPONSIBLE PRODUCTS

We buy products for many reasons, running from physiological needs to aspirations and beliefs.[7] For our purposes, two reasons will help us to ap-preciate the special marketing challenges faced by mission-driven compa-nies: product performance and emotional bonding with the company. Let's first work through these in turn, because each is different in the world of mission-driven companies.

Product Performance: Breaking
Through Green Product Trade-Offs

All products that companies bring to markets embody trade-offs. Consum-ers are familiar with trade-offs that appear in conventional markets. Walk into one of Carrefour's hyperstores in France, and you'll be overwhelmed with products at reasonable prices. But the service here or at other big box retailers won't begin to approach the level that you would receive at a neighborhood store.[8] If you are willing to swap that service for lower price, then the hyperstore is the place for you. There is nothing new about this trade-off, which has been a fact of commercial life in an increasing number of countries for decades. But using the case of green products, we can understand that some of the trade-offs are new. And finding innovative ways to overcome them can generate marketplace success.

PRODUCT PERFORMANCE FOR GREENNESS   If there's one trade-off that turns customers off, it's losing product performance for the sake of environmental improvement. In the early days of green consumption, customers were often willing to put up with products that didn't meet the performance standards of conventional goods. Remember some of the early green cleaners? For customers who used most of them, the memories aren't fond. This category is where initial product offerings often enter, attempting to be first in a new niche. Over time, competition and research and development improve products. The problem is the long memory that consumers have after giving an underperforming product a trial run.

Most of the original environmentally sensitive cleaners and detergents were easier on the environment than they were on stains. And like an ink spot, that reputation didn't fade quickly. Nonetheless, after several decades, a new generation of cleaners has emerged that meets tough environmental standards while making wash days just a little bit less blue. Although less publicized, greener commercial and industrial cleaners had to overcome these same reputational impediments. Coastwide Laboratories, which makes and sells janitorial and sanitation supplies, was able, after years of research, to create an entire line of environmentally sensitive cleaners.[9] Its Sustainable Earth line features products that clean up to 65% better than conventional products, based on independent tests.[10] Thanks to the conservatism of its competitors, Coastwide faced no competition for a number of years, enjoying expansion in an industry known for snail-paced growth.

Similarly, the original organic wines were not favorites among oenophiles. Reasons included that most of the grapes were not grown in choice vineyards and that some of the early wines excluded sulfites, which help to stabilize and preserve wine. The more recent thrust has been to move the attention away from a single additive to a more holistic view of growing and harvesting grapes. A 2007 cover story in *Wine Spectator* proclaimed "Wine Goes Green," and the writer discussed biodynamic practices and other methods for making vineyards more like functioning ecosystems. The article featured an honor roll of wines whose tasting scores and prices suggested that the green movement had overcome the sour reputation of the original organic wines.[11]

CONVENIENCE FOR GREENING   Although they may meet or exceed the quality of conventional products in appearance, longevity, flavor, or any number of product dimensions, green products can be inconvenient. The inconvenience can be manifested in a number of ways. For example, concentrated refill formulas save materials and space but require on-site mixing by consumers; electric vehicles have limited ranges; and design for recycling requires postuse efforts to achieve a positive environmental impact.

The classic case of an inconvenient green product is cloth diapers.[12] Ask any parent. There is just no getting around the issue: Whether a diaper service or your own washer and dryer are put into service, it's a hassle to use cloth diapers compared to disposables. And some parents believe that more frequent diaper changes are necessary with cloth. But the use of disposable diapers has a mammoth impact on the waste stream. Purchase concentrated soap and you will reuse bottles and save some materials that would be used for containers. Move to cloth diapers and you'll keep some 5,000 diapers out of the landfill during the life of the average child.[13]

gDiapers, first developed in Australia, offers a product that breaks through this trade-off with its single-use diapers. The diapers consist of a cotton outer pant that can be washed when necessary and an inner liner made from Forest Stewardship Council certified farmed wood fluff pulp, cellulose rayon, and a safe absorbency agent. Here's the twist: The liners are flushable. One simply places them in a toilet, gives them a whirl with the giant swizzle stick provided with a diaper kit, and flushes them. It turns out that even the flushing has synergistic effects, as local municipalities report that the ingredients in the liners help them to cleanse water before its return to nature.[14]

If the liners are just wet, they can be composted in the backyard. And in fact, even tossing them out is an improvement over conventional disposables. According to gDiapers' online video, the diapers will completely disappear in less than two months in a landfill (unlike the conventional diaper, which will fully return to nature sometime around when a newborn's fifteenth generation is in nappies). Being the first consumer product in the world to receive an environmental certification from MBDC (McDonough Braungart Design Chemistry) supplies assurance to customers.

Car-sharing services, such as the Netherlands' Greenwheels, overcome much of the inconvenience of being car-free while creating greater utilization of scarce assets like raw materials and urban space. Urban residents who rely on public transportation have long had to deal with the hassle of occasionally renting automobiles for reaching odd places in town, going out of town, or making a round-trip to the local hardware store. Yet the inefficiency of owning an automobile is manifest: From rapid depreciation of an expensive asset to insurance, fuel, and parking charges, the cost per mile of urban car ownership can be prohibitive. The answer: car sharing. Such services, which originated in Europe, provide for a system of shared automobiles that are owned by a third party. Typically, the cars are kept at a central location, where an electronic key permits access. No counter, no forms, no pressure to buy a damage collision waiver. The cost? There are variations, but typically fees include a monthly subscription plus a charge for mileage and/or time of utilization.

PRICE FOR GREENNESS   It's no secret that many products with environmental features are expensive. Especially where they confront national brands backed up by companies that enjoy efficiencies in all phases of the product stream, it's difficult for small and medium-size mission-driven companies to sell products cheaply. This is not the end of the world. In the previous chapter, I described how these companies can command higher prices in the marketplace. But some customers still feel priced out of the market for many of these goods. It may be an affordability issue or merely that the willingness to pay on the part of a particular customer does not rise to the requisite level. In either case, a trade-off exists and therefore an opportunity.

Natural Value is a Sacramento-based producer of more affordable organic food and paper goods. It broke through the price trade-off by reconfiguring its supply chain in a way that leveraged co-owner Gary Cohen's thirty years of experience in the organic foods industry.[15] Most organic canned and dry goods travel to the grocer from canners and packagers after two stops, first at a large warehouse and then at a distribution center. Cohen's innovation was to arrange for manufacturers to ship directly to distribution centers. This would have been impossible without a network of trusting relationships with his many friends in the organic foods growing, packing, and canning industries. These connections facilitated fluid communications, shortened product development times, and ensured on-time deliveries. Cognizant that such a model may attract imitators, Natural Value tries to further its advantage by keeping costs to an absolute minimum. Cohen and his wife and co-owner, Jody Stephens, run the company out of their home in Sacramento, California. And only family is involved: the third and only other employee is Cohen's daughter, Beki.

The design and construction of a new house, a vastly more complicated purchase, requires an entirely different approach. Architect Michelle Kaufmann's goal is "thoughtful, sustainable design that's accessible."[16] A native Iowan, Kaufmann has a Midwesterner's down-to-earth manner and sensibilities, including the idea that accessibility has a cost component—homes should be designed with broad affordability in mind. Sitting in her conference room surrounded by the fascinating visual array that adorns any architect's walls, she explains how she's worked to move away from one-off designs to preconfigured homes and communities. Popularizing green design demands hardheaded decisions about selecting materials that respect many, sometimes competing requirements about initial impacts on the earth, maintenance, longevity, beauty, efficiency, and of course cost. Over time, architects in her office have developed a number of systems approaches to bring costs down with, for example, factory-built homes. Through meticulous design and long-term learning, Kaufmann's team has created a portfolio of six preconfigured homes from which a buyer can choose, reserving a few final choices to customize the home. Kaufmann's work has made her a favorite of the media, but serious observers have noticed her too. A full-scale replica of her preconfigured homes, the Glidehouse, was displayed in the National Building Museum.[17] Another home, the mkSolaire, appeared at the Museum of Science and Industry in Chicago.[18] The surprising part: Kaufmann can build a design for a mere 3% cost increment over conventional construction. But that's just the initial cost. When the energy, water, and utility cost savings are accounted for, the home actually is cheaper to build and own.[19]

By challenging assumptions and capitalizing on their own experience, relationships, and learning curves, companies can bring down costs and expand the reach of more sustainable products to segments of consumers who are less willing to pay additional costs for green products. Thus they can expand the total market.

GREENNESS FOR GREENNESS   Nobody's perfect, as the last type of trade-off—greenness for greenness—signifies. And these types of trade-offs, in which environmental impacts of one type are reduced while impacts of other types rise, are ubiquitous. TerraChoice, a Canadian environmental marketing consultant, identified this trade-off as the most prevalent greenwashing sin in a 2008 report.[20] Examples are everywhere, from office equipment that promotes energy efficiency without attention to hazardous material content to paper products that contain recycled content but ignore many manufacturing impacts. In-depth analyses of product comparisons can be revealing.

One greenness for greenness debate that has raged across the globe involves the familiar paper or plastic query we all have received at the checkout stand. Many consumers, given the choice, take groceries home in paper sacks, often believing that this is the correct environmental choice. In 2007, San Francisco became the first municipality to ban plastic,[21] and in early 2008 Whole Foods Market removed them from all of its stores.[22] Yet doubts linger about which of the options is better, based on careful life-cycle analyses. A 1990 study by the well-regarded Life Cycle Assessment Group at Franklin Associates found that paper bags required more energy to produce and were more difficult to recycle. Perhaps saving on petrochemicals created offsetting issues?

One way to break through this trade-off is to avoid it altogether by using *neither* paper nor plastic and replacing the single-use bag with a cloth one. Enter Sharon Rowe, who founded Eco-Bags in 1989 when a friend brought a string bag back from Europe for her.[23] Like its competitor, the ChicoBag, the Eco-Bag is light and "scrunchable" and fits in a purse.[24] Reusable bags have their own issues (Rowe's are sourced in Asia), but the product does break through a good part of the greenness for greenness issues embodied in the paper versus plastic question and, long after reaching acceptance in Europe, has clearly reached the tipping point in America.

The punch line for green products, then, is that the situation is more complex than for conventional products. Green products must create the type of product performance benefits that will win in the marketplace in precisely the same way as conventional products. But to truly excel, a product must also overcome the types of special trade-offs that environmental sensitivity creates.

FORGET TRADE-OFFS! CHANGE THE BUSINESS MODEL   I'm in downtown Oakland talking with Joel Makower, whose GreenBiz Web site provides news, links, blogs, and a number of commercial offers. Makower didn't become the leading journalist in green business by being shy, but he knows how to diplomatically offer a contrasting perspective. He reminds me that it isn't all about trade-offs. Many green products win by changing the business model altogether. Fulfilling needs through services rather than with products helps. The key insight of car-sharing services is the notion that people really need mobility, not a large, costly asset that declines in value over time while sitting idle more than 90% of the time.[25] Similarly, we don't really need to own solar panels on our roofs—we just want the electricity. Even after the raft of tax incentives, solar panels still are a dicey economic bet for most homeowners. But instead of selling panels, SolarCity leverages a tight relationship with U.S. Bancorp to offer to lease a system that saves the homeowner money from day 1. Staples and SunEdison have partnered in a similar way, working with retail landlords who are willing to have SunEdison own the solar panels on stores and distribution centers and sell the power to Staples.[26] The same general idea is in force at Earth Friendly Moving, which rents out moving boxes (from recycled plastic), saving some 250 pounds of cardboard purchased for the typical home move.[27]

You also can change a business model by reconfiguring a supply chain, as Tom Szaky did with TerraCycle. Instead of treating waste as a problem, Szaky founded a company that makes products exclusively from garbage. He started with fertilizer created by worms chewing through compost, selling it in reclaimed Pepsi bottles. Now he's creating products from a variety of snack packages, from chip bags to yogurt containers to cereal boxes. Because his materials cost is negligible (and negative in some cases when individuals pay him to remove garbage), his products are priced below his competitors.[28] That's been fueling growth and attracting the attention of major retailers that are carrying his products.

Designing products from the ground up is a key to staking a claim with customers who care about social and environmental criteria. But forging an emotional link to customers can build loyalty and deepen the product experience for them.

Emotional Bonding with the Company: Creating Natural Attraction

The second key to customer value for green products is building an emotional bond to customers. Emotions are a key to understanding the behavior of consumers, as decades of marketing research shows.[29] They are separate from the rational, calculative dimensions of decision, such as cost per use, efficacy, and longevity. But it turns out that using feelings to guide purchasing is surprisingly rapid and consistent.[30] That is, it can be more effective to rely on the gut than on the gray matter when shopping.

This may well be one reason that green brands can be so powerful in markets: They elicit purchases based on emotion at least as much as those based on rational dimensions. Studies of so-called green marketing validate this emotional element. One robust result is that when consumers believe they are making a tangible difference on environmental or social criteria, this belief strengthens their commitments to products.[31] A particularly provocative result was that when consumers sense that the character of their values and a company's values overlap, their propensity to purchase increases.[32] Furthermore, this effect rises as the consumer's commitment to social responsibility rises.[33] Think back to those LOHAS consumers I described in the last chapter, and you can understand why emotional bonds can create customer value and continued loyalty.

So here again, we see that for mission-driven companies, the content of the emotional bond is distinctive because it is so closely linked to the selling company. It is surely true that some conventional companies create emotional bonds with consumers. In products from companies as diverse as Harley-Davidson and Rolex, the brand images resonate with delighted customers. And although the image for many conventional products frequently does reflect the company (and often its founders), for mission-driven companies the company and its story are a central part of creating emotional ties to customers.

The ways in which mission-driven companies create these emotional ties to customers are varied, but the best ones leverage values and even elicit customer input into product and company decisions.

DEVELOPING THE BRAND'S STORY   Chip Conley and Eric Friedenwald-Fishman, in their book *Marketing That Matters*, include a chapter titled "Emotion Trumps Data." They urge mission-driven companies to "connect with the heart first, and the mind second."[34] Their point is that the emotional bond with customers can forge the type of loyalty that product attributes simply cannot. A key to this emotional bond is communicating the company's vision for social and environmental change and especially its own story of specific actions. For mission-driven firms, this story can take on many plot lines. The Ben & Jerry's brand story has touch points that include the $5 correspondence course on making ice cream that Ben Cohen and Jerry Greenfield took, the company's progressive social programs, and its many innovative flavors. Think for a moment about how these elements each connect with powerful emotions:

- The $5 correspondence course: entrepreneurship, starting from humble roots, self-reliance.
- Progressive social programs: philanthropy, empathy, connectedness.
- Innovative flavors: innovation, creativity, individualism, fun.

The emotional bond does require opening up a bit about the roots of the company. Vincent Ben Avram launched Organically Happy, a Maryland Web-based business that sells natural cleaning supplies. A tall and burly 40-something father, Ben Avram had a defining moment when he was bathing his infant son and reviewed the ingredients of the soaps and shampoos he was using. His dissatisfaction led him to natural skin care products.[35] His fledgling Web site is professionally done, filled with carefully chosen products, and even includes "Lucy, our on-line esthetician and skincare maven." Like just about all Web sites, the Organically Happy site includes a tab titled "About Us." But the information there doesn't include any discussion of Ben Avram's aha moment. His disappointment with the site's low traffic can be the result of many influences, but having a more personal story about founding the company (perhaps with a photo of father and son) could help to create feelings of common emotion with potential customers by serving to put a human touch on his Web site.

Of course, you have to be willing to tell the story. Egg is a boutique advertising agency in Seattle. Led by longtime industry pro Marty McDonald, the agency works exclusively with sustainable brands and organizations. In their office near Pioneer Square, McDonald and partner Hilary Bromberg talked with me at length about the roots of what makes people buy. Bromberg, who studied neuroscience at Harvard and MIT, talked about the difficult of selling in 2009, as the world faced a "pullback from consumption."[36]

Bromberg is also the ad agent for Canadian cereal manufacturer Nature's Path, which is reticent about aggressively advertising that it is the last large producer not owned by a larger parent. The company has been relatively inwardly focused, and its slogan, "Nurturing people, nature, and spirit," wasn't very lighthearted for a company that was quirky, independent, and playful. The solution, for Bromberg, was to "give them permission to be themselves" in a way that underscored their uniqueness without being combative.[37] The solution was a simple tagline: "Eat well. Do good." If it works, Nature's Path will broaden its appeal to mainstream cereal fans while staying tight with core customers.

CONNECTING THE PRODUCT TO THE COMMON GOOD   As the marketing studies mentioned so far indicate, when consumers believe that they actually can affect a social or environmental cause with their purchasing behavior, they can bond with a company. It can be a matter of providing information at the point of purchase, so that consumers are educated about the effects the company has on its chosen points of impact. Accounting in the aggregate can help. Newman's Own certainly gets enormous mileage out the quarter-billion dollars the company has given to charities since its 1982 birth in Paul Newman's basement. But personalizing such impacts can create a stronger emotional punch.[38]

TOMS Shoes works to do just that. Since 2006, the Santa Monica–based seller of stylish casual shoes has had a straight-on social mission: For every pair of shoes sold, the company donates a pair of shoes to children in need.[39] One for one: simple and powerful. As its founder Blake Mycoskie parsimoniously states, "The design is not in the shoe but in the business model."[40] In 2008, TOMS Shoes expected to deliver 200,000 pairs of shoes to children in locations across the globe.[41] Led by Mycoskie, TOMS has been able to leverage this social mission to create a powerful brand. The choice for casual wearing by Keira Knightly, Renée Zellweger, and other Hollywood luminaries, TOMS misses no opportunity on its Web site and in its sales materials to connect a consumer's purchase with footwear for disadvantaged youth.

For many in the growing middle classes in newly emerging economies, supporting the common good means doing more for their compatriots. So some mission-driven companies in those settings stress local content and connect it to their brands. From its original location in Mexico City's trendy Condesa neighborhood, Sustenta Soluciones has grown into a fifteen-person company with annual sales of more than $1 million. The company works with companies that are launching campaigns to create memorable gifts made and grown by local artisans and farmers, frequently using high levels of recycled content.[42] Taking a page out of Freitag's book, Sustenta Soluciones took past advertising banners from Coca-Cola and fashioned them into bags, wallets, and even aprons while providing employment to indigenous Mazahuan women. The company provides seeds and seedlings from local trees to Banamex to be distributed by the company in a campaign to encourage customers to grow with the bank. It also engages in significant philanthropy—for example, donating a portion of proceeds from sales of beautifully packaged spices to Naturalia, a nongovernmental organization that promotes species protection in Mexico.

Sustenta's founder, Santiago Lobeira, returned to Mexico after receiving his MBA from Duke University, determined to create a meaningful business. In person, he's able to project a blend of confidence, caring, and competence that goes over well in meetings with business leaders. Lobeira and partner Manolo Ruiz have developed a brand and a set of relationships so powerful that companies are now coming to Sustenta with further questions about social and environmental issues. Branching into green communications and consulting may be possible, if Lobeira can avoid the greenwash he fears. As he says, "Everything comes from this positive energy" of giving something to fellow Mexicans.[43] If Sustenta can grow without endangering this asset, it will convert its bright prospects into greater profitability.

COCREATING SOCIAL VALUE   A new and potentially powerful way to create emotional ties to customers is to actually bring them into the process of channeling benefits to social and environmental causes. The idea of cocreation of value has its roots in the service literature,[44] although it has recently gained currency as a way to describe Internet models of serving customers.[45] The essential idea of cocreation is that customers are integrated into the process of product development and sales so that the final products actually reflect their real-time preferences. The idea benefits greatly from the Internet, which can break through the trade-off of "reach and richness," by presenting a more personalized experience to a large population.[46]

Cocreation can apply to social and environmental missions of companies, especially to the targets of their philanthropy.[47] An excellent example is the company Nau, a division of Horny Toad. Nau lost its independence because of operational issues and some marketing mistakes I'll discuss later. But one can predict that a part of Nau's social mission will be copied by others. Nau donates 5% of sales to charitable causes, an admirable practice consistent with a number of mission-driven companies.[48] Nau's innovation was to allow customers, at the point of purchase, to direct the donation created by their purchase to one of six charities. Thus the glow associated with the company's philanthropy is a little brighter for customers. Recall that studies show that emotional ties to customers are strongest when they feel that the company's social and environmental policies are consistent with their own. What better way to forge this link than to empower them to set a small slice of company policy at the checkout stand?

Web-based businesses are particularly well suited to this task. And they can push the envelope even further. For example, when a customer purchases carbon offsets from CarbonFund.org, a special screen cues them to select the type of project that will be used to create the offset. Support reforestation? Then have your funds used to plant a new stand of trees. Other options include energy efficiency and renewables development.[49] The use of customer choice avoids other, perhaps more difficult approaches, which might include surveys that permit well-meaning but opportunistic representatives of causes to "stuff the ballot box" to have their organizations funded. Employing customer cocreation in these ways can create an emotional bond (especially when the customer receives notice of the exact number of trees planted for their particular offset purchase), and the interaction works to forge an emotional link by involving customers directly and specifically. Such customers are also more likely to answer surveys and provide other information that permits a company to serve them with greater specificity and understand their motivations. As in other settings, this customer intelligence is highly prized and can lead to a competitive advantage for a mission-driven company.[50]

THE RISKS OF EMOTIONAL ATTACHMENT   The emotional side of developing customer value has a dark side, however, one that companies must respect. When individuals invest their personal commitments in companies that they see as representing their higher-order values, a rapid and harsh backlash can occur when they smell hypocrisy and dishonesty on the part of companies.[51] The media are full of truth police, and although popular outlets can build up mission-driven companies, they can also expose gaps between claims and reality. The issue for marketing is clear: Doubts about the authenticity of the company or its initiatives can lead to customer resentment and even organized boycotts.

This doubt then presents mission-driven companies with an important challenge. They must somehow communicate their marketing message while avoiding a chin-jutting approach that can set the stage for a backlash. They must also be smart in how and where they present their goods to potential customers.

CHOOSING THE RIGHT CHANNELS

Choosing where to sell can be almost as critical as choosing how to sell. Mission-driven companies that have succeeded were able to get products to consumers, and not just any segment of the consuming public, as Julie Lewis discovered. Several principles of selling can be identified, and I illustrate them with examples.

Meeting Customers on Their Turf: Finding the Right Customers and Avoiding the Wrong Ones

It's no secret that the Internet is a method for reaching out to customers far and wide. That's especially true at Dolphin Blue, a seller of environmentally preferable office supplies. Based in the not terribly green city of Dallas, Texas, the owner of Dolphin Blue, Tom Kemper, relies not at all on local sales.[52] Instead he has built an Internet-based business model that is able to outcompete the large, slow-moving giants in the industry. Because the bulk of this market is almost exclusively price based, Kemper is able to operate at its fringe, catering to customers who desire recycled paper, envelopes, and other accoutrements of the modern office. Essentially a network company, Dolphin Blue relies on a constellation of distributors that can bring to customers the products Kemper identifies as meeting his standards. At $2 million in sales, Kemper is clearly flying well under the radar of the big boys of the industry. But the company's annual growth suggests that Kemper's approach to order fulfillment allows him to provide customer value in ways that offset the higher costs of his products.

Freitag's approach also matches this strategy. It sells through boutiques with names like Modern Artifacts (San Francisco, California), Area 51 (Wellington, New Zealand), and Mr. Goodfun (Zermat, Switzerland). The choice of just which boutiques to sell through is a topic of intense discussion at Freitag. According to marketing director Filippo Castagna, when the advance team sees brands such as Prada and Gucci, that's a "red light." A boutique near an American Apparel outlet, by comparison, gets Freitag's motor running.[53]

As important as it is to find the right customers, mission-driven companies must also pay attention to avoid the wrong ones. Partly because of their own ambitions and partly because their venture capitalists pushed them to do so, Deja Shoe, the maker of footwear from 100% recycled materials, took on any retailer that wanted to stock its trendy recycled shoes. It sold through many outlets where one would expect the shoes to meet receptive eyes, such as The Nature Company and Whole Earth Provisions.[54] And when Nordstrom's and Bloomingdale's asked for the line, Julie Lewis, the founder of Deja Shoe, and Scott McGregor, a longtime industry professional whom Lewis recruited to operate the company, jumped at the opportunity. As it turned out, they should have been more cautious. All start-ups have problems, but manufacturing the first line of shoes from all-recycled content created a batch of peculiar challenges. Larger retailers simply were not terribly compassionate about Deja Shoe's predicaments, leading McGregor to observe that if a mission-driven company is going to make mistakes, it is better to do so "in a limited distribution with a consumer base that is sensitive to what you are trying to accomplish and will be forgiving of those mistakes."[55] By starting out large, Lewis and McGregor had to "bet the farm," and unfortunately poor sales by conventional retailers contributed to their demise.[56]

Expanding Channels: The Right Direction and Tempo

For products that are at the cutting edge of style, just as for their conventional counterparts, there can be a certain value in growing more slowly than they could. Freitag's deliberately measured growth in outlets keeps products "just a little bit hard to get," like the other hip brands in the marketplace.[57] A more cautious expansion also permits the company to go further with internal funding. Because a leading reason for selling equity in firms is to fuel such growth, a slower pace can also help a company retain a greater degree of independence and avoid some of the governance issues I'll address in Chapter 9. The rapid rollout by Deja Shoe was also in part dictated by its funders, led by several conventional venture capital firms.

Measured growth is not generally associated with meeting the ambitious targets they demand in return for equity stakes.

It is also important to validate the channels that are used, especially when distance to markets and transportation are involved. At Nau, an innovative method of fulfillment that the company thought was carefully validated turned out to create tension when it was rolled out. Here's how it worked. The company had a dazzling Web site through which it sold widely. But it also created a number of "Web-front" stores that had a limited supply of its goods. For example, for a given sweater it might have a small and medium in one color and a large and extra large in another. Thus a customer was able to decide which sweater color and size he or she desired. If the right combination was in the store, the customer could take it home. But all customers were encouraged to order through the Web site and have the good shipped to their home. A 10% discount added an inducement.

But customers may have wondered how such an arrangement could make ecological sense, adding to Nau's difficulty in establishing its green credentials. The company had conducted extensive studies to validate that the combination of the efficiencies of more centralized distribution and smaller store footprints actually offset the impact of shipping to customer homes. But it had not succeeded in *communicating* these benefits to a group of customers that can be skeptical of product claims. This episode thus spotlights the importance of communication in the world of mission-driven companies.

360-DEGREE COMMUNICATIONS

For all companies, but especially those that sell to end consumers, communicating with customers, stakeholders, and the public at large is paramount. I've addressed the importance of the company story, but it is also critical to have a clear strategy for conveying this information. Here are some touch points of effective communication for mission-driven companies.

Don't Forget That the Product or Service Matters . . .

Do bear in mind that ultimately the product or service being sold must meet the customers' needs in a traditional sense, and a central thrust of communications strategy must reflect that. The United Kingdom's Innocent is a company devoted to making and selling great smoothies and other related drinks. Its Web site features (in an understated manner) its social and environmental responsibility initiatives.[58] But the company's main thrust is to reinforce the quality of its products, which are made with high-quality natural ingredients. The same product-first strategy goes for Patagonia, where the high performance of its clothing and equipment is elemental.

. . . But It's the Social and Environmental Credentials That Secure Free Publicity

Nonetheless, the company's story does matter. I noted earlier the importance of telling the company's story. And to the extent that the company's mission can attract free advertising, literally thousands of dollars of expenditures can be avoided. In 2007 alone, TOMS Shoes was able to land articles in *People, Time, GQ, Teen Vogue, Women's Wear Daily,* and *O: The Oprah Magazine,* among others.[59] Later, TOMS and Mycoskie were featured in an AT&T national advertising campaign. In every single case, the company's social mission was highlighted. The social mission also was a key factor in TOMS beating out 330 nominees to win the Cooper-Hewitt People's Design Award in 2007.[60]

Blogs: The Power of Real-Time Communications

All companies know that for many if not most of their customers, the Web site *is* their company. Customers expect to be able to locate information about products, compare alternatives, and make purchases in a seamless, hassle-free way. But for mission-driven companies, blogs are essential to maintain a dialogue with companies, customers, stakeholders, and the public. The rise of blogs as a method of real-time communication is important for four reasons.[61] Blogs and other open forums can (1) create dialogue that can personalize a company and build trust with customers, (2) elicit feedback and new ideas from customers and stakeholders, (3) lead to viral effects that promote brands, and (4) provide a method for addressing threats to a company's reputation and otherwise address criticism. These advantages are real, and an examination of blogs maintained by mission-driven companies and observers illustrates them with some specificity. As we'll see, some elements of blogging match those of conventional firms, whereas others reflect the importance of maintaining and even defending the social and environmental reputations of companies.

Customer blogs and other open forums can produce a stream of information that tells a company about its product, how it's being used, and what social and environmental issues its customers care about. gDiapers uses a Facebook site where parents ("gMums" in the company's Australian lingo) can exchange messages.[62] In November 2008, a run through the site revealed two potential opportunities for the company from postings: entering the Canadian market and making a larger size for big babies. On the one hand, this information might have come from letters or phone calls, but on the other hand, both of those may require more effort than parents with infants can afford. But another topic demonstrates how blogs are so much more valuable than traditional modes of feedback. The gDiapers Facebook site also revealed that the company's products were challenged by "heavy wetters." Here, the advantage of the blog comes though, because unlike the one-way or two-way communication of traditional modes, a forum is created where other parents and gDiapers addressed the issue together. And here again we see an advantage of the blog: Compared to something formal that might come back from a company on letterhead from an impersonal source, the informality of the blog serves to encourage involvement on a more equal basis.

Blogs, because they are more spontaneous and less rule bound, allow for rapid reaction to ideas, events, and new information. In mid-2007, Joel Makower's GreenBiz.com posted a story about a report from Climate Counts that rated "major consumer brands on their climate commitments and performance."[63] Within days, comments were posted by *Fortune* writer Marc Gunther and by Dave Stangis and Bob Langert, who headed up corporate responsibility at Intel and McDonald's, respectively. This type of instantaneous forum provides real-time reactions to news and can identify emerging issues that create opportunities for mission-driven companies.

The rise of blogs can stimulate viral marketing that also can promote brands. The story of Shayne McQuade provides an example.[64] McQuade invented a backpack called the Voltaic, with built-in solar panels that let hikers keep their cell phones, iPods, and other gadgets powered up. As part of his prelaunch plan, McQuade asked a friend who ran a green design blog called Treehugger to mention the product. After seeing the product on Treehugger, bloggers at CoolHunting gave the Voltaic a plug, followed by Gizmodo, a gadget-oriented site. The expanding network of viewers pulled out their charge cards, and a surprised and not particularly prepared McQuade saw orders start popping up in his inbox.

Seventh Generation's blog, Inspired Protagonist, is worth viewing for seeing how the site is used to anticipate and address criticism. Most of the company-provided blog entries come directly from Jeffrey Hollender, and in October 2008 the blog featured topics that ranged from favorite books to initiatives by conventional and mission-driven companies to workplace democracy to reflections on the twentieth anniversary of the company.[65] Perhaps most provocative was a posting by Hollender discussing his decision to sell Seventh Generation products through Marketside, a chain of small and upscale stores created by none other than Wal-Mart. The blog was issued the weekend that Marketside debuted with four stores in Arizona and explained in terms that went well beyond a press release (which surely would have been the wrong mode) the thinking behind the decision and how Seventh Generation viewed Wal-Mart's corporate citizenry. According to the blog, this was a difficult decision for Seventh Generation, which knew it would get plenty of heat for a decision to do business with a company it had long considered a social and environmental bottom feeder. One commenter ranted:

It's not so much that any company's decision to work with another for (perceived) mutual gain is at issue—that should be protected. It's just that your latest statements continue to stink of self-righteousness and worse. To think that you actually believe that "I . . . have worked to help make (Wal-Mart) better" is laughable, and positioning the fact that your products are not in their supercenters as a process for socially responsible action to "help us decide whether we should even think about taking a next step" is dubious.[66]

Ouch. Should the posting be treated as a random case or evidence of a serious issue management challenge? Arguably, it really doesn't matter because the key is that the engagement has taken place on Seventh

Generation's blog. And by virtue of that location, the nature of the posting must be viewed alongside other entries that, by comparison, support the company, such as this one:

Sounds like Marketside is similar to Fresh 'n' Easy, and would be an appropriate fit. While Wal-Mart's supply chain and facilities management activities are nothing more than waste reduction and applied lean thinking, I do applaud them on their expanded category mgmt for sustainable products. Any retailer should do the same. My main problem with distributing to Wal-Mart stores is their perpetual penny pinching on everyday suppliers' prices and the dangerous situation it places on them as production volume % to WM increases.[67]

Thus, as the reader scrolls through the comments, both positive and negative reactions are posted, guaranteeing at least some exposure to differing viewpoints. A further advantage of working through such an issue within a company's Web site is that it may restrict critics from filling the blogosphere with attacks that can cause enormous damage to a brand.[68] Regardless of whether or not one believes Seventh Generation sold out with its decision to do business with Wal-Mart, if the dialogue takes place on its blog, the company is far more likely to get its side of the story out. Hollender chose not to respond to the previous messages, which can be a mistake. Even if the posting is extremely negative, it deserves some response, if for no other reason than to defend Hollender's assertion that he influenced Wal-Mart's thinking.[69]

TAKEAWAYS FOR ENTREPRENEURS
A lot of ideas have been presented in this chapter, with much to guide enterprising individuals who are interested in mission-driven companies. A couple of key threads are woven through all these ideas.

Product First
A product is a bundle of attributes that provide value to customers. One can't pick and choose these attributes, selecting the price of a Kia, the drivetrain of a Prius, and the styling of a Porsche. Products of mission-driven companies present a new source of value to the customer, but if that socially or environmentally oriented attribute comes bundled with other

characteristics that underperform compared to conventional counterparts, it can be problematic. And consumers, even responsible ones, aren't crazy about making trade-offs to purchase products.

And not all trade-offs are created equal. It's most difficult to overcome lower performance, to the point where it is inadvisable to pursue such products without a substantial social or environmental payoff—and even then the product may be doomed. Somewhat less difficult to overcome is inconvenience, but given the lack of time that characterizes modern society, the same caveat applies there. If the product meets or is superior to conventional offerings across all its attributes, there may be hope for capturing a higher price by means of the company and product effects discussed earlier and through savvy marketing.

The companies described here have worked to overcome these trade-offs, and in so doing, they have created market space for themselves. One takeaway is that a product should not leave the workbench until it can "win in a white box" against conventional wares. In the best of all worlds, products of mission-driven companies embody no trade-offs, not even carrying a higher price. As I noted, one way to leapfrog trade-offs is to rethink the business model. A prime approach is to find ways to succeed by envisioning ways to meet needs through providing services rather than by selling physical products.

But in a highly competitive marketplace, no matter what the product or service, a company must build its brand.

Psychographics, Not Demographics
Richard Seireeni, in his book *The Gort Cloud*, advances the idea that it's a mistake to look at demographic categories such as age, sex, and educational level.[70] Focusing on such categories is a blunt approach that can exclude as many individuals as it mistakenly includes. Instead, psychographics, which directs attention to how individuals think and behave, is far more important for marketing purposes. To use a simple example, it may be valuable to advertise in publications read by higher-income individuals living on the West and East Coasts and in the Midwest. But it would be far more valuable to sell through outlets whose readership is typified by dynamic and socially aware individuals who are unafraid of change and innovation.

Thinking in terms of psychographics also helps us to understand why stories are so important to the marketing of products and services offered by mission-driven companies. These stories resonate with psychographic variables such as attitudes and values—which can create the types of bonds I've noted here. Further, many customers of mission-driven companies are highly involved individuals who are more likely to volunteer in their communities and engage in environmental activism. They are more likely to read package covers and learn online about companies with which they interact. LOHAS consumers are significantly more likely to use online social networks.[71] That's why high-involvement modes like blogs and chat rooms are extremely important for mission-driven companies. Although the individuals who participate in these platforms may be a tiny percentage of customers, they are enormously valuable as a way to assess a company's social and environmental performance.

A CONCLUDING THOUGHT

Developing and marketing any product is a challenge. In this chapter I've tried to spotlight some of the unique and particularly challenging issues that are likely to emerge in mission-driven companies. Some of the points of contention can serve as a diagnostic for one's view of the mission-driven movement. The difficulties in obtaining clear distinctions between green and brown can be viewed as perplexing, frustrating, and even a point of entry for hypocritical products and product claims. But they can also be viewed as signs of maturity, as indications that the move toward more social and environmental responsibility does not always cross bright lines and that society and enterprise still have much to learn. This doesn't diminish the tremendous opportunities in the marketplace. But it does suggest that each company must strike its own balance between aggressive product claims and failure to fully leverage product and company stories that can win customers.

5 CRAFTING THE MISSION-DRIVEN ORGANIZATION
The Human Dimension

You can feel the pulse of the city while striding down U Street in Washington, D.C. Walk up the stairs from the Metro, past historic Lincoln Theatre, where Duke Ellington, Paul Robeson, and Billie Holiday once performed, and on the next street you'll come upon a nondescript doorway with an intercom for visitors to use. Upstairs are the offices of Community IT Innovators.[1]

Founder David Deal seems an unlikely entrepreneur in a neighborhood that is still home to a number of originally African American Baptist and Catholic churches.[2] Born in North Carolina, Deal married into a Mennonite family and adopted its religious faith. His gentle manner, more sensitive than streetwise, would seem out of place in most urban settings. Yet here he has built an admirable small business based on providing information technology services to nonprofit organizations.

His company went through an unusual rite of passage: It originated as the philanthropic arm of a larger IT firm and was spun off when times grew tight. When he was offered the opportunity to strike out on his own by purchasing the division that he had managed, Deal took a chance and rechristened his new company Community IT Innovators—CITI for short. Through 2008, the company was growing 20% annually, making money, and enjoying minimal turnover. In early 2009 CITI was strong enough financially to double its line of credit (at that point still untapped) and explore new opportunities.[3]

But wait a minute.

How could a company like CITI possibly assemble and keep the IT talent necessary to run a viable business? IT pros, after all, work in a field marked by intense competition for talent, high salaries, and rapid turnover. And how would Deal replace the cross-subsidies of a successful parent company? Appreciating how he addressed these critical issues by keeping close to his mission is an instructive—even noble—lesson in entrepreneurship. It illustrates some of the management challenges and opportunities that we'll explore in this chapter. Here, I focus on the organizational issues confronting managers, including managing human resources, making decisions, and growing the company.

Before touching on these points, however, it's important to start with the values on which a company is founded. Values form a DNA strand that is woven into the fabric of the organization.

VALUES DRIVE THE CULTURE

Executives use the term *values* frequently but often without the benefit of a clear definition. Lynn Sharp Paine, of Harvard Business School, provides a definition that finds a bright line between what values are and what they are not.

Values are not a "management tool" or a special type of management system. . . . Nor are they bits of ethereal matter. . . . [They are] beliefs, aims, and assumptions that undergird the enterprise and guide its management in developing strategies, structures, processes, and policies. They constitute an "organizational infrastructure" that gives a company its distinctive character and ethos—its moral personality.[4]

Looking at a couple of sets of values from mission-driven companies will help.[5] First, there are the values of ShoreBank Corporation, which is based in Chicago, Illinois. The company, launched in 1973 to overcome pervasive discrimination in residential lending, lists these as its values: integrity and excellence, respect and inclusion, "collaborative and local," a triple bottom line, and innovation.[6] Green Mountain Coffee Roasters, of

Burlington, Vermont, lists no less than fifteen principles, including a passion for coffee, sustainability, appreciation of differences, business success, a vibrant workplace, and world benefit.[7]

In these and other examples, values go well beyond the social and environmental elements that are critical differentiators of these companies. With respect to values that are reflected in internal operations, it's important here to recognize that mission-driven company values support employees and seek to build robust cultures. Some of these values include work-life balance, fun, individuality, and spirituality.

Let's go back to the question originally posed. How is it that David Deal attracts and keeps employees? Actually, it's pretty simple: He gives them their lives back by sticking to a forty-hour workweek. Work-life balance is a keystone value of his company. To appreciate that this value contributes to his mission, consider that the typical IT job involves enormous pressure to complete complex jobs, often in a time-compressed world. Burnout is common—one reason that the average person stays in a given IT job only eighteen months, according to Deal.[8] Although there are plenty of IT professionals who would willingly put in hours reminiscent of the Industrial Revolution, there are plenty who would gladly trade off the higher salaries that go with that world for the slower pace at CITI. According to Deal, the typical IT consulting firm expects $150,000 in revenue per employee annually. For CITI, the amount is about half that number. Naturally, this means lower salaries must go along with lower hours. But the payoff is a workforce that experiences far less turnover than its competitors. Because Deal's business model calls for steady, sustainable growth, he is able to maintain a workplace based on a key value of promoting personal growth while limiting burnout.

As the CITI example beautifully illustrates, values, if consistently reflected in decisions, can create a unique and supportive culture that can fuel financial, social, and environmental success. For example, if "respect and inclusion" is a primary value at Chicago's ShoreBank Corporation, then the organization can attract employees who are good listeners and who appreciate the importance of hearing arguments from all sides. This then contributes to a culture of collaboration that will serve the long-term interests of the company by reducing interpersonal friction and encouraging consideration of alternative ways to make a loan feasible. By contrast, lending institutions that do not share ShoreBank's values are more likely to house cultures in which standard operating procedures are the bible.

Similarly, the value of "world benefit" at Green Mountain Coffee Roasters means that the company, in order to contribute to its culture, must draw new employees who believe in the importance of changing supply chain practices to promote human development in growing regions. To strengthen its culture, Green Mountain tracks not only the amount of fair trade coffee that it sources but also how many of its employees have visited coffee-growing communities, making the latter a metric in its responsibility reporting.[9] Surely encouraging such visits strengthens the link from values to culture.

That a strong company culture can then drive its economic performance is not just a theory. Studies by researchers at Harvard Business School found that the stronger the culture, the higher the economic performance.[10] A follow-up study from MIT found that companies with stronger cultures had more stable performance over time.[11] Although no study has considered how the cultural implications of a social and environmental mission influence the triple bottom line, I believe that values and culture can be a magnet to attract great applicants, help assess the fit for potential hires, and facilitate personal growth through empowerment.

THE IMPORTANCE OF KEEPING
VALUES IN BALANCE

Developing and inculcating strong values is enormously important, but so is making sure that they don't take on a dysfunctional character.

Remember the Soup Nazi on the television show *Seinfeld*? The character was based on Al Yeganeh and his soup kitchen on West 55th Street in Manhattan. The Soup Nazi's expectations for customers were exceeded only by their love for his soups. One misstep in ordering proved you unworthy and . . . "No soup for you!" The episode illustrates one organizational pathology that can materialize when mission-driven companies build cultures in which one set of values dominates others.

Patagonia learned this the hard way in 1989. The company always had ties to environmental stewardship, but perhaps its most central core value was a commitment to functional excellence in its products.[12] Style was well down the list of imperatives. A culture that grew out of these values tended to see clothing in a similar light as equipment: to be designed first for strenuous use and extreme weather.

This may have been the reason that some in Patagonia took umbrage when a broader, far less thrill-seeking class of consumers began wearing their products. This came to a head when President George Bush appeared on the cover of *People* magazine wearing a Patagonia jacket.[13] This was a manifestation of the mainstreaming of customers that came with the increasing success of the company, a broadening of the customer base that did not sit well with all its employees.[14] Kristine McDivott, a Patagonia executive at the time, said, "Part of the problem is that some of us in the company have actual disdain for this ever-increasing segment of the customer base."[15] Like some of the customers of the Soup Nazi, yuppies were unworthy of such performance gear! An aggressive downsizing resulting from a crisis of organization in the company served to put this issue to rest and reminded employees that yuppies who bought Patagonia products for their look also delivered bottom-line stability. The lesson for managers: Maintain balance among the values to which the company ascribes, one of which must be to remain financially strong.

HOW PEOPLE AND THE MISSION SUPPORT EACH OTHER

Mark Albion's book *Making a Life, Making a Living* is an honest, poignant, and ultimately inspirational account of how individuals overcome the contradictions of living and working by different sets of values.[16] In the book, Albion chronicles case after case of people who got fed up with conventional business and struck out in completely different directions. Many started their own companies, to try to bring their work life into balance with their values.

No one should doubt that crafting a strong business model is supremely important to an entrepreneur. But entrepreneurs who also can master the human side of the management equation can attract committed individuals who are loyal to their company and highly productive in their positions. It is they who implement business plans and carry ideas into practice. It is they on whom success ultimately depends.

A simple model of how a company can succeed through its people appears in Figure 5.1. By building culture on a bedrock of mission-related values, companies can attract, hire, and empower great employees. The organizational effects of such practices are displayed both in traditional organizational outcomes, such as lower turnover, and in triple bottom line effects such as the company's social performance. Naturally, these organizational and triple bottom line outcomes then buttress the company's values.

The reader will note that if the environmental and social impacts are removed from the model, the result looks similar to a model that might be in use for a conventional business. The provocative issue is how having goals that go beyond simple financial returns to explicitly include social and environmental goals generates intrinsic rewards that are unique to mission-driven companies. An intrinsic reward is "a natural reward associated with performing a task or activity for its own sake," according to a leading management textbook.[17] Many intrinsic rewards appear in mission-driven companies. They might include being part of an organization that tries to balance financial, environmental, and social goals; creating products with lower social and environmental costs; feeling a sense of accomplishment from meeting social and environmental goals; and knowing that along with others in the organization, you may have sacrificed

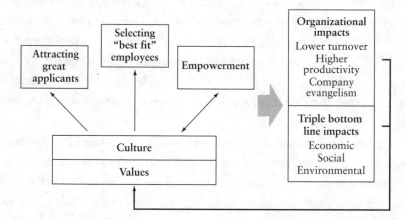

FIGURE 5.1
Building a mission-driven organization through people.

some of the compensation you could receive elsewhere for working in a company whose goals more closely match yours. Intrinsic rewards can be contrasted with the more familiar extrinsic rewards, such as pay and other compensation that is tangible, visible to others, and dependent on working effectively.[18] The connection between an authentic mission-driven strategy and intrinsic rewards that galvanize commitment to the company is one of those key human resource advantages that these companies use to create high-performing organizations.

A run through the model will illustrate its applicability to mission-driven companies. In doing so, I'll leverage underlying research that has revealed consistent relationships among work-related factors, but most of the argument is built from my many observations of and interviews and interactions with mission-driven companies. The resulting framework is broadly consistent with human resource management practice but reflects the unique challenges and opportunities faced by mission-driven companies.

Attracting Great Applicants

The process of attracting good job candidates begins with their giving a second thought to applying to a company. This second thought is frequently based on the reputation of a company. But does a strong reputation for social and environmental responsibility elicit better job seekers?

Fortunately for mission-driven companies, this question has been the motivation for several studies that collectively have revealed a clear answer. A couple of studies are worth noting, because they were planned and executed with the care necessary for publication in top journals. In 1997, two University of Missouri researchers analyzed how corporate social performance influenced how prospective employees felt about a company.[19] The management researchers sampled 633 large companies that were rated on corporate social responsibility by Kinder, Lydenberg, and Domini, a leading social investment firm. They found that the higher the scores, the more attractive the firm was judged to be as a place to work, even after accounting for the company's profitability and size. A follow-up study published in 2000 found an even stronger influence of corporate social responsibility on the intention of individuals to seek employment with better rated companies.[20]

A completely different study was completed by marketing scholars at Boston University.[21] In this study, the investigators worked to isolate the effect of corporate social responsibility performance on intentions to seek employment with companies. To accomplish this, the researchers surveyed students (and potential job seekers) after an announcement of a major philanthropic gift by a company to their university was made. Students aware of the gift reported a greater likelihood of desire to work for the company than those who were unaware of the gift.[22]

For our purposes, it would be better to have studies that focus on small and medium-size companies. Even more important, it would be preferable to have studies that analyze where job seekers actually landed, rather than jobs they might take. But the results of the studies are consistent and highly plausible. All else being equal, people *do* prefer to work in companies that promote not only profits but also loftier social and environmental goals.

The managerial implications of these studies are clear: Wherever and whenever a company is looking for employees, it should include reference to elements of its mission-driven qualities in all literature used in hiring. Further, it should use the right outlets to advertise for employees for its more senior positions, which may expand the applicant pool. Many of these outlets are online, sponsored by publications such as *Sustainable Industries* (until recently *Sustainable Industries Journal*) (sustainableindustries. com) or theme organizations like the Social Venture Network (svn.org). Of course, a mission-driven company should not ignore traditional industries, which may have people with the right values who are ready to leave positions in conventional companies. Josh Hinerfeld, president of Organically Grown Company, a major Northwest distributor of organic foods, was plucked from the food distribution arm of PepsiCo. He was ready to take a job that reflected his personal values, and he was able to bring with him decades of experience in the food industry. A search that simply focused on the mission-driven community would have missed him.

Selecting "Best Fit" Employees

When reviewing applications and candidates, the role of company values is critical in the selection process. In the many interviews with company executives that were part of the research for this book, I asked whether they had ever passed up a more traditionally qualified candidate for another whose values were more consistent with those of the company. The answer was always yes. Even if candidates have the right educational background, for example, they are wrong for a company if they don't understand its greater mission. Just ask Reto Ringger, until recently the CEO of Sustainable Asset Management (SAM) in Zurich. SAM created a proprietary system for assessing the environmental risks and opportunities of a large group of global companies. It manages a number of specialty funds using this information.[23] Being in the finance field, there is a clear pecking order of MBA programs whose graduates seek jobs in the investment field. Yet SAM does not always make the conventionally predictable choice, as Ringger points out. The difference between working for SAM and other firms is how SAM's decision making reflects passion for the natural environment.[24] Absent that, it's pointless to go further in an interview.

But how does an interviewer judge whether a candidate's values resonate with the company? Lots of ways. The methods cover a wide range. Dave Williams is CEO of ShoreBank Pacific, ShoreBank's West Coast offspring. Williams is a longtime Oregonian who seems to personify the state's values. Rugged looking even in a necktie, he's in the business of assessing risk, whether his attention is directed to making loans during business hours or negotiating rock cliffs on the weekends. ShoreBank pursues relationships with companies to which it lends, requiring commitments to the triple bottom line but following through with assistance where necessary. The company has deep ties to the values of Oregonians, which include a life that is more intimately interwoven with the natural world than many other locations. When interviewing, Williams has a basic system that serves him well. He simply asks what an applicant is doing on the next weekend.[25] The answers transition conversation into a discussion of how the applicant sees his or her connection to the outdoor environment. By appreciating their passions, Williams can better ascertain whether the applicants complement ShoreBank's mission.

KEEN Footwear's Kate Lee, who directs global human resources for the hip casual footwear manufacturer, takes a different tack. The company has grown in giant steps from a standing start in 2003. But from its birth, it has instituted policies for social and environmental engagement.[26] Now institutionalized as its Hybrid Life program, KEEN maintains a Web site that collects stories of individuals nominated for awards that the company funds.[27] In addition to two days of volunteer activities sponsored by the company, each employee receives five paid days to volunteer for just about any cause they support. KEEN works to weave this commitment into its brand, and this "mission-driven mentality," argues Lee, under-girds its product strategy and its selection of workers.[28] But rather than probe applicants as Williams does, Lee prefers to see if they'll initiate a dialogue that probes her about KEEN's level of commitment. She wants employees who display a high degree of expectations about the company's social and environmental programs. Occasionally, that won't be the case: "If they ask us why we have a volunteer program, they're telling us they don't understand our culture."

High expectations reflect a commitment by employees to push the company toward higher levels of social and environmental achievement. This type of positive feedback is shown in Figure 5.1, where these practices influence values and culture.

A more structured approach to selection is taken by David Deal at CITI. He will usher potential employees into a room where the following is posted on a wall, and then discuss the applicant's reaction.

Community IT Innovators' Dream
We are Community IT Innovators, a beacon for socially responsible business,
and a catalyst for the transformation toward a loving, equitable, and non-
violent society.
We dream of working side-by-side
as one engaged team of gifted and caring experts,
in a company that esteems a healthy work-life balance
and promotes sustainable business practices.
We foster a collaborative culture,
encourage mutual respect and dialogue amidst diversity,
and nurture leadership, innovation, and professional development in all
employees.

We dream of a work environment that is diverse, physically inviting, and spiritually nourishing. Our workplace is filled with joy, constantly transforming individuals and organizations, both in and out of work hours. We grow only in service to our dream: the creation of a more just and peaceful world.[29]

Recall that this is an information technology consulting firm. The boundless aspirations in the statement are not those normally associated with a crowd known more for pocket protectors than Peace Pops. On the other hand, CITI's proposition to potential employees is so radically different from the typical employer that there are bound to be some IT professionals who view it as the type of company they've been waiting to work for all along. And because CITI leads with its values and not compensation or office size or some other conventional comparator, the company offers the chance for an emotional bond right off the bat.

A vow to recognize a wider set of stakeholders than the stereotypical group of conventional business—investors, customers, suppliers, and employees—is true of all mission-driven companies. For this reason, employees may have urges that are often found in nonprofits but that are reflected in the company's values. Gregory Dees, who has been studying nonprofit enterprises for many years, sees a continuum that runs from "purely philanthropy" to "purely commercial" among the greater group of social enterprises.[30] The key is that mission-driven companies, although much closer to the commercial end of the spectrum, nonetheless seek employees who are energized by their social mission in many of the same ways that employees in the nonprofit world are. Thus, if there were an optimal job candidate for the prototypical mission-driven company, it would be someone who combined the passion for social change with an acute knowledge of the essentials of effective management.

The Salary Question

The issue of compensation is a difficult one to approach when speaking with interviewees, but it is clearly important for mission-driven companies. Some, like Switzerland's Freitag, do actually pay below prevailing wages and believe that their workplace conditions make the company attractive (sure enough, one manager who left for a raise at a large corporation was soon calling

Daniel Freitag to try to get his old job back).[31] When interviewed, though, most other companies reported salaries within sight of industry norms.

But all good managers know that the human resource issue does not begin and end with salaries. Or even salaries plus benefits. This is because good managers know in their heads—and in their hearts—that the contribution they receive from an employee must be a part of the equation. And the contribution of employees in mission-driven companies may well be higher than their conventional counterparts. Although there are no studies that can confirm this, reports from these companies suggest that turnover is lower. When all the costs of turnover, which include recruiting, training, and other start-up expenses, are added up, replacing an employee may cost close to one year's pay.[32]

Then there's the productivity side of the equation. Lower turnover means higher productivity. But there's another source of productivity for these firms. For a given wage, an argument can be made that mission-driven companies will attract more productive employees. Evidence presented here supports this assertion. This enhanced productivity may originate from an employee bringing a higher level of skills or experience to the job for a given level of compensation, but it also can be rooted in the warm glow that comes from being immersed in a positive culture.

Empowerment
Let the cooks cook!

"We are not interactive with our tasks," protests Grace Pae, criticizing larger companies that routinize food preparation down to an act of mass production.[33] Pae started Artemis Foods in 2000 in Portland, Oregon, with a commitment to a catering service that stressed local foods, organically sourced whenever possible, and sustainable business practices. The company, which has grown to include a small café, is the type of place where a mild case of dyspepsia strikes when a review of ingredients for "localness" shows that pumpkin seeds, a current favorite for a crunchy, nutritious salad additive, actually are grown in China. Although organic, they'll have to be replaced with seeds from local farms or a different type of seed.

At a company like Artemis Foods, cooks are allowed to experiment, to create new dishes that might make it onto a menu already filled with

creative entrees that often name the local farm where the ingredients originated (e.g., "Roasted delicata squash and Rogue Creamery blue cheese
salad, with Millennium Farms greens, pine nuts, and horseradish apple
cider vinaigrette").[34] Many cooks, even those working in companies the
size of Artemis, simply aren't allowed to explore their ideas about what
might be an exciting new dish made with local ingredients. It's easy to see
how the ability to have an impact helps Artemis Foods stay on the knife's
edge of the local food movement: Cooks are already working under constraints that conventional caterers may soon face. If the movement for increasing local content accelerates, Artemis Foods will be well positioned
by empowering its cooks to be cooks.

This story is a classic illustration of workplace empowerment. Although
this term is tossed around, academics have worked to define and study
empowerment carefully. Working on early ideas about how to carefully
describe empowerment, a University of California study was able to show
that there are four elements to the concept:

1. Self-determination: an employee's sense of having choice and autonomy in meeting their responsibilities.
2. Impact: the degree to which an employee can influence strategic,
   administrative, or operating outcomes at work.
3. Meaning: a fit between the work role and an employee's value
   system.
4. Competence: employees' belief in their ability to perform their work
   with skill.[35]

To varying degrees, the Artemis Foods story illustrates all these elements. Each supports the others, and together they produce a self-sustaining
blend that generates empowerment. The model does not mandate that
all ingredients of empowerment be present, but it is easy to see how having gaps in one or more elements will impair this goal. For example, if
an employee's role in the company does not match his or her values, this
mismatch can defuse commitment to the job and the organization.[36] This
lessened commitment could be manifested in detachment from processes
that can affect outcomes, one of the other elements.

Many mission-driven companies favor a strong form of promoting impact, by introducing meaningful workplace democracy. South Mountain Company, a construction business on Martha's Vineyard, is known for exquisite designs and execution. The company creatively deploys recycled materials wherever possible and is so concerned about site design that it has declined to build projects that it thought would dominate their surroundings.[37] The company faced the prospect of losing key employees if it didn't provide them with more than an hourly wage. Owner John Abrams discovered the answer in a network of worker-owned cooperatives in the Basque region of Spain.[38] Under the Mondragón Cooperative model, employees can become owners, but only after a tour of duty with the company. Employee-owners found that although they had a voice in the company, their role as owner provided even greater empowerment. As one stated, "Sharing ownership of this company has given me a greater sense of community. . . . I feel empowered by this chance to help guide the company. I have increased my commitment, discovered more opportunities, assumed more responsibility, and acquired more influence. . . . I belong here."[39]

Abrams is clear that employee ownership may well create some worries in the future (e.g., ensuring that new ideas and change are introduced or facing the prospect someday of too many owners to practice management effectively). But there is no doubting the empowering effect it brings to the company.

Even the more typical approach of profit sharing (also popular among conventional companies) can have empowering effects. At Mal Warwick Associates, fully 35% of pretax profits are placed into a fund for distribution to employees. The company's board studied the program's impact on company performance and found a "significant role in bolstering" economic performance.[40]

A different type of cooperative is worth mentioning for its wonderful approach to using empowerment to drive change in its own supply chain. The Association of Consumers' Cooperative in South Korea was created to aggregate the many cooperatives and secure some bargaining power for its members. Over tea on an October afternoon in Seoul, the Cooperative's general secretary, Hang Sik Oh, described how his members decided to take matters into their own hands when it came to sourcing coffee.[41] Although the Cooperative had been a leader in stocking organic produce, it lagged somewhat on coffee and other imported goods. Several members took initiative and went to East Timor, where they contracted directly with villagers for coffee. Then it was on to the Philippines, to another village that would sell the Korean cooperative sugar. The members created a program in which a portion of the sales of these goods went back to the villages directly, which amounted to a $30,000 donation each year. If members had encountered resistance from the Cooperative or other actions that would have curbed their influence on its policies and practices, such a program would never have been attempted.

You'll notice in Figure 5.1 that there is a double-headed arrow running between values and culture and empowerment. This arrow represents a virtuous cycle wherein greater empowerment deepens the shared values of employees and strengthens the corporate culture. This in turn enhances empowerment, the product of that strong culture. For example, employees won't need to ask for guidance in a particular situation but rather will intuitively understand the right decision because it will reflect and build on the company's culture.

A strong, positive culture is particularly valuable in guiding and promoting ethical behavior. The alternative approach, a set of rules, would be of little use in this regard in preventing unethical behavior, because by definition unethical employees violate rules. Social pressure to adhere to behavioral norms can be a far more effective tool for eliciting ethically consistent and organizationally beneficial practices.

Outcomes

ORGANIZATIONAL EFFECTS   As I've described, the organizational effects of visionary human resource policies in mission-driven companies can reduce turnover, increase productivity, and galvanize commitment to company goals. Creating a tightly knit team of employees can also elicit evangelists who share enthusiasm about the product and the company with friends, relatives, and a broader group of associates. Writing in *Entrepreneur*, marketing consultant Kim T. Gordon describes how company evangelism can fire up customers and create new sales leads, as it has for Green Gear Cycling, seller of foldable Friday Bikes that are perfect for travel.[42] But evangelists also have profound internal advantages when they can circulate through the company and raise employee performance to still higher levels.

ECONOMIC PERFORMANCE   We've traced how a strong mission can attract and empower great employees. But are there bottom-line benefits to excellent human resource practices? Here, fortunately, a number of studies can connect so-called high-performance work practices (HPWPs) to profitability. HPWPs typically include employee participation. There are so many studies in this area that an analysis summarizing all of them, known as a meta-analysis, was published in 2006.[43] The study found that, when analyzed as a group, the ninety-two studies in this area validated that HPWPs boost profitability.

SOCIAL AND ENVIRONMENTAL PERFORMANCE   Throughout this book, stories and other evidence show that mission-driven companies do make a difference compared to mainstream competitors. How much of this difference can be traced to human resource policies and practices? A moment's thought reveals that it *must* be central to these efforts. The internal factor must be critical to a company's social and environmental thrusts—in our model, empowerment is key and this guarantees a voice in the company's deeds and active consideration of ideas.[44] One interesting study conducted at Canada's University of Western Ontario focused on two United Kingdom companies. The investigator found that when employee concerns and organizational values meshed, better environmental responsiveness resulted.[45] Thus hiring with an eye toward fit with a company's values does lead to better environmental outcomes.

So, how is this different from conventional companies? This model reveals a way to view the human side of the equation for mission-driven companies in a way that helps them appreciate where their approach matches that of their mainstream competitors and where it diverges. The key point of divergence from the traditional model is the strength of the feedback from social and environmental outcomes to values and culture. There may be some of this in mainstream companies as well. Companies such as Hewlett-Packard or Henkel often are lauded for their social and environmental deeds, and this praise no doubt buttresses their value system. But social and environmental values are not nearly the big drivers for larger companies as they are for the smaller, mission-driven companies. This reinforcing cycle of values, human resource practices, and triple bottom line outcomes creates, reifies, and elevates the authenticity on which their companies are based.

DECISIONS AND HANDLING DISSENT

Managing for a single bottom line is challenging enough, but managing for the triple bottom line can be a minefield. No writer who claims that managing a mission-driven company is easy should be trusted; in fact every single person interviewed for this book reported at least one episode in which a tough choice between economic realities and social and environmental principles had to be made.

Executives at KEEN Footwear were worried. Sales for their shoes were running ahead of schedule. Great news, right? Absolutely—except KEEN then faced the difficult prospect of speeding up its delivery schedule to put shoes into the hands of distributors. It turned out that the company could do so, but only at a significant cost of up to several dollars per pair and only by using air freight from its factories in China. The issue spotlighted a clear tension between KEEN's economic goals and its environmental goals. To maintain its market position and increase profits, KEEN had to boost its carbon emissions by using a mode of transit that was far more carbon intensive than its preferred mode, ocean-borne transport.[46]

The decision to use air freight may have kept the shelves full and its vendors happy, but it upset many of KEEN's employees. That it had to resort to air freight, at a hefty financial and environmental cost, was largely a function of the intensely competitive market for shoes. But that didn't mean that KEEN couldn't try to avoid such a thorny decision in the future, especially given the heightened awareness of carbon impacts among its employees. Communicating this to employees was critical. The challenge, according to former director of sustainability Kirk Richardson, was for employees to "understand that it's a journey" toward sustainability.[47] Issues like the one faced by KEEN are discussed in "town hall" meetings that the company holds regularly. Although the sections of these meetings devoted to values tensions have been difficult, they promote a more nuanced understanding of the difficulties of managing for multiple bottom lines.

A different approach was used by Seventh Generation when it faced these tensions. The seller of natural home products created a group specifically to address such issues, called the Values and Operating Principles (VOPS) Committee. The committee consisted of employees and a senior management representative. An example of a tough decision that Seventh Generation faced came in 2003, when a supermarket that it sold through, Albertsons, was the target of a union strike.[48] The company's dilemma: Should it continue to ship its products to Albertsons markets or honor the strike, which it felt was a just action? Failure to ship could result in the loss of shelf space, which it had fought to secure. It would be a long way back into Albertsons if the grocer was upset with their actions.

After lively debate, the VOPS Committee, cognizant of the difficulty of balancing social values and profitability in this situation, came up with a novel solution. Seventh Generation would continue to ship its products to Albertsons but would contribute all profits attributable to sales at the stores to the union's strike fund.[49] In this way, shelf space was preserved and Seventh Generation did not put itself in the position of tacitly opposing the strikers. Although this move could have backfired by angering Albertsons, CEO Larry Johnston later told Seventh Generation's Jeffrey Hollender that he found the move (paraphrasing here) "gutsy."[50]

It is commonly agreed that some level of dissent is good for organizations—in fact, companies sometimes incorporate designated skeptics to ensure that there is some respect for opposing viewpoints and to avoid groupthink. One study by researchers at Oklahoma State University and Hong Kong Polytechnic University explored the link between dissent and the quality of decision making.[51] The researchers found that to gain from dissent, parties to a decision must believe in the competence of fellow decision makers and together share loyalty to the organization. If it is felt that the dissent is being disregarded or that dissenters are being co-opted, then the gains evaporate. In the extreme, widespread dissent in a decision process can create chaos and feelings of being ignored altogether on the part of those in the organization.

Thus, far from undermining the culture within mission-driven companies, attacking difficult decisions head on actually can strengthen the culture and deepen employee commitments. But there are some rules that can be used to guide the process.

First, there must be *engagement*. Employees must have a seat at the table, even if it is just to observe. Engagement was weaker at KEEN, where an executive decision was delivered, than at Seventh Generation, which explicitly delegated the decision to a committee dominated by employees. It may be that managers at KEEN didn't expect the reaction from employees, but that might indicate that the decision would have benefited from their input. As Jason Graham-Nye of gDiapers puts it, the consensus model leads to a "collective intelligence" that can elicit buy-in as well as deliver good judgment.[52]

Second, there must be a *clear communication* of the decision. Executives must articulate the rationale behind the decision. When companies are small, this of course is much easier and sometimes can be done in person. Depending on the magnitude of the decision, it may be valuable to have several forums to discuss it. But for all, clear communication should at least include why the executives had to make a difficult decision, what trade-offs they had to address, how they decided what to do and who would be involved in the process, what the decision means for employees, stakeholders, and the natural environment, and how they will avoid a recurrence of the problem. Engaging employees in the communication stage is highly valued. "Two-way communication is always more powerful than one-way communication," as leadership guru John Kotter puts it.[53]

Finally, leadership demands that, to the extent that personal burdens are associated with a difficult decision, these *burdens should be shared*. Again, in the words of Kotter, "Nothing undermines the communication of a change vision more than behavior on the part of key players that seems inconsistent with the vision."[54] For some mission-driven companies that faced downturns in late 2008, economic belt tightening that could have threatened their social and environmental goals was necessary to keep the businesses afloat. Organically Grown's Josh Hinerfeld, faced with this need to slim down in the late 2008 slowdown, had to communicate to his employees that "shared sacrifices" would be necessary. But some elements of the company's compensation that were targeted to all its employees were to be preserved. An employee stock ownership plan that distributed shares based much more than usual on seniority rather than on status in the organizational hierarchy was preserved.[55] Sticking with this plan in the face of a turbulent economy was a way to signal to line workers that they would not suffer asymmetrically.

THE GROWTH PUZZLE

Gary Erickson walked away from $60 million when he wouldn't sell his energy bar company, Clif Bar, to a large food conglomerate. Faced with the culmination of months of work and practically with pen in hand, he gave his gut equal time, went for a walk, and told his partner, "Send them home. I can't sell the company."[56] But although Erickson remained in control, he faced serious internal challenges. Because rumors about the sale had been floating through the halls and warehouses of Clif Bar, the culture of the company had taken a hit. Erickson was worried that the company was beginning to lose its mojo, the values-driven magic bag of intangibles that motivates employees, stimulates marketplace reception, and makes success the norm. He asked employees what might cause the company to lose its mojo. Most of the responses focused on the culture of the company, but many spotlighted growth.[57] Growing while retaining and serving core values challenges many mission-driven firms whose products and services have been so successful that managing the growth itself proved a challenge greater than scaling a cliff wall.

Determining the direction and speed of growth may be the single most profound management challenge facing mission-driven companies. There are so many advantages of growth for mission-driven companies. Larger size can mean giving more grants as net profits rise, hiring more disadvantaged or physically challenged employees as human resource needs expand, or saving more trees as market share in relation to conventional competitors grows. But growth all too often comes with problems that overwhelm these good works.

Two classes of growth issues face these companies. The first, held in common with conventional entrepreneurs, is operational challenges. From cash flow management to quality control, growth creates a steady stream of obstacles for small and medium-size businesses. But the second, unique to mission-driven companies, is rooted in values-related challenges. I focus on this second set of issues here.

Mission-driven companies can lose their mojo in many ways. One way is when employees learn that the practices of the company aren't what they are claimed to be, as when *Business Ethics* magazine published revelations about The Body Shop (I'll review this episode in Chapter 6).[58] But the decline of the mission focus of these companies is usually not so sensational. The commitment to core values can be eroded through two primary means that slowly sink the organization's culture and performance. The first is growing so fast that values get lost in the shuffle. The second is depending on investors who are primarily concerned with financial returns, which can subordinate social and environmental values.

Misplacing Your Values, Losing Your Mojo

As growth takes place, managerial attention can migrate away from the triple bottom line to issues consistent with more conventional firms. One cautionary tale comes from AND 1 Basketball Company, which promotes its products with basketball exhibitions focused on inner city neighborhoods. But AND 1 also had a culture of supporting inner city youth through employment and an appreciation that teamwork occurs not only when people work together in an organization but also when they play hoops on the playground.[59] The maker of footwear and clothing simply began growing so fast that it was not able to socialize new employees to its values.[60] Although still growing, the situation contributed to the sale of the company.

Growth also can dull commitment to financial performance by creating a flabby organization. This happened to Rejuvenation Hardware, a $30 million Portland, Oregon, seller of period lighting and salvage hardware. One of its values was first-class employee relations, and it was loath to fire people. Gradually, this turned into a situation where founder Jim Kelly thought the workforce had grown "fat and stupid" and less customer responsive.[61] In 1992, in a campaign called "Find the Asshole Within," the company somehow made light of the need for a cultural renewal and handled the necessary terminations with aplomb.[62]

More recently, Rejuvenation Hardware felt a need to once again stress accountability. Looking back, current president Alysa Rose, thought that the message that the company cares about employees was being misinterpreted, and she instigated a new program intended to "send a message to supervisors that they do really need to set a high bar of performance and manage to that." Further, "Being a socially responsible company—caring about your people—doesn't mean you don't effectively manage them, doesn't mean you don't give them negative feedback, doesn't mean you don't hold them accountable."[63] True to its irreverent nature, Rejuvenation Hardware added a new core value to its list, alongside the entries for personal growth, compassion, and integrity: "ass on the line."

The housing slowdown in 2008–2009 brought a different reality to Rejuvenation, prompting the layoff of twenty-five employees, 15% of its workforce.[64] But the company remains independent and hopes to recall the workers when conditions improve. Absent the moves the company made to introduce accountability during good times, however, it may have delayed difficult decisions when growth slowed.

Bringing in Single Bottom Line Investors

It is typical for mission-driven companies that are in a growth mode to face the need for more cash than they can generate internally. I'll discuss one extreme response to this—selling the company outright to a well-heeled suitor—in Chapter 9. But a less extreme course of action is staying independent while attracting outside investors. But new owners, even minority owners, bring their own set of expectations for returns and may not truly appreciate the triple bottom line heritage of the company. Consider this story from gDiapers, recounted by its founder Jason Graham-Nye. The company is growing in a way that rivals the newborns it serves, doubling sales each year since launching in the United States in 2004. Under these conditions, gDiapers simply cannot generate the required cash internally, so it must attract additional investments. In the course of discussing equity infusions with a variety of investors, Graham-Nye was questioned by one about one of its in-house perks, an on-site day care center. "You're not in the day care business," the investor argued.[65]

Stop and think about this for a moment. A *diaper company* closing a day care center? First of all, as I've argued throughout this book, companies frequently see programs such as on-site day care as a portion of their commitment to work-life balance. So do many companies that don't have a mission-driven nature but see this as a valuable perk that draws better employees and thus is a smart investment. But wouldn't a company that makes diapers simply *want* its own day care center, if for no other reason than to test its products? Needless to say, discussions with that investor went into the hamper.

Aspire, a United Kingdom start-up that employed homeless people in a door-to-door catalogue business, wasn't in a position to say no to any investors when it needed a cash infusion in 2002. But its investors insisted that the year-round catalogue business be reduced to the Easter and Christmas seasons only, a total of only eight months. This of course put tremendous pressure on Aspire's social objectives, because it could not underwrite employment in the other months. This conflict between the social and economic missions contributed to the collapse of the company shortly thereafter.[66]

Naturally, a company can stay small and grow slowly using internal funding. Founders need to appreciate that their aspirations for growth can necessitate some level of outside ownership as a way to underwrite that growth. Readers should understand that once again, there is tension between the economic goals and the social and environmental goals here. This is especially true in industries where scale is critical to reduce costs, such as in manufacturing. By growing quickly, a company can bring its costs down to a level where it can broaden its market reach and draw more customers from cheaper mainstream products.

Interviewees were reticent about discussing their investors, but one takeaway that is clear is that in the same way that the concept of fit is key to drawing employees, fit is also key to seeking investors. In her perceptive book *Getting to Scale: Growing Your Business Without Selling Out*, Jill Bamburg offers shrewd advice to small mission-driven companies.[67] Her first point is to exhaust all forms of bootstrapping, from using personal and employee resources (e.g., working for stock in lieu of pay) to creating a culture of frugality to conserve capital. But if outside capital is necessary, Bamburg advises a diligent search for nontraditional investors who will respect a company's multiple bottom lines. Choose the wrong investors, and your mission will come under intense pressure.

RECOMMENDATIONS FOR ORGANIZATION BUILDING

At this point, it is worth offering a few observations. First, each human resource policy must be measured against the company's core values. In the same way that potential consumers will reject the company if they smell hypocrisy, so too will potential employees reject the company if it adopts policies antagonistic to its espoused values. If an entrepreneur finds that a company is adjusting its core values to fit the reality of its practices, often that's a danger signal.

A second parallel, between a company's market strategy and its human resource policies, also can be drawn. The type of differentiation pursued by mission-driven companies will succeed if their (frequently) higher costs can be more than matched by the higher prices they can charge for their goods and services. In a similar way, if the higher costs of a first-class human resource management system are not outweighed by the contributions of those employees in terms of productivity, creativity, and longevity, it could threaten the viability of the company.

Having said this, however, I would caution managers. With respect to human resource strategy, the costs to the company of health plans, paid volunteerism, on-site day care, and a host of other benefits are likely to be easy to tabulate. The benefits, by contrast, accrue only circuitously to the bottom line and may frustrate efforts at quantification. An undue concentration on costs without efforts to account fully for what great employees can do for the company may tragically undervalue their seminal contribution to its mission and profitability.

. . .

So far in this book, I've identified a number of challenges that managers of mission-driven companies must confront. Through issues such as building and communicating authenticity and developing responsible organizations, the company itself is essential to the brand. So when dissent about the true nature of the company is voiced, it is a threat to the very essence of the business. In the next chapter I discuss strategies for dealing with threats that can rock a mission-driven company to its core.

6   EVERYBODY TALKIN' 'BOUT HEAVEN AIN'T GOIN' THERE
Building Credibility and Avoiding Scandals

In 1976, Anita Roddick established The Body Shop in Brighton, England, as a purveyor of personal products—soaps, oils, scents, and the like. Starting with neither business training nor substantial capital, she nonetheless led the company through opening many storefronts, eventually going public, and capturing worldwide renown.[1] Her vision was reflected in the company's mission statement, a 1995 version of which included these elements:

- Our Reason for Being: To dedicate our business to the pursuit of social and environmental change
- To Creatively balance the financial and human needs of our stakeholders: employees customers, franchisees, suppliers, and shareholders
- To Courageously ensure that our business is ecologically sustainable: meeting the needs of the present without compromising the future
- To Meaningfully contribute to local, national, and international communities in which we trade, by adopting a code of conduct which ensures care, honesty, fairness, and respect
- To Passionately campaign for the protection of the environmental, human, and civil rights, and against animal testing within the cosmetics and toiletries industry

- To Tirelessly work to narrow the gap between principle and practice, whilst making fun, passion, and care part of our daily lives.[2]

Yet despite its public pronouncements and accumulating accolades, The Body Shop's backstory was considerably less rosy. In 1994, *Business Ethics* magazine printed an exposé by a determined reporter, Jon Entine.[3] Although not the first to criticize the company, Entine's piece was the most comprehensively researched—and merciless in its assault. According to Entine, among the many serious transgressions by The Body Shop were the use of ingredients that did not square with company statements that opposed the use of petrochemicals and toxic compounds as well as the practice of animal testing; only minimal sourcing of ingredients from less developed countries, despite its promotion of a "Trade, not Aid" program; and unfair practices toward franchisees. In addition, Entine discussed the accusations that the chain's name (and some of its products and their descriptions) was lifted from the original Body Shop in Berkeley, California, and that it romanticized and sometimes fabricated stories about the origins of ingredients in its products.

These strong statements were not appreciated by The Body Shop. Setting out to tell its side after the *Business Ethics* story, the company hired the public relations firm Hill & Knowlton.[4] The PR firm was reported to have created a sham charity in order to obtain the magazine's mailing list and then sent out a rebuttal letter to its 12,000 subscribers.[5] Even in an audit paid for by The Body Shop, Kirk Hanson, its consultant, gave the company a single star out of a possible five for "Reaction to Criticism."[6] Noting its use of legal saber rattling and other defensive actions, Hanson panned The Body Shop, writing that it had "reacted poorly to criticism even from 'friends,' franchisees, and employees."[7]

The credibility lost from this episode had tangible results. Franklin Research and Development, a leading socially responsible investment company, sold its entire holdings in The Body Shop, explaining itself by devoting an entire issue of its company newsletter, *Insight*, to the controversy.[8] And Entine's impact was long-lived; his exposé was discussed at length on America's National Public Radio by commentator Scott Simon upon Roddick's death in 2007.[9]

An experience at natural home products maker Seventh Generation provides a sharp contrast to The Body Shop's reaction to a revelation.[10] In 2004, the company was faced with a difficult decision. Its contract manufacturer decided that its orders for baby wipes made according to Seventh Generation's specifications didn't justify the expense of making changes to its manufacturing lines for the company. Seventh Generation decided to use the manufacturer's standard formulation, after an outside consultant determined that it was safe.[11] But at the time, the company did not double-check the consultant's decision against Seventh Generation's own higher standards for ingredients. So the company started shipping the baby wipes.

It took a while, but customers started calling Seventh Generation to complain about the new wipes. Many of the calls were directed to its new chemist, Martin Wolf. Struck by the passion of the calls, he and Sue Holden, Seventh Generation's consumer service manager, brought together the management team to discuss what to do. The company's president at the time, Jeffrey Hollender, decided that it would stop shipping the baby wipes immediately. Significant revenue was lost, and the company risked losing shelf space after the product sold out and before Seventh Generation could find a manufacturer to make a reformulated wipe. But Hollender saw the decision as a gut check of the company's values and acted forcefully.

We can question how the decision to ship conventional wipes could have been made in the first place and even question the decision not to clear the shelves before those wipes sold out. But Seventh Generation took customer complaints seriously, realized and publicly admitted its faulty procedures, and acted. The episode served to deepen the values held by the company, and by putting principles ahead of short-term profits, it likely boosted long-term performance. The reader may not have heard of this brief episode at Seventh Generation, but that's the effect of skillful management of possible crises, isn't it?

As these vignettes indicate, the increasingly sophisticated socially and environmentally conscious marketplace can push a company into a sharply focused and sometimes uncomfortable spotlight. And with a worldwide audience available to anyone through the Internet, a single person can create what's known to academics as an information cascade, in which an issue can pick up steam and take on its own momentum.[12]

It is thus essential that companies build and bolster a credible brand, one that customers appreciate and trust.[13] As we'll see, part of that process is addressing criticism in a direct and forthright manner. In the remainder of the chapter, I take a step back and focus on three elements of building, validating, and promoting shared social and environmental claims: (1) the need for comprehensiveness in social and environmental performance, (2) how companies build credibility, and (3) how industries build credibility.

COMPREHENSIVENESS: THE ELECTRICITY PRINCIPLE OF SOCIAL AND ENVIRONMENTAL PERFORMANCE

For mission-driven companies, social and environmental issues present opportunities for differentiation, but they also create risks, because customer expectations for mission-driven companies with respect to these issues are so very high. And the hurdle is still higher: It is not just that these expectations are elevated but that they apply to a wide variety of social and environmental issues, from work-life provisions to recycled content. Mission-driven firms, like no others, are expected to excel on all relevant criteria. So one of the reasons that credibility with respect to social and environmental values is so difficult to attain is that, unlike the more strategic dimensions frequently studied (price, quality, service, etc.), consumers are not always willing to make trade-offs among social and environmental dimensions (workplace conditions, organic content, etc.). Kmart is not expected to have low prices and consistently high quality; Green Mountain Coffee Roasters is expected to both have fair trade organic beans and pay fair wages. The commitment to multiple responsibility goals must be comprehensive.

A brief refresher course in electricity provides an analogy. Consider a set of lightbulbs wired in parallel versus a set wired in series, as shown in Figure 6.1. In the set that is wired in parallel, a separate circuit runs through each bulb, whereas for the set in series, a single circuit runs from bulb to bulb before returning to the battery. Here's the upshot. For lightbulbs strung in parallel, if one burns out, the others continue to glow, but for lights strung in series, the situation is different. When strung in series, if one lightbulb burns out, it opens the circuit running through the bulbs and all of them go dark.

And so it is with social and environmental issues, which operate like those lightbulbs in series.

Series connection    Parallel connection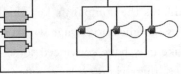

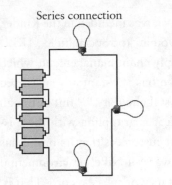

FIGURE 6.1
The electricity principle.

From the world of larger corporations, Nike provides a good example. The company's mission is focused on sport: "To bring inspiration and innovation to every athlete in the world."[14] But its reputation in several social and environmental areas provides an interesting example of the electricity principle. With respect to a key social issue, overseas manufacturing, Nike has struggled mightily to overcome its reputation for ignoring abusive behavior by its suppliers.[15] Yet, with respect to environment, it has taken a leadership role. Its Considered line of shoes won a *Business Week* design award.[16] Nike led other shoe manufacturers in removing PVC materials from shoes and introducing water-based glues. Nike's equivocal performance was reflected in *Business Ethics* magazine's 2006 listings of the 100 best corporate citizens, in which the company enjoyed the highest environmental assessment while finishing ninth from the bottom in employee relations and seventh from the bottom in human rights.[17] Because of strengths in such areas as environment, community, and diversity, the overall assessment was positive: Nike reached number 13.

But in terms of whether or not its social and environmental elements influence demand for its products positively, it's not clear. Back in 1996, a Nike-sponsored survey found that among 13–25-year-olds (its target market), the list of what Nike meant to them was topped by (1) "athletics," (2) "cool," and (3) "bad labor practices."[18] In the intervening years, the company did much to burnish its social credentials. It actually has been placed into portfolios of some socially responsible mutual funds. In

December 2005, for the first time, Nike's stock was included in the Kinder, Lydenberg, Domini and Company's (KLD) Domini 400 Social Index.[19] KLD cited evidence of positive change: "On supply chain management, which remains the company's key challenge, Nike has substantially increased its willingness to engage with a number of stakeholders."[20] But although Nike may have convinced some critics that it is grappling with these issues, there is no evidence among concerned customers that its brand has recovered. Many of these consumers are aware of Nike's environmental accomplishments but are still worried about its workplace record. That is, its social and environmental performance may have worked as a defensive strategy, but it has not drawn customers to the brand.

For mission-driven firms this issue is even more pressing. Unlike mainstream companies, mission-driven companies do not have the luxury of adopting a defensive strategy toward social issues. This is because their social and environmental policies are the centerpiece of their differentiation strategies. They may not have distinctive product-related attributes as the key to their value propositions. Instead, they may be leveraging their company authenticity and its supply chain. Companies have been seriously damaged when customers perceive that they have not delivered on one or more social or environmental dimensions.

Mission-driven companies are expected to excel at many points, including but not limited to workplace conditions, natural product ingredients, responsible supply chains, environmental stewardship, and energy efficiency. Add to this the need to keep the business's doors open by earning profits, and you've got a tall order. Can any company realize these great ambitions? Not many have. The difficulty of meeting such obligations has even created incentives for some entrepreneurs to create elaborate myths about themselves and their companies. In several cases this has led to inevitable embarrassments. But how can the more typical mission-driven company square the gritty reality of business viability with the need to communicate to a broader public in a way that promotes credibility?

HOW CAN A COMPANY BUILD CREDIBILITY?

If a company loses credibility, the results can be catastrophic, as the case of Arthur Andersen vividly illustrates. When an auditor is retained by a company, as Arthur Andersen was by Enron, essentially it produces no physical products or value-added consultation for companies. Its job is to review statements and attach a stamp of legitimacy. And if the auditor has no credibility, its service and therefore its company are worthless. Thus, when Arthur Andersen was indicted for obstruction of justice in the Enron case for knowingly shredding key documents, its business evaporated. Even after having its conviction reversed by the United States Supreme Court, it had to sell off its operations to competitors. When the product is credibility itself, the loss of that credibility is corporate suicide.

And when a major point of differentiation concerns the company and its supply chain and not the more easily evaluated product and service criteria we are used to, then the company's credibility is paramount. As The Body Shop found out, embellishing or fabricating stories about the company and its products is risky business. If authenticity lies at the core of the mission-driven company, threats to that authenticity are attacks on the very essence of the business. Mission-driven companies must build and protect their credibility in the marketplace through a number of mutually reinforcing actions.

Resist the Pressure to Stretch the Truth

Mission-driven companies recite their stories habitually. The tales can be an important source of marketing—the press can take a feel-good story and run with it. A company that appears to be financially successful without compromising its social or environmental goals can be an irresistible magnet for reporters and bloggers. If there's a record for most stories about one of these companies, it's probably held by Ben & Jerry's Homemade Ice Cream, founded by two Vermonters who started out making ice cream in an old gas station with the help of a $5 correspondence course and $12,000.[21] The company and its founders have consistently won awards for their social and environmental actions and have been treated to the media's favorable spotlight.

The company's creative flavors have always won acclaim, and it sometimes tied flavors to its values. In 1989, Ben & Jerry's launched Rainforest Crunch, which it said was stocked by nuts from a Brazilian rainforest cooperative. Unfortunately, demand outstripped the cooperative's abilities quickly, and few of the nuts in the ice cream actually were sourced from the cooperative. Perhaps worse, there were reports that the cooperative received little of the profits that Ben & Jerry's promised to send it.[22] Sadly, the company could have avoided these embarrassments in the press if it had simply been more honest about the challenges it had faced and how it decided to act. Surely, many customers would have lauded its intentions and understood that it was breaking new ground in dealing with such supply partners. Under such conditions, mistakes are bound to happen.

A more instructive experience is offered by Excellent Packaging and Supply, a Richmond, California, seller of plates, utensils, containers, and other food service necessities. The company has been able to create quite a business for itself by selling bio-based packaging and potato-based utensils in a line it calls Spudware. Allen King, one of the company's founders, received a call one day from the Canadian Food Inspection Agency, which had found that one product actually consisted of 40% polypropylene, a substance the company wanted no part of. Within a day Excellent had sent a memo to customers explaining the situation and then forced its supplier to take back the phony product. Its customers understood the company's position, dealt with what was "a gaping hole in the product lineup," and within time a genuine product was procured.[23]

Admit Mistakes

Nobody enjoys being wrong. But as the example of Excellent Packaging and Supply demonstrates, it is imperative that mission-driven companies get out in front of problems when they arise. For an entire class of organizations that in large measure owes its market openings to the mistakes of conventional businesses, to repeat some of those mistakes is disappointing enough. To suppress or deny them is reprehensible.

Be Transparent

Another element linked to credibility is the importance of promoting transparency. Without substance to back up public statements, a company risks media glare. KEEN Footwear for years had promoted its social and environmental values, and its foundation had a number of philanthropic endeavors. But it began to worry that some of its statements were beginning to outstrip its documentation. So in 2009, KEEN released its first sustainability report under a Global Reporting Initiative format. The report offered a publicly available backstop of information to boost credibility, but it had an important side benefit. The process of measuring its status and progress on environmental performance made KEEN far more cognizant of its own shortcomings in this area and therefore more humble. The more humility throughout a mission-driven company, the lower the chance that it will overstate its position or accomplishments.[24]

Link to Prominent Players

Many start-ups lack credibility. Customers that might do business with them are wary, particularly other businesses that might purchase their product. One method open to companies is to pursue relationships with other companies and organizations that have higher status and visibility. This actually turns out to be true in a wider set of situations. For example, bio-technology start-ups that had strategic links to important partners earned higher valuations when they went public.[25] In a world where credibility isn't obvious, the reasoning behind these salutary effects becomes apparent. Third parties rely on signals—and one of these is a link to a trustworthy partner. An excellent example of this is TerraPass's 2006 partnership with Expedia, the online travel service. Book a flight on Expedia, and with a few clicks you can purchase carbon offsets. Aside from the obvious source of new customers and profits for TerraPass, though, the deal puts a clear stamp of credibility on that company.

Build Organizational Capabilities

The last item is emblematic of a much larger need for companies, that of building organizational capabilities to deal productively with stakeholder issues that can arise from suppliers, the media, customers, and even activist groups.[26] Often, these challenges present companies with nettlesome decisions. Even a simple issue such as a company's philanthropy can elicit media attention if someone who was denied support believes that inconsistent treatment was responsible. Problems such as these are symptomatic of the absence of an overarching set of organizational capabilities for dealing with stakeholders. Companies will serve their interests by consciously viewing these interactions as opportunities for learning and developing organization-wide capabilities.

Figure 6.2 displays some of these sharp contrasts between ad hoc and integrated strategies. Companies with an ad hoc approach to stakeholder issues tend to view each as a sample of one—an episode that is unique to itself and offers no enduring lesson for the firm. Not surprisingly, the tactical approach to resolving such issues is simply to deal with them—to put out the fire and move on. The skill-building potential in an ad hoc system like this is minimal, because there is no institutional mechanism for learning from each episode. Overall, there is a certain immaturity to the stakeholder skill set under an ad hoc approach, which can be manifested in some of the following responses to credibility crises: refusal to appreciate the gravity of problems, refusal to take responsibility for problems, evasiveness, and defensiveness.

By contrast, an integrated approach appreciates that these issues actually are interconnected and demands managerial attention as part of a strategic whole. For companies with an integrated strategy, learning is cumulative. Companies in this category are good listeners. Over time, they appreciate, for example, what turns the media on and off. They are better at understanding precisely why particular challenges rise to the level of significant credibility risks. Add it up, and you obtain a much more mature, fully formed skill set.

	Ad hoc strategies	Integrated strategies
	←——————————————————————————→	
Perceived nature of issues	Unique	Deeply interconnected
Tactical approach	Deal with	Manage
Learning	Transitory	Cumulative
Maturity of skill set	Underdeveloped	Fully formed

FIGURE 6.2
Continuum of stakeholder capabilities.

HOW CAN AN INDUSTRY BUILD CREDIBILITY?

Forging the bonds of trust isn't the sole responsibility of companies. It's important to think at the industry level as well. This makes sense for businesses that have strong social and environmental missions. In fact, sociologists claim that most industries start out as social movements and thus are plagued by low levels of credibility at first.[27] At various times in their history, socially and environmentally oriented industries from microlending to wind energy needed to establish credibility for their whole industry. A review of their histories suggests a number of paths to greater credibility for nascent industries.

Standardizing Benefits and Certifying Practices

If an industry has no standards, it has no credibility. I do not mean that products should be standardized. Rather, the processes used to determine social or environmental benefits from the product need to be standardized. In this sense, it is difficult to obtain information from the Web sites for many, if not most, products.

Certification of benefits has gone some distance in establishing credibility for many products. The Marine Stewardship Council (MSC), which was formed by an alliance of Unilever and the World Wildlife Federation, had an ambitious goal: to create a global certification scheme for sustainable fisheries. The partnership had its share of misadventures, stemming frequently from difficulties the members experienced in building up trust.[28] But after a number of years and near-death experiences, the MSC began making headway, and by early 2009 it had succeeded in certifying forty-two fisheries containing thirty-seven different species.[29] It estimated global retail sales of MSC-certified products at $1.5 billion. That's still a minnow's share of the worldwide market, but with major sellers such as Wal-Mart coming onboard to join long-standing MSC advocates such as Whole Foods Market, its future is bright. One reason that MSC did finally achieve traction after its own crisis of credibility was its push to strengthen credibility by improving transparency, demanding consistent interpretation of its standards, and documenting environmental benefits of the processes it introduced into fisheries.[30]

The experience of the Marine Stewardship Council provides an important corollary to our story: Certifications will carry more weight if they involve third parties. This axiom can be extended to the wood products industry. One of the reasons that the wood product industry's Sustainable Forestry Initiative has been so harshly criticized is simply because it is an industry creation. The Forest Stewardship Council, by contrast, is the offspring of a nongovernmental organization that does not have to confront issues of perceived conflicts of interest.

Taking Collective Action

United we stand. This bromide applies to infant and adolescent industries such as many of the ones I've been discussing here. This second industrywide approach to improving credibility is to work collectively not just to achieve goals, such as increasing demand for a product, but also to aggressively work to improve the standing of the industry in the eyes of policy makers. The ways in which socially and environmentally oriented industries have acted together illustrate the many avenues toward successful collaboration.

ADOPT COMMON STANDARDS The first way that collective action can provide credibility is by adopting common standards. Common social and environmental standards offer a slew of benefits to industries, including defusing complaints that an industry has no shared sense of mission, removing a source of intercompany conflict, signaling to consumers that the industry has matured, and reducing risks to consumers using company products.

It probably is not helpful to the carbon offset industry that its companies and nonprofit organizations use a dozen different certifiers.[31] Several of the benefits just mentioned would accrue to companies if a set of common standards were in place. But the current situation, which includes some standards that are proprietary and therefore not open to public scrutiny, will likely give way to a common set of standards at some point. This may be painful, but it is clearly in the interest of traders in the voluntary carbon offset market.

BECOME AN INFORMATION CLEARINGHOUSE Peak organizations in many industries develop their own information gathering and dissemination capabilities, bolstering their credibility by becoming go-to nodes for information. Consider the European Wind Energy Association, which stocks a Web site full of statistical, political, and technical information.[32] Being a repository for industry information can lead to a sense of expertise that can lend legitimacy to policy debates and further market acceptance.

LOBBY FOR INDUSTRY BENEFITS   Most industries require government assistance of one type or another, perhaps through direct subsidies, as in the case of the German and Spanish solar and wind energy facilities, which benefit greatly from so-called feed-in subsidies.[33] These subsidies pay alternative energy generators above the going rate for electricity they produce. Or government assistance may come in the form of indirect support, as when makers of nontoxic cleaning materials lobbied school boards to include sustainability in the specifications when they bid out for supply contacts.[34] Such support is mandated by explicit allowances in bids for green cleaners. But whatever the support sought by an industry, speaking with one voice is essential. And to ensure that the various voices harmonize, a collective organization is vital.

ALLY WITH STAKEHOLDERS   To the extent that an industry can reach out and engage other stakeholders, it helps to build a network that can protect its flanks and create synergistic possibilities. Formed in 1998, the Organic Federation of Australia faced a number of challenges by 2001, including the fact that "industry networks and linkages between various stakeholder groups are currently very weak."[35] The federation laid out a strategy that will bring together its industry stakeholders, universities, governments, and other constituencies to help them overcome problems of "industry cohesion and professionalism."

It may be that industries full of mission-driven companies will grow out of the credibility deficit they often face. Industries must take steps to promote the establishment of their credibility, or like the fledgling carbon offset industry, they may face uncomfortable questions. And once attained, credibility must remain a critical contingency for industries. But the taken-for-granted status of such industries as organic produce or car-sharing services indicates that the long-term effect of credibility is to help nurture and promote the growth of entire fields of enterprise.

A FINAL THOUGHT

The final point reiterates my central theme: If a mission-driven company can attain—and maintain—credibility across a number of social and environmental dimensions, it can erect a significant barrier to direct competition from established conventional companies. If instead a mission-driven company blurs the distinctions between itself and these other companies or falls below the standards of conventional competitors, it risks the essence of its value proposition. A company must protect and enhance its credibility, the foundation on which it communicates with its customers.

And if mission-minded entrepreneurs can fashion authentic triple bottom line companies, they can provide lessons for mainstream companies. What and how these organizations can learn from their mission-driven counterparts forms the nucleus of the next chapter. We'll see that there is much opportunity for mainstream companies to observe and work with mission-driven companies as well as to leverage their own considerable strengths to broaden and further democratize the trails blazed by mission-driven pioneers.

LEARNING FROM

THE LEADING EDGE

Lessons for Mainstream Businesses

A WORLD OF COLLABORATION

"I don't believe that any company intentionally sets out to do the wrong thing," asserts Priya Haji, one of the founders of World of Good, a distributor of responsibly sourced goods from the developing world.[1] But she reckons that only about 1% of the $55 billion informal economy is fair traded.[2] So there's plenty of room for goods that are sourced "thoughtfully, with good principles and also with fair prices" paid to artisans. Haji's mission is to build a far larger market share for responsibly sourced goods, by bridging the gap between these craftspeople and the consumer.

Haji's resolve springs from a lifetime of activism. The daughter of two doctors from East Africa and India, she helped her father organize a free clinic in Bryan, Texas, when she was still in high school. Sipping tea in her Emeryville, California, office, she jokes that she filed her first set of 501(c)(3) forms while still in high school. In 1992, Haji took her passion to East Palo Alto while at Stanford University, building a network of social services in a city that at the time had the highest murder rate in the country.[3] Shifting to a traditional business surely would have frustrated her, so she fashioned a company with a mission beyond profitability.

In surveying opportunities, Haji found one that captivated her. She felt that as a group, the various fair trade organizations were doing an admirable job of delivering a wider slice of the economic pie for artisans and improving workplace conditions, but there was a need for a company that could reach back to the villages and urban enclaves where the informal economy thrived and take these fair trade goods directly to the consumer—with certifications intact. Her gamble was to try to popularize fair trade goods to a broader group of consumers, such as "Joe American, who does shop at Wal-Mart, who has never traveled internationally, but who is a thoughtful, kind person and would like to think about things he buys differently."[4]

Doing so meant getting to the mainstream eventually. And that meant getting to scale. Haji started with a local Whole Foods Market, whose decentralization permitted a store manager to carry her goods straightaway. Meeting success, she was offered regional exposure and was carried nationally within two years. At the same time, the company was finding success selling through urban boutiques, campus bookstores, and other outlets, which in early 2009 numbered 1,200 points of sale. But getting to Joe American was still on her mind. Haji was still thinking about her grand strategy of "building a huge distribution pipeline" for fair trade products.

That's when mutual friends introduced Priya Haji to Robert Chatwani, an eBay marketing executive. They had much in common, from their Indian ancestry to their love of travel. And they both believed it was the responsibility of business to make a difference. Chatwani recalls, "We realized right away we had a shared vision, that we could use commerce as a force to alleviate poverty."[5] But eBay had a problem. It had no way "to organize the ethical inventory," as Haji puts it, and this revealed a perfect opening for her company. After eighteen months of development—aided by generous terms extended by eBay—the World of Good eBay site was launched in 2008.[6]

World of Good demonstrated to eBay a number of innovations about how to create and deliver "the trust structure." Because World of Good is relatively agnostic about the companies that certify goods, importers that wish to sell through eBay can be certified by any of more than thirty "trust providers," such as the International Fair Trade Association, Green America, or the Rainforest Alliance. The presentation of this information to shoppers also is innovative. Each producer's story appears to the left of its Web page, with its "Trustology" and "Goodprint" on the right. Trustology refers to the trust provider; the Goodprint refers to specific product impacts on people, the natural environment, animals, or philanthropic causes. Online instructions guide potential sellers through a sign-up process for the site, which in 2009 topped 10,000 items.

The World of Good site provides the giant auction and shopping site with an entirely new and credible source of goods from the informal economy, which might attract shoppers who are outside eBay's typical profile. For World of Good, which desires to reach out to these more typical eBay buyers, the site serves as a portal to an enormous new set of customers who can help it meet its goal of democratizing fair trade. Who knows, maybe Joe American has just located an Indonesian Xanadu necklace for his wife, Jane.

The World of Good story illustrates how innovative mission-driven companies are influencing mainstream business. Larger companies have much to learn from these smaller, nimbler enterprises. Just as World of Good taught eBay about the latest in transparency, mainstream companies could learn from their mission-driven counterparts about handling other social and environmental challenges and opportunities. And just as eBay partnered with World of Good, mainstream companies can bridge the gaps in their social and environmental profiles by engaging with mission-driven companies. In this chapter I also address a related topic. Can small companies whose histories have not highlighted social and environmental missions take up the cause? I review the experiences of two companies, drawing lessons for managers intrigued about more responsible business. I finish up by trying to weigh the collective impact of mission-driven companies on society and enterprise in general.

WHAT CAN A MAINSTREAM BUSINESS LEARN FROM MISSION-DRIVEN COMPANIES?

The Importance of Moral Reflection

If you had an imaginary moral compass of many companies in the palm of your hand, short-term profit maximization would be true north. Worse, many corporate executives know that composing their company's mission statement is an exercise in creative writing. The poster child is Enron, whose mission statement proclaimed, "We treat others as we would like to be treated ourselves. . . . We do not tolerate abusive or disrespectful treatment. Ruthlessness, callousness and arrogance don't belong here."[7] Although extreme, Enron is not an isolated case of a morally—and now financially—bankrupt company.

Setting aside delusions or intentional misrepresentations, most larger companies generally don't appreciate how powerful a moral element is to their reason for being. Corporate consulting guru Nikos Mourkogiannis spotlights morals in his book *Purpose*.[8] He forcefully argues that to attain greatness, a company must have a "moral DNA" that represents core beliefs—such as discovery, excellence, altruism, and heroism. Purpose guides behavior in an implicit, uncalculative way. Rather than being an empty mission statement that is subordinated to the bottom line at the "first sign of crisis," purpose is most evident at those times and guides behavior.[9] Recall Seventh Generation's decision to continue to ship products during the Albertsons strike and send profits to the striking union. It didn't involve a cost-benefit calculation about the odds of Albertsons dropping the company as a supplier if the action was taken. The decision, taken after a period of reflection, was guided by the company's moral DNA.

Of course, we should not overstate the case that traditional firms are moral laggards. Plenty of large companies have a purpose, and this purpose *has* guided behavior. When Johnson & Johnson cleared shelves of Tylenol after a deadly case of tampering, it didn't run the decision by accountants. But it surely appealed to its moral DNA, as manifested in its credo. But in so many other cases, opportunities to deepen commitment to a company's mission are instead replaced by short-term thinking. For example, in 2007, Circuit City fired its best paid salespeople to trim costs, an action that is hard to square with the company's self-described commitment to innovation, the closest thing that comes to a stated purpose in a review of its annual reports from 2006 and 2007.[10] By 2009, Circuit City had declared bankruptcy and was liquidating its assets.

Many of the companies studied here describe frequent methods by which they remind employees of their social and environmental commitments, running from KEEN's town hall meeting to Timberland's provision for forty hours of paid leave for community service.[11] Among other indications that values are meaningful, actions that allow senior leaders to teach employees about values "at every opportunity" are particularly meaningful.[12] It is simply not possible to do this without an authentic commitment that is based in the company's moral DNA.

One attempt to promote moral reflection at a conventional company had the further advantage of being deeply personal in nature. One of the least known aspects of Wal-Mart's attempt to introduce sustainability into its operations was its engagement of consultants to work with employees in its Personal Sustainability Project. Through training workshops, consultants taught employees about environmental sustainability and healthy living. The project is the leading edge of a program in which Wal-Mart will ask employees to take a pledge of improvement.[13] Speaking of her own experience with the project, which compelled her to stop smoking and lose weight, one associate said, "I realized that what I was doing to my body, we were doing to the planet."[14]

Talking about a company's moral basis can be awkward, frustrating, and a dozen other adjectives that wouldn't describe a discussion of why profits matter. But as discussed in previous chapters, when employees develop a bond to the greater purpose for which the company stands, many benefits—even financial ones—flow. Chip Conley, in his book *Peak: How Great Companies Get Their Mojo from Maslow*, provides insight here.[15] Conley, founder of Joie de Vivre Hotels, believes in Abraham Maslow, a psychologist who developed the human "hierarchy of needs," from simple physiological and safety needs up to esteem and self-actualization. Applying the idea to employees, Conley explains how he tries to go beyond the basic needs of the workplace, such as decent pay, to create a type of experience that meets employees' aspirational needs for meaning in their jobs. Clearly, one way to infuse meaning into the workplace is to create a workplace where those values are taken seriously. Done in sincerity, commitment and employee loyalty follow.

An Early Warning System for Social and Environmental Expectations

The importance of moral reflection is only one clue to take from mission-driven companies. Another key takeaway for conventional companies is that mission-driven companies serve as a type of early warning system for social and environmental issues. In case after case, these companies have anticipated environmental and social trends and have positioned themselves to avoid costs of eliminating ingredients or practices that were on the fringe of acceptability. In so doing, they also reduced risks to their brands.

INGREDIENTS   Few of us knew what trans fats were ten years ago. But behind the scenes, mounting scientific evidence pointed to trans fats as the culprit behind up to 30,000 additional coronary events a year.[16] The FDA finally proposed labeling trans fat in 2000, and in January 2006 the new labels appeared on foods.[17] Many makers of conventional foods that relied on trans fats hadn't spent those years trying to replace them in formulas, or worse—were busy lobbying against the FDA-mandated labeling.[18] By contrast, most natural foods had little or no trans fats, so the change meant only that these products were more attractive in the marketplace. The natural foods companies were free to concentrate their energies on reminding consumers that their products were trustworthy.

Additives to consumer products also seem to have led a secret life until recently. It's interesting to spotlight phthalates, a set of industrial compounds that have been used in a wide range of applications, from health care products to toys. Phthalates are suspected to be endocrine disruptors that could undermine human reproductive and neurological health.[19] The European Union banned the manufacture and sale of some forms of phthalate in 2005. The United States followed suit, banning phthalates in toys starting in 2009.[20] The presence of phthalates in a broader group of products, such as cosmetics and shampoos, may next draw the attention of regulators. Procter & Gamble would no doubt argue that its products are perfectly safe, but it has also made decisions that suggest that it sees an issue coming—an issue that many sellers of natural cleaners had anticipated for some time.[21] Procter & Gamble recently banned some phthalates from its products, citing regulatory concerns rather that any health risk.[22] Colgate-Palmolive appears to be a bit further behind the curve on this one, continuing to use phthalates, which it states "have an excellent safety profile and are present at very low levels."[23] Method, a rising seller of natural cleaners that have never contained phthalates, will not be distracted by this debate.[24]

Mainstream companies are well advised to keep an eye out for emerging issues of ingredients. It is not necessarily true that they must replace ingredients immediately. But mainstream companies should at least have contingency plans in place for replacing ingredients if social or legal mandates (or both) require it. An example might involve trans fats in America. Many products tout having "0 grams trans fats." This means that they could have up to but not including a half-gram of trans fat and still claim 0 gram, because of FDA rounding allowances. But this has not stopped brands from publicizing that their 0 gram is less than their competitors' 0 gram.[25] Because the amount of advisable trans fat is generally quite low, the issue is not minor. Smart companies are positioning themselves for future policy in this regard, which might include listing trans fats in a decimal format (e.g., "0.4" rather than "0").[26]

TRANSPARENCY   Bangkok, Thailand, 2001. I've been given a tour of a Nike facility on the outskirts of town by one of the company's overseas manufacturing experts, Phil Berry. Berry needs to stay behind to attend to some other issues, so he has his driver take me back into town in time for an early evening presentation I will be making. I have forgotten my notepad, but I still would like to record my observations during the trip back. Berry searches for a blank side of paper, but keeps coming across sheets that have supplier information on the reverse side. At the time, the identity of these suppliers was highly sensitive for Nike, which treated its network of far-flung manufacturers as a key competitive asset. By 2005, though, the company had decided to reveal to the world the identity of its entire stable of first-tier suppliers. Nike realized that its stakeholders' expectations for transparency outweighed the strategic cost of making this information public. Many of Nike's worst environmental impacts may well be farther up its supply chain (e.g., tanneries that treat leather that is then sold to a first- or second-tier supplier). But this action represented a major shift for the company, and it continues to list suppliers.

There are many reasons for Nike's initiative, which it continues with periodic updates to its list of first-tier suppliers.[27] Pressure from activist groups and the media undoubtedly had a role. But the earlier initiative to list suppliers by Levi Strauss, a larger company than most we've studied here but one with a long history of social responsibility, must have been noticed by Nike.

Years ago, transparency was still anathema to conventional companies. For strategic and legal reasons, the idea of revealing information seemed highly questionable, even naive. Yet, for years mission-driven companies have pushed the bounds of transparency. Seventh Generation has listed functional names of ingredients since it first sold cleaners in the mid-1990s. The actual chemical names were listed on its Web site in 2002 and on product labels in 2006.[28] So far, the Procter & Gambles of the world have not come clean about what's in their bottles, boxes, and tubes. But the pressure's on. Non-governmental organizations such as Green America's Responsible Shopper Web site have fingered Procter & Gamble for "failing to remove unsafe and potentially carcinogenic ingredients from its personal products."[29]

Companies wondering where transparency is headed can take heed of World of Good's representation of certifications on their Web site. But an entirely different Web-based information system addresses labor compensation in a way that responds to Priya Haji's annoyance that embodied labor and pricing of goods often have little connection in emerging economies. In these markets, where spot pricing dominates, there can be enormous power differentials between artisans and their buyers. Often, the greater the artisan's need for cash, the lower the price he or she will accept for a good. After a natural calamity, such as a drought, "you'd see Bangladeshis that were selling baskets that had taken them two or three weeks to weave, and they're selling them for pennies because they *just* needed the money.[30]

So World of Good's nonprofit subsidiary convened a council of nongovernmental organizations and artisans to create an impressive Web site that works as a resource for any company purchasing piecework. The site, fairtradeguide.org, includes information in English, Spanish, and Thai for 120 countries.[31] Prospective buyers can select a country and insert what they are paying the artisan for a good and how long the good took to produce.[32] Even with this simple information, the site will report how this piece rate compares to the country's minimum wage and poverty line, providing invaluable support to companies trying to establish whether or not their supply chains are exploitative.

This type of social innovation typifies the diligence of many mission-driven companies in unveiling new ways to make supply chains transparent. Part of the value of World of Good's initiative is advancing a new, welcome tool for companies, but it also points to a new area for further innovation. What will be the next step in this process of revealing information about the supply chain?

HOW CAN A MAINSTREAM BUSINESS LEARN FROM MISSION-DRIVEN COMPANIES?

In the areas that we just explored, mission-driven companies have been leaders. This is not to say that all their initiatives have diffused into the mainstream, although many have. Taken with the topics we've covered throughout the book, the examples point to a few recommendations for conventional firms.

Pay Attention!

You may see mission-driven firms as lying on the periphery of commercial reality and unimportant, even puny, in the big scheme of things. If so, you're mistaken. It's true—mission-driven companies contribute only a bump-up to a nation's GDP, but they represent a growing phenomenon. And they generate media and new product buzz that far exceeds their aggregate size. Most important, they have repeatedly gotten it right well ahead of other companies.

You might say that mission-driven companies have frequently provided *proof of concept* for social and environmental initiatives, demonstrating the operational soundness of their innovations.[33] They serve to remove excuses that block progressive initiatives at mainstream companies.

Now, many of the ideas of mission-driven companies would translate uneasily to conventional companies. In fact, as argued, this is one reason that their strategies can create a competitive advantage over the long haul. But that doesn't mean that larger companies can't observe how their mission-driven counterparts address emerging social and environmental issues and position themselves for the future. If mission-driven companies act as an early warning system for issues, it is managerial malpractice for mainstream executives to ignore them.

Paying attention also allows companies to benchmark across industries. Environmental and social issues are almost never wholly industry specific. Companies can observe and specify best practices in business activities where their business generates significant environmental and social impact. As noted, using some type of third-party certification for overseas manufacturing or growing is becoming an expected attribute of products. But which standard to use? Keeping an eye on what leaders are doing can help a company understand which standards share the key attributes of boosting its authenticity and which ones can be implemented within its organization.

Lead Where You Can

Mainstream companies don't always have to be followers. Often they can marshal their resources to go beyond what many mission-driven companies can do. Four areas are important. The first is developing metrics and measures, and this is particularly true with respect to environmental impacts. (The other three areas are reporting, purchasing, and conducting research and development, discussed later.) The sheer size of many companies allows them to apply resources to measure variables from recycling rates to water usage. Vancity, Canada's largest credit union, lists hundreds of measures it uses to track its triple bottom line performance in its 171-page 2006–2007 accountability report.[34] Reporting at the Global Reporting Initiative A+ level of detail allows Vancity to include measures running from greenhouse gas emissions per employee to the percentage of employees who are comfortable expressing dissent to the dollar value of community leadership materials. Whether the organization has improved or declined on each metric is also reported.

The ability to develop metrics has a symbiotic relationship with another area where conventional companies can lead: reporting those figures. Since 2003, the Carbon Disclosure Project (CDP) has reported carbon emissions associated with many of the world's largest companies. The CDP is growing both in terms of reporting companies and in terms of the depth of reporting detail. No one has documented the costs of reporting to the CDP, but given that the questionnaire asks companies to report three levels of emissions (from energy sources, from their own operations, and by their suppliers), few small companies can shoulder the full costs of compliance.

By taking initiative in developing metrics and reporting, conventional companies can claim leadership in at least some area of the social and environmental reputation space. And to the extent that pressure continues for further formalization of social and environmental performance, they will find that, to paraphrase hockey great Wayne Gretsky, they will have skated to where the puck was going.

A potent impact also can be made through purchasing. Mainstream companies, because they generally command much larger segments of the market than their mission-driven counterparts, can change the nature of upstream markets. When Staples, the office products giant, decided to try to eliminate file folders made wholly from virgin materials, its supplier told it that inconsistent small-lot purchasing from a collection of insubstantial players was keeping prices for that material high. By quickly moving all its tonnage to 30% postconsumer content, Staples was able to secure price parity.[35]

A final area is research and development, where resources of larger companies can be brought to bear on problems that require a scale going beyond that of many mission-driven companies. Some needs are seemingly small, such as replacing the typical five-microlayer potato chip bag with something more ecologically sound.[36] The benefits of success in these endeavors are clear. If Frito-Lay can leverage its considerable research capabilities to invent a recyclable or compostable potato chip bag, the Kettle Foods of the world are sure to want to license it for their products.

Sometimes it makes sense to follow where you can. From Safeway's O brand organics to Clorox's Green Works line, mainstream companies are finding that it's not just the LOHAS consumers who are interested in purchasing responsible products. They are betting that lighter shades of green buyers (those Naturalites and Drifters in Table 2.1) also are interested in better products but keep an eye on price. The result may be less about competition between the products of mission-driven and conventional companies and more about meeting the broader demand in the marketplace.[37]

Too frequently, mainstream companies look first to the marketing function as a way to play up their social and environmental credentials. It would be far better to lay a foundation of achievement in areas where they have built-in advantages and humbly draw attention to their achievements as a way to build trust with customers.

Use Partnerships as Learning Tools

Strategists have always viewed learning as a prime motivation for alliances.[38] Consider the Dow Jones Sustainability Index, now over a decade old (actually, it's now a family of indexes—eleven in all as of early 2009). The index is a partnership of Dow Jones and the Swiss firm Sustainable Asset Management. Reto Ringger, founder of SAM, approached Dow Jones about creating an index that would use SAM's social and environmental databases to create a screened index fund. Ringger was surprised when Dow Jones readily agreed to move forward with SAM to create an index.[39] But with perfect hindsight, it's easier to see the advantages to Dow Jones, which can use the partnership to access the considerable depth of knowledge at SAM about assessing social and environmental performance of firms. Tapping into SAM's reputation in the area also created value for Dow Jones.

The World of Good–eBay partnership also shows how parties bring together strongly complementary assets and skills to promote learning. With luck, the partnership will create spillover benefits for eBay as it engages in other selling platforms where social and environmental assurances must be credible.

Resist the Temptation to Look for Faults

Just as the press builds up many mission-driven companies, so too will it tear them down when they fail. There *have* been cases of hypocrisy in the movement, The Body Shop being exhibit A. But conventional companies must not look for reasons to dismiss an entire population of mission-driven companies. Instead, they should look beyond bad actors and their self-believed mythologies to appreciate the essence of what mission-driven companies are trying to do.

It may not be that these companies will grow to a size that can truly threaten a mainstream competitor. Rather, the threat is that the bedrock values of mission-driven companies will be incorporated by that mainstream company's large competitors. Then, by improving environmental and social performance, these companies will engage more customers, attract better and more loyal employees, and sidestep the risk of clinging to outmoded ideas. These evolved mainstream companies will not be up to the standards of first-class mission-driven companies, but they'll certainly outclass slow-moving competitors of their own heft.

TRANSFORMING THE MISSION

Change is hell. Ask anyone who has been through reengineering, reinventing, downsizing, rightsizing, or any other euphemism for company upheaval. For companies that choose to transform their social and environmental missions, in many ways it's no different. Moving from long-understood, easily articulated financial goals to a new set of goals that reflect society and the environment can provoke pushback ("What other trends are we going to buy into?"), defensiveness ("But we already recycle!"), and insecurity ("Will we still promote based on performance?"). But the histories of two companies that have infused new values into their cultures and business models offer lessons on what it takes to succeed.

Calvert-Jones

Stan Peregoy has the personality of a bartender and the conviction of a preacher. He's part-owner and president of Calvert-Jones Company, an Alexandria, Virginia, contractor that specializes in mechanical, environmental, and energy services for commercial buildings. His unkempt hair, earring, and open-collar shirt suggest that if he was going to manage anything, it wouldn't be a 63-year-old company in a tradition-bound field.

A far cry from an installer of HVAC systems (heating, ventilation, and air conditioning), Peregoy has refashioned Calvert-Jones to offer a more holistic roster of services that includes energy audits and design consultation, often under the eyes of its LEED-certified professionals. In fact, these days, when nearly half a building's utility costs can come from mechanical systems, Calvert-Jones is working to transform itself into a full-line services company. "We've been a traditional mechanical contractor for sixty years. What's a traditional mechanical contractor going to look like in twenty?" asks Gerry Rodino, Peregoy's more closely cropped marketing chief. "Mechanical contractors have always been in the energy business; they just didn't know it."[40] Yet as simple and elegant as it may seem, moving this $110 million company in that direction has been no small task.

Here's where the conviction comes in. You'd need rock-solid belief to stick with the company's green strategy. Peregoy recalls the incredulity of his fellow investors. "OK, where's the return?" they asked as his 3-year-old initiative continued to lose money. Simply put, building owners and developers are reluctant to try new ideas, especially those with long pay-backs at today's energy rates. Maybe it's just being on the East Coast, where customers and regulations both lag their West Coast counterparts in demanding energy conservation. But the frustration is evident. "So what I hear is you're not going to have any tenants in ten years," Peregoy blurts out to the owner of a building who refuses to appreciate how energy costs borne by tenants will become ever more critical in choosing commercial space.[41] For the owner, it's still all about initial costs.

Undaunted, Peregoy is pushing ahead. It's now taking not "five or six" but a couple of meetings to gain access to the decision makers who can commission improvements to existing buildings, the largest segment of Calvert-Jones's business. But it may ultimately depend on the nature of the economy. Unseen renovations that are not absolutely essential in the short run may be one more casualty of tight credit. On the other hand, given the long-run trend of utility costs (which compared to gyrating fuel costs have increased more steadily), time is on its side.

Coastwide Laboratories

Over on America's left coast, a quite different history emerged when a main-stream company instigated change. Based in Wilsonville, Oregon, Coastwide Laboratories formulates, manufactures, and sells janitorial and sanitation supplies for industrial and commercial applications. Under the leadership of partners John Martilla and Grant Watkinson, the company continues to innovate and has created ripples that moved outward and across its supply chain. So powerful is Coastwide's business model that it has survived multiple recessions, and recently, its 2006 purchase by Office Express and the subsequent purchase of that company by Staples in 2008.

Martilla and Watkinson trace their awakening to the 1980s, when the company heard concerns from customers in Oregon's nascent semiconductor industry. When additives used in its cleaners entered the fluid waste stream, they complicated an already difficult industrial waste situation at chip-manufacturing plants.[42] Further, there were some human health and safety concerns in their use. The partners encouraged Coastwide's top chemist, Roger McFadden, to devote increasing hours to inventing environmentally sensitive cleaners.

The government in Oregon, unlike Virginia, took a leadership role in promoting sustainability, and Martilla and Watkinson served on several state task forces that shaped state policy in the years around 2000. The policies that emerged from this process laid the foundation for standards that would promote greener cleaners by mandating purchasing practices that rewarded environmentally friendly products.

Meanwhile, back in the lab, McFadden's experiments were beginning to yield new products. It turned out that in just about all cases, less toxic cleaners presented the best of all worlds. In addition to their environmental benefits, they were more effective and cost no more than conventional products.[43] Coastwide's Sustainable Earth line was born. When it won a BEST (Businesses for an Environmentally Sustainable Tomorrow) Award from the City of Portland, the sense of pride in the company deepened. Then Watkinson hired a sustainability chief, signaling that he was "damned serious" about greening.[44] Employees were ready for a change they readily accepted. The entire workforce attended Natural Step training. Workers launched a green team to explore how they could reduce waste at work. A contracts supervisor became a certified recycling expert. Employees formed carpools and purchased hybrid cars.

Outside the organization, Martilla and Watkinson decided that they would start pushing their suppliers for improved environmental performance, vowing to get on a first-name basis with the presidents (*not* the shipping managers) of their dozen largest suppliers. When you realize that these suppliers include such giants as Rubbermaid, 3M, and Rohm and Haas, that sounds ambitious, even quixotic. But those companies listened. And they learned from Coastwide.

Sales picked up after a series of educational seminars at industry events. The first event, expected to draw 15 people, instead played to a packed house of 150. Initial attendees would return to future events, but with their managers. Sales and market share improved for Coastwide, and the company became an attractive acquisition target as Martilla and Watkinson neared retirement. So powerful is the Sustainable Earth line that Staples, the new owner of Coastwide, has retained the Coastwide name for its cleaning products and extended the Sustainable Earth brand to nonchemical products that meet sustainability criteria.

But for Martilla and Watkinson, perhaps the greatest source of pride concerns the end users of the product. A vast, generally invisible army of janitors work in factories, offices, and schools. An estimated 6% of janitors are injured each year by the chemicals they use, making the profession more hazardous than most would guess.[45] Watkinson leans forward to make his point. "The people that use our products are for the most part at the bottom of the economic scale, and have precious little influence over the products they use. There's a lot of pride in the fact that . . . we've really improved the work environment for folks." Martilla reminds us that these workers "are exposed to (hazardous) chemicals for 40 hours a week," not just now and then as in a household. Coastwide has improved social equity in the janitorial profession, a deeply satisfying legacy for Martilla and Watkinson.

A Few Lessons

The two companies profiled here have much in common. Both Calvert-Jones and Coastwide Laboratories were long-lived companies that could trace their roots back many decades. They also were in traditional fields removed from end consumers where price competition was fierce and many sales were made after an open bidding process. Coastwide Laboratories has enjoyed great success from its initiatives, whereas the jury's still out for Calvert-Jones. What might account for their differing experiences? These are only two companies, yet their experiences suggest a pair of questions that must be answered if a company is to successfully recreate itself as a mission-driven company.

IS THE MARKET READY?   First, although Coastwide Laboratories and Calvert-Jones have some similarities, they also have sharp distinctions. With respect to price, both can show advantages. But there is a wide gulf between a product that is bought and used quickly and one that represents an investment that will pay off over time. In Northern Virginia, the market is relatively blind to the advantages of energy efficiency. It also is a market in which owners flip properties on average every three years.[46] So few owners are willing to lay out the dollars for improvements that might not inflate the building's selling price. In this neck of the woods, tenants aren't yet used to inquiring about energy costs when they rent space, another barrier to greening.

One way out of this dilemma is, of course, to sell into appreciative markets. And Calvert-Jones is pushing out to try to take advantage of nearby markets where energy costs do receive the attention they deserve. In that sense, it's lucky. Not 10 miles away from its home office is Washington, D.C., where all buildings, public and private, must now be LEED-certified. Partnerships that bring together a local D.C. presence with Calvert-Jones's strong technical skills are an important way in which the company could grow sales of green products and services.[47]

Another approach is to prime the home market. Here, Calvert-Jones began by offering to conduct energy audits for older buildings that are candidates for retrofits. According to Gerry Rodino, the original response was, "I don't know what you're trying to sell me but you're going to sell me something if you come in my building." After several years of efforts, the tone changed to "When can you do it?" and "When can you meet with my board of directors?"[48]

IS THE COMPANY READY? Internal resistance must be confronted and overcome. Sometimes gentle persuasion must be used to convince a company's owners. Both Coastwide Laboratories and Calvert-Jones were privately held, with fewer than ten shareholders each. But acceptance of sustainability proved more of a challenge for Calvert-Jones. Speaking of Stan Peregoy's mission to bring owners on board, Gerry Rodino observes how Peregoy "has had to get out on a limb with the other owners. . . . When we started doing this, he wasn't getting a lot of support from a lot of people. So we've had to work through this together as a company and as a team, educating our own people and helping to educate the company investors that this is going to take a while."[49] At Coastwide, the situation was much simpler: Martilla and Watkinson held a controlling interest in the company, the central reason they felt no pushback. On the other hand, they never had to explain themselves to minority owners, because none of them voiced concern over their plans.

Down in the trenches, the idea of sustainability seemed to get a warm reception in both workforces. Calvert-Jones also worked the social side within its workforce, with a generous philanthropy program and an active employee health initiative. The difference on the internal dimension may well be the advantage that Coastwide has in its location: Oregon's general level of awareness and commitment with respect to sustainability meant that the process of greening was much more likely to take on its own momentum. This was manifested in the company's private initiatives to push greening in the office, but the personal commitment must have made product marketing easier.

Sending its employees through training similar to the Natural Step seminars might be one way for Calvert-Jones to invigorate its culture and promote sustainability. But the costs for that training might raise eyebrows in the boardroom. So Calvert-Jones has hosted some volunteer events, such as its quarterly recycling days, where it invites the community to bring recyclable goods and fluorescent tubes in. In time, the culture of the company may evolve, which might result from the type of external recognition won by Coastwide, or the effect of a slowly changing workforce may become apparent. But as the culture changes, so too will Calvert-Jones's ability to excel as a company that can promote social and environmental goals along with financial ones.

WHAT'S BEEN THE COLLECTIVE IMPACT OF MISSION-DRIVEN COMPANIES ON THE MAINSTREAM?

Having looked at some of the provocative implications of mission-driven companies for their mainstream counterparts, it's time to take a few steps back to ask a big picture question. In concluding the chapter, I want to reiterate that the vast majority of mission-driven companies, like companies in general, are small—even tiny. Many struggle to stay afloat, and each year a large number fail. Together, their impact as, say, a percentage of GDP in developed and emerging economies is the size of a rounding error. Detractors focus on this small collective size. They also find it easy to dismiss the contributions of mission-driven businesses when leaders in the movement oversell the ease with which a triple bottom line approach to business can be successful. Despite the value in providing a primer for launching such a business, longtime leaders Ben Cohen and Mal Warwick give their critics a target when the subtitle of their book *Values-Driven Business* bills its focus as "how to change the world, make money, and have fun."[50] Worst of all, expressions of enthusiasm and optimism that sometimes are manifested in shallow simplicities are not helped by scandals that several companies have had to weather. It can be easy to denigrate the movement as having a trivial impact on enterprise, society, and the environment.

But such a harsh assessment would be a mistake for several reasons. For one, many in the movement do not view growth and shear size as their yardsticks of success. More important, although the movement of mission-driven enterprise has been oversold by some, its impact goes far beyond the boundaries of those in the movement. Mission-driven businesses have set in motion an important virtuous cycle. What is this cycle, and how is it created?

As conventional firms raise their social and environmental performance levels, distinctions between them and mission-driven companies will not melt away—far from it. More and more, customers in markets for many products are increasingly active—and activist. This indicates that even nuanced differences between mission-driven and more conventional firms are not going unnoticed. Societal expectations will create further opportunities for mission-driven companies as they open up new frontiers for social and environmental initiatives that are rewarded by socially and environmentally astute citizens.

At the same time, the notable steps taken by many larger companies toward social and especially environmental stewardship owe much to the mission-driven enterprise movement. And as companies in that movement continue to challenge themselves to take on new social and environmental goals, conventional companies trying to stay within sight of best practices will find themselves challenged by greater expectations. The relationship between mission-driven companies and their mainstream counterparts is

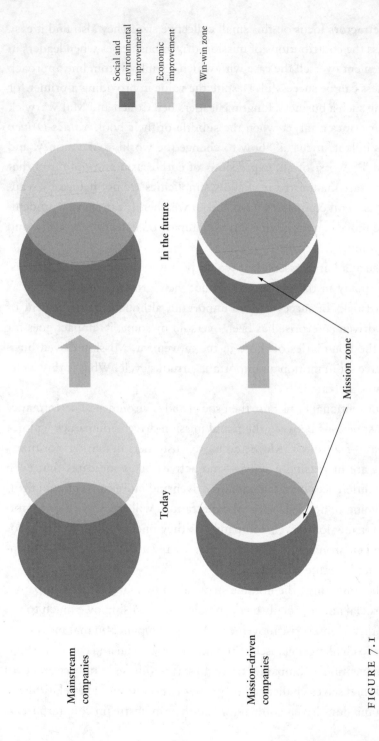

Social and
environmental
improvement

Economic
improvement

Win-win zone

Mainstream
companies

Today

In the future

Mission-driven
companies

Mission zone

FIGURE 7.1
Dynamics of the win-win zone and the mission zone.

becoming symbiotic as the two groups interact in ways that push each other to exceed current performance norms.[51] A virtuous cycle results.

To illustrate this effect, let's recall the idea of the win-win zone and the mission zone introduced in Chapter 1. I add the dimension of time in Figure 7.1. What this figure shows is that there is a dynamic nature to the overlapping domains as society's expectations shift and mission-driven companies prove and publicize the viability of new initiatives. Although the effect has a certain ebb and flow to it, over the long haul it has produced greater opportunities for meeting triple bottom line goals simultaneously.[52] For this reason, the win-win zone expands for mainstream companies, as shown in the upper right-hand corner of Figure 7.1. But as the mainstream company positions itself to take advantage of greater opportunities, a shrewd mission-driven company hasn't stood still. It will have been constantly innovating in the social and environmental area and will expand its own win-win zone, triggering another round of cyclical improvements.

The impact of mission-driven companies on mainstream businesses thus goes far beyond their modest collective size. The ways in which they pursue their social and environmental missions are difficult for those mainstream companies to replicate, although if those in the mainstream pay attention, there is much to learn. In the next chapter I look at the geographic clustering of mission-driven companies. As we'll see, one of the advantages of being in a hotbed of this type of enterprise is the ability of mission-driven companies to learn from one another as they anticipate societal expectations and position themselves for marketplace opportunities that result.

VALUES CLUSTERS
Portland and Other Hotbeds of
Mission-Driven Companies

After purchasing the North American rights to produce and sell its flushable diapers from a company on the Australian island of Tasmania, Kim and Jason Graham-Nye looked for a home for their infant enterprise. They picked Portland, Oregon, settling into a beautiful converted Victorian in the northwest sector of the city. Their company, gDiapers, has grown faster than a newborn baby and has just moved to a new location to accommodate its rapid expansion.[1]

gDiapers isn't the only company that relocated to Portland in the last several years. Vestas Wind Systems, the world leader in what it shrewdly terms modern energy, placed its North American headquarters and a manufacturing plant there in 2002. KEEN Footwear, known for its hybrid sandals and distinctive urban vibe, came in 2006. And then there are the start-ups, from green carpet cleaners to marketing consultants to "social-impact bankers."[2]

Why have so many businesses chosen to grow in Portland? Why Portland and not Las Vegas or Long Beach, two cities close to it in population?

The answers to these questions are telling, because they show that the movement of mission-driven companies has developed distinctly from the ordinary clustering behavior of companies. In terms of catchphrases, it's snappy to call Portland the Silicon Valley of Sustainability, but as we'll see, this is a facile comparison. In this chapter, we'll have a look at what is driving this colocation and also examine the dense network of mission-driven companies in Portland, Oregon, in some depth. In so doing, we'll appreciate why a variety of locations have become hosts to mission-driven companies. But first, let's review the theory behind industrial clusters, the starting point for our strategic exploration.

WHAT CREATES AN EFFECTIVE CLUSTER OF COMPANIES?

In a now classic treatise, *The Competitive Advantage of Nations*, Michael Porter advanced a model that explained powerful industrial clusters within nations.[3] Porter explained the national advantages enjoyed by Japanese robotics, Italian ceramic tile, American movie making, and many other country-specific industrial sectors. Although Porter's focus was on nations, readers quickly saw that the framework he advanced could be much better applied to regional advantages. After all, is it America's cinematic leadership or Hollywood's? So development professionals and planners everywhere focused on Porter's framework, which is based on four interrelated factors that together explain regional concentration of industries.[4]

Porter's model consists of a diamond of four factors. The first, factor conditions, represents skilled labor, raw materials, or infrastructure. If workers in an industry are more highly skilled, they can be a foundation of competitive advantage. The second factor, demand conditions, represents how sophisticated and assertive customers are for the industry's product. The more discerning the customers, the more the companies in an industry are pushed toward excellence. The third factor is firm strategy, structure, and rivalry, which represents the intensity of rivalry within an industry. Typically, the more companies compete within their cluster, the more they are ready to take on competitors elsewhere. The fourth and final factor, related and supporting industries, represents supply and other industries that connect to the main industry and are highly competitive in their own right. These complementary players are vital to the focal industry. Without premier machine tool or robotics producers, Japan's strengths in many manufacturing industries would evaporate.

Porter's assertion is that the points of the diamond act as a self-reinforcing system. Each point, on its own, can contribute to a competitive advantage, but when the four factors depend on and buttress each other, systemic excellence is created. For example, when sophisticated buyers demand goods that only a highly productive workforce (one of the factor endowments) can deliver, both dimensions must be present for success.[5] Once in place, the two work together to create more innovation.

Porter went on to take the idea of national competitive advantage and bring it down to the level of geographic areas, such as Northern California's wine industry or Hong Kong's fashion apparel industry.[6] But his focus is always on industries or fields consisting of groups of tightly linked industries.

Does the Porter diamond model explain the colocation of mission-driven firms? No, primarily because his intent was to explain single industries. Because socially and environmentally oriented companies don't occupy just one industry, the Porter model cannot explain their agglomeration. Essentially, this is because all four factors that make up the diamond are unique to each industry. For example, firm strategy, structure, and rivalry are different for differing industrial sectors. In one industry, dominance by one firm can retard the frothy innovation that occurs when many smaller competitors colocate. Demand is also different across industries. The acutely discriminating Swiss populace demands leadership in premium watches, but that same consuming public does not drive excellence in athletic footwear. And the idea of related and supporting industries loses its meaning when one is studying clusters that are not limited to a particular industry.

But perhaps a more important issue is Porter's home discipline, economics. Just as the single economic bottom line cannot capture how these companies are managed and succeed, the simple application of economics will not explain clustering of mission-driven companies. Instead, it is critical to introduce social and environmental factors.

In the remainder of this chapter, I piece together data where they are available, refer to in-depth interviews with a great many individuals in Portland, Oregon, and elsewhere, and leverage some published research to try to appreciate what drives clustering by mission-driven companies. But first, let's answer a basic question.

WHERE DO MISSION-DRIVEN COMPANIES CLUSTER?

The first task is to explore where mission-driven companies are placed and to link this to one likely factor: responsible consumers. To complete this task, I gathered data for numbers and locations of mission-driven companies and other data that could track concentrations of responsible consumers. Needless to say, gathering this information was difficult, and outside the United States the data were unavailable. Even in the United States, the information was far from an easy download from the Chamber of Commerce or Bureau of Labor Statistics.

Fortunately, however, other less traditional organizations have compiled data that can help us.[7] First, to locate mission-driven companies, I turned to the *National Green Pages*, created by Green America, which serves as an information clearinghouse for these companies. One can have some confidence that the companies listed actually are trying to meet triple bottom line goals, because Green America actually screens them before adding them to its roster.[8] It turned out that in 2008, there were 2,885 such companies in the *National Green Pages*, including 1,088 in the largest fifty urban areas.[9] I took the number of listings and divided these totals by population to put the numbers on a consistent basis.[10] Table 8.1 shows the tabulation.

The table reveals a number of hot spots for mission-driven companies. The cities at the top of the list are home to a great many of these companies—far more than the average and clear evidence of agglomeration. What is also interesting is the geographic distribution of these values clusters. The movement is not exclusive to the East and West Coasts, although cities there are at the top of the list: The top ten cities include a Midwestern city and two Southern cities too.

With that question answered, the next step is to establish how key social, economic, and environmental forces explain the location of mission-driven companies.[11] To do that, we must think about what creates the local conditions that make launching such a business a better bet.

TABLE 8.1

Concentrations of mission-driven companies in the fifty largest metropolitan areas

Metropolitan area[a]	Green Pages listings per 100,000 residents	Metropolitan area[a]	Green Pages listings per 100,000 residents
San Francisco–Oakland	4.97	Cincinnati	0.33
Portland, Oregon	3.08	Richmond	0.33
Washington, D.C.	2.69	Sacramento	0.33
Austin	1.56	Milwaukee	0.32
Seattle-Tacoma	1.54	Providence	0.31
Minneapolis–St. Paul	1.50	Cleveland	0.29
San Jose	1.00	Atlanta	0.28
Boston	0.98	Hartford	0.25
San Diego	0.84	Charlotte	0.24
Tampa–St. Petersburg	0.84	Virginia Beach–Norfolk	0.24
Chicago	0.66	St. Louis	0.21
Raleigh	0.57	Rochester	0.19
Baltimore	0.56	Miami	0.18
Salt Lake City	0.55	Birmingham	0.18
New York	0.54	Dallas–Fort Worth	0.18
Kansas City	0.50	Detroit	0.13
Denver	0.49	Houston	0.12
Pittsburgh	0.47	Las Vegas	0.11
Los Angeles	0.47	Orlando	0.10
Columbus	0.46	Memphis	0.08
Louisville	0.41	Oklahoma City	0.08
Nashville	0.39	Buffalo	0.00
Phoenix	0.36	Jacksonville	0.00
Indianapolis	0.35	Riverside	0.00
Philadelphia	0.34	San Antonio	0.00

a. The cities actually represent metropolitan areas. For example, Washington, D.C, includes businesses from the Washington-Arlington-Alexandria area. For brevity, I've shortened most of the metropolitan area names to the main city.

BUILDING A BETTER DIAMOND
Indigenous Regional Values

Porter's work assiduously avoids sociocultural factors. In fact, in *The Competitive Advantage of Nations*, the index shows that "social norms and values" are mentioned on 2 of 813 pages of text and notes. "Culture" is missing entirely.[12] One can argue that more than a passing mention of social norms, values, and culture is compulsory in a book about the emergence of clusters of internationally competitive industries—or even their regional counterparts. If our aim is to appreciate the emergence of clusters of mission-driven companies, the role of indigenous values must be addressed far more forthrightly. This is because social and environmental goals are intimately tied to local society and culture; Figure 8.1 explicitly recognizes the indigenous regional values within which this diamond is set. What are some of the elements of this context that will influence the development and emergence of what I call values clusters?

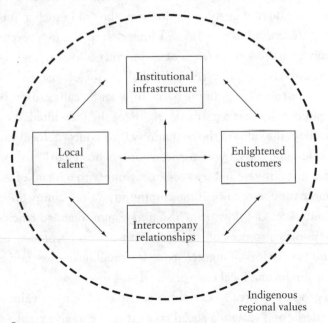

FIGURE 8.1
Determinants of values clusters.

Local values that could be reflected in the structure of enterprise in a geographic area include environmental stewardship, social justice, care for the disadvantaged, entrepreneurship and private enterprise, local sourcing, faith and spirituality, and inclusion. But other values are not so obvious and may be rooted in history. For Dave Williams of ShoreBank Pacific, the history of enterprise in Oregon begins with collective activities (e.g., fishing, agriculture, and forestry) that dominate the commercial landscape. These enterprises depend on cooperation, because they frequently draw on common resources before the arrival of larger companies.[13] Without cooperation, the "tragedy of the commons" can be invoked. That's where many individuals, each pursuing their own self-interests, can draw down commonly shared resources faster than the rate at which they are replenished.[14] For Williams, it was obvious: People must cooperate when facing a commons problem. Historically, the business culture that developed in the state and in Portland was dense with social networks, which favored local partners and collaborative solutions.

Some values militate *against* the rise of mission-driven companies. Adherence to values of gritty individualism (the "old rancher and oilman mentality," according to one Texan I interviewed)[15] may prevent a local population from thinking in terms of social and ecological benefits that do not accrue directly and privately to themselves. Sociologist Amitai Etzioni has written extensively about the perils of what he calls radical individualism, a philosophy that regards the rights of the individuals as supreme and downplays the value of the community.[16] By contrast, local values that stress communitarianism will attract people who regard mission-driven companies in a different light: as organizations with a blend of goals that can promote the community. If the community values competition, many positive outcomes can flow from a shared commitment to efficient organization. But it's also possible that competition can become an end in itself, leading to the loss of market space for small businesses and a lack of interest in supporting local enterprise.

Each geographic area has a unique portfolio of seminal values that together underlie and sustain a social context that can give rise to mission-driven companies. Environmental concern may top the list of values in Seattle, whereas for Chicago it might be social justice. The mixture of businesses that arise in these cities reflects their indigenous values. Thus more companies with sustainability orientations may be situated in Seattle and companies more focused on social justice may locate in Chicago. Seattle is in one of the most "unchurched" states in the union, whereas Illinois is closer to the norm, so the role of faith will be more prominent in Chicago.[17]

It's important to recognize that although indigenous values are deeply ingrained, they do evolve over time. Chicago's long-standing social justice movement has meant that its greening trajectory has been especially inclusive. For example, ShoreBank, the Chicago bank that lends with social goals in mind, was founded in 1973. Later, in 2000, the bank "expanded its focus to include environmental issues, believing that communities cannot achieve true prosperity without also attaining environmental well-being."[18] Bianca and Michael Alexander, tired of preaching to the sustainability choir in Los Angeles, took their production company, Conscious Planet Media, to Chicago in 2009. The company distributes its media products through several markets and also produces videos for companies seeking to tell their stories online and elsewhere. Although the Alexanders left the sunshine of Southern California for the frigid Midwest in February, they were surprised by the warm reception they received in Chicago. For Bianca Alexander, Chicago was close to the tipping point for sustainability values, a city where receptivity to change was escalating. Equally important, the city offered a chance to "meet people where they're at" and "bring the movement to the people."[19] Alexander is particularly energized about her series of videos, *The Soul of Green*, which explores the nexus of social justice and sustainability.[20]

Indigenous regional values are the foundation for clusters of mission-driven companies. But whether these values will incubate mission-driven companies depends on four interrelated factors: (1) local talent, (2) enlightened customers, (3) the institutional infrastructure, and (4) firm networking, collaboration, and cross-purchasing.

Local Talent

The availability of talent is essential to the growth of any enterprise, but why is *local* talent preferable? Of course, for practical reasons costs and risks are lower to both the company and the prospective hire if the prospective employee is close by. New local hires won't need to change their housing situation or have to confront new customs, make new friends, or be exposed to new allergies. Locals also have a ready-made social network that serves as an informal sounding board for new products and services and stimulates thinking about the next generation.

Furthermore, it is so much easier to connect with local talent for the purposes of recruiting. First, prospective applicants are more likely to know about the nature of a company and its prospects for success. Newspaper stories about a growing company generate buzz that can enhance prospects for hiring. With millions of Web sites, locals are more likely to view outlets that focus on nearby opportunities. And of course, the dense social networks that I've just mentioned form the circuitry through which information flows from person to person. The social network also has the important function of promoting good behavior. If a worker is a star, his or her reputation will be known locally. Searching locally for those with the right stuff is far easier when there is a large local talent pool.

To explore the connection between local talent and the presence of mission-driven companies, I used a measure of local talent created and tabulated by urban geographer Richard Florida. From his book *Cities and the Creative Class*, I obtained rankings of talent for the fifty largest cities in the United States.[21] Unfortunately, there aren't measures of potential employees with the mission-driven companies, so we have to assume that the more talent is available, the more of these potential employees there are.

The results are shown in Figure 8.2. What the chart shows is that there is a reasonably predictable relationship between the talent index rank (in which a lower rank means more local talent) and the concentration of mission-driven companies: The more talent, the greater that concentration.[22] On the left-hand side of the chart, we see that almost all the cities with high concentrations have top-10 talent indexes. Only one of the ten cities with the highest concentrations of mission-driven companies is not a top-20 location of talent.[23] There *are* hotbeds of mission-driven companies, and one contributing factor is the quality of local talent.

Having lots of talent in and of itself creates further opportunities for green business. In Portland, Jim Morris has created quite a practice for himself and at MBL Group in the area of executive placement of individuals into mission-driven businesses in Portland. A classic jeans-and-jacket

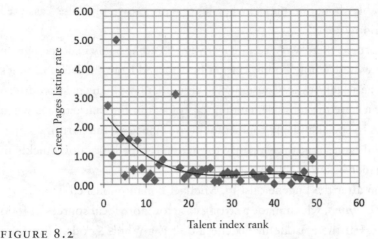

FIGURE 8.2
Concentrations of mission-driven companies versus Florida's talent index.

professional, if Morris looks like he owns a guitar shop on the side, it's because he does. His passion for music runs deep, and he looks for that level of fervor when he recruits. He evaluates candidates beyond education and even work experience, hunting for a passion for social and environmental causes.[24] In 2009, Morris saw enough potential to strike out on his own, trusting local demand for his services.

Enlightened Customers

The second factor in clustering, related to the first, is the presence of enlightened customers. In late 2005, Whole Foods Market announced that it wanted to come to Eugene, Oregon. It picked out a site that could help revitalize a corner of the city's struggling downtown with a constant flow of shoppers. But it appealed for help, asking the city to invest $7 million in a new parking garage to serve it and surrounding businesses.

That's when a conflict erupted in the otherwise laid-back town.

Eugene's city council voted in favor of the garage in March of the next year, but not before nearly 100 citizens delivered three hours of public testimony on the project, the content of which was overwhelmingly negative.[25] Complaints were lodged about the city unfairly subsidizing a competitor to its many natural foods stores, but also—and for our purposes more telling—about Whole Foods' lack of local purchasing. "What's so sustainable about organic strawberries that are grown in Chile?" asserted opposition leaders.

Of course, there was a certain irony here: Perhaps only in deepest green Eugene would Whole Foods Market be attacked from the left. But that's the teachable takeaway. Consumers in cities that host many mission-driven companies are the most demanding customers in the marketplace when it comes to social and environmental performance on the part of companies. And issues that they identify for action can gain traction quickly in the broader business context.

Soon after the Eugene dustup, Michael Pollan published *The Omnivore's Dilemma*, which made a strong case for more local sources of food supplies.[26] If the episode in Eugene didn't get Whole Foods CEO John Mackey's attention, Pollan's book and his accompanying media campaign certainly did. Pollan charged Whole Foods with hypocritically marketing itself as sustainable and organic while purchasing from "industrial organic" giants Earthbound Farm and Cal-Organic/Grimmway Farms as well as distant providers. A well-publicized exchange between the two then took place online.[27]

By July 2006, Whole Foods had reacted to the issue of localness (and perhaps the much hyped move into organics by Wal-Mart) by introducing a number of new policies at its stores, giving $10 million annually to help small local farmers and producers humanely raise animal products, raising standards for how farm animals were raised generally, and even hosting farmer's markets in some of its parking lots.[28]

The point of the story, of course, is *not* about Whole Foods. It's about enlightened customers in a progressive town and their expectations that a new company stand up to the standards set by its own group of home-grown natural foods stores. The story teaches us that, whether for stylish clothing in Milan, country music in Nashville, or organic food in Eugene, demanding consumers will bring out the highest possible performance in local companies based on what matters to the local population. And when the population chooses to demand higher social and environmental performance, it can create companies that lead.

Customers in places where mission-driven companies locate exert pressure and constant vigilance on those companies by demanding superior triple bottom line performance. But although the relationship is one of tough love, it is one of love—love in the sense that those customers will buy locally when they can, love in the sense that they may be willing to pay a premium for goods sold by local companies whose values match their own, and love in the sense that they will give the company every chance to succeed when it meets competition in the marketplace.

Portland's Stumptown Coffee Roasters demonstrates how strong local demand can create mission-driven companies that can extend their geographic reach. Duane Sorenson, its founder, decided that Portland was the place to fire up the espresso machine. And even in the Northwest, where neighborhoods are thick with java joints, customers took to his coffee. Although it was mostly for flavor, the company's social mission mattered too. Sorenson was a pioneer in direct buying, bypassing middlemen and even cooperatives to purchase directly from the farmer. Customers in the Portland area, especially wholesale customers, have pushed him and Stumptown toward greater levels of transparency.[29] That type of experience has helped Stumptown and its founder gain a reputation that is serving them well as they expand into the Seattle and New York markets.

Growing up in Portland also is elemental to the success of *Sustainable Industries*, a magazine that chronicles green business on the West Coast and increasingly elsewhere in the nation. It's now headquartered in San Francisco, a more prominent media town than Portland, but it still bears the stamp of its early years in the Oregon sustainability culture. Owner, editor, and publisher Brian Back recalls, "Portland is really the backbone and foundation of the authenticity we bring to the table."[30] The trust Back sees in his readership is based on this endowment of authenticity. If a business enjoys authenticity among the most enlightened and demanding customers, it has a worthy competitive asset.

As with the pool of local talent, when it comes to enlightened consumers, there is also a family resemblance to Porter's factors. Where local talent parallels factor conditions, enlightened consumers parallel demand conditions.

The last two factors in this model, institutional infrastructure and networking, collaboration, and cross-purchasing, are unique to mission-driven clustering and put distinctions between industry-based clusters and values clusters in sharp relief.

Institutional Infrastructure

Institutions grow from and reflect the shared values in a geographic area. They include but are not limited to the emergence of supportive civic and business leadership, policy-making organizations, and educational and skill-building resources. All can create and sustain momentum that elicits foundings of mission-driven companies.

CIVIC AND BUSINESS LEADERSHIP Spencer Beebe takes the long view, looking to the future but also to the past. In a state full of recent arrivals, his roots go deep: All eight of his great-grandparents were native Oregonians. In his life, Beebe has seen the loss of habitats and species but also the return of peregrine falcons to the Columbia Gorge after careful stewardship efforts. An accomplished ornithologist who jokingly claims a "bird gene," his understated demeanor revs up a bit as he describes two falcons that he raised. Brother and sister, they developed unique personalities and put the lie to the "mechanistic" view of nature espoused in economic models, where living creatures "do as their instincts require" with no room for "personality, character, fun, or joy of learning."[31] Beebe had other problems with economics, despite having some training in the field. He grew increasing concerned about the ecologically ignorant tendencies of economics (and cranky landlords) and decided to nest in a place where he could nurture businesses and organizations with more sound practices.

After some search, in 1998 Beebe came across a dilapidated century-old railroad storage building on a siding in Portland's Pearl District. His goal: "Take an old building that helped distribute the goods of an industrial economy, and turn it into a marketplace for the goods and services and ideas of a conservation economy." Early in the amazing gentrification process that transformed the neighborhood, Beebe's Ecotrust purchased the building. Twelve million dollars' worth of LEED-certified renovation later, the result was the Jean Vollum Natural Capital Center, named after its most generous benefactor. Today, the Ecotrust Building (as it's popularly known) houses a range of thriving businesses and organizations. Downstairs there's a Patagonia store, an integrated natural health center, and the ever popular Hot Lips Pizza, known for its local sourcing of ingredients and reuse of oven heat to warm the building. Upstairs, among many others, there's the city's Office of Sustainable Development, Portfolio 21 Investments (home to a major ecologically oriented fund), and of course, the offices of Ecotrust.

Beebe is not alone in terms of the civic and business leadership he's shown in Portland. A large number of mission-driven businesses, especially green ones, have grown into national and even global leadership positions here. Companies in the green building industry in particular reflect these indigenous values.[32]

The town hosts the leading green office and high-rise housing development company in the country, Gerding-Edlen Development. Following Bob Gerding's retirement, the company has been led by Mark Edlen, who has continued to question standard practice in architecture and design. Aided by his ecoconsigliere, Dennis Wilde, Edlen has developed offices, apartments, and condominiums with an aim toward so-called net zero buildings, which produce as much or more energy than they use. In pursuit of this goal, he has incorporated energy measures from bioswales to rooftop wind turbines in buildings. Edlen laments that investors won't provide better terms for his buildings. But even in 2009, in the midst of what was shaping up to be a disaster in the construction field, he refused to bargain away his long-term focus. And it's understandable, given the rewards he's captured from taking risks in green design and learning along the way. A building certified at the LEED platinum level will cost a conventional developer 10% more to build, but for Gerding-Edlen that number is 2–3%—an enormous advantage.[33] Edlen's firm, a living repository of green building expertise, anchors a movement that has made Portland number 1 in green building, according to the online resource SustainLane.[34]

Green building in Portland also encompasses small-scale residential building. The city is home to Neil Kelly Company, which for more than forty years has served the metropolitan area. When the industry's leading publication, *Professional Remodeler*, named Tom Kelly the 2008 Remodeler of the Year, it described him as having "the aggressive nature of a world-class athlete, the passionate soul of a rock star, and the wily personality of a high-stakes gambler."[35] Kelly chuckles as he reads the passage, but for those across the country who follow the $27 million company, the description rings true. And in the same way that Gerding-Edlen has benefited from a history of green innovation, Neil Kelly also has learned that building in a green way generates many advantages that make their way circuitously to the bottom line. These advantages may meander by the eyeshades of most accountants, but Tom Kelly knows they're real and contribute to his mission, a powerful asset that serves to "expand opportunities well beyond what it looks like on face value."[36]

Through innovation and leadership from Edlen, Kelly, and many others, a large community of related businesses in Portland has materialized. Companies across the spectrum from environmentally sensitive paint producer YOLO Colorhouse to energy specialist ECOS Consulting to sustainable landscape designers GreenWorks, the city is packed with supporting players. If there is a Porter-style industry cluster in Portland, it's the green building sector.[37] For our purposes, the key is that this sector produced civic leaders who collectively articulated a vision for triple bottom line business and broadcast this vision beyond the city. This strengthened the brand effect for the city and drew other entrepreneurs to it.

It certainly helps to have local venture capitalists who understand the nuances of sustainable businesses. Called the Oracle of Oregon by *Sustainable Industries*, David Chen works within many social and business networks in a world that somehow defies the 24-hour day.[38] He also demonstrates the key linkages between elements of the values cluster diamond by straddling private enterprise and government. When not building Equilibrium Capital, a venture capital fund devoted exclusively to later-stage sustainability-oriented companies, he chairs two important public associations, the Oregon Innovation Council and the Oregon Nanoscience and Microtechnologies Institute. Chen's venture capital practice reflects an intimate understanding of its local context, confirming that location matters.

Here we are in Oregon, where we have something that money can't buy: We have a population that seems to be genuinely, for the long-term, predisposed to this. We have companies that have been practicing this ethos as a competitive advantage for many years. There is a supportive environment. There is expertise that has been accumulated over years across many of these sectors. As the world is recognizing some of the things we've done here, now is the time to continue to drive our leadership in these areas—especially because the world is listening. Let's take full advantage of what we have to push ahead.[39]

Civic leadership *legitimizes*, *popularizes*, and *publicizes* a city's mission-driven community. It helps to create a receptive environment for other businesses, particularly when a geographic area hosts businesses that are willing to place early bets that receptive customers will support their initiatives.[40] Policy initiatives can help to keep the momentum going.

RIGHT-MINDED POLICY INITIATIVES   What is the proper role for government in eliciting mission-driven companies? On this topic, studies of traditional clusters provide some insight. For the most part, writers from academia and government tend to frown on direct subsidies and targeting. In one two-year study on regional clusters across the globe, the investigators asserted, "Our case studies clearly show the foolishness of directive efforts to organize" them.[41] Similarly, a report for the U.S. National Governors Association concluded (with more circumspection, given its source), "It is important to recognize that states rarely, if ever, have the ability to create clusters out of whole cloth."[42]

Yet all sources see a positive role for policy makers that is less about jump-starting groups of companies than it is about promoting interactions, implementing progressive tax policies, streamlining regulations, and purchasing local goods and services. In the case of Portland, it's important to appreciate that steps taken by policy makers reflect the unique history of the city and also the state. Oregon has a long history of environmental stewardship, manifested in its progressive land-use laws and the nation's first bottle bill. Many of its initiatives are associated with Tom McCall, who was governor of the state from 1967 to 1975.[43] Portland's city government parallels this history. In the 1970s, after local opposition killed the inner city Mount Hood Freeway, the city redirected most of the project's federal construction budget to mass transportation.[44] In 1990, Portland became one of the first cities to ban Styrofoam containers, and more recently it has been pushing for aggressive new energy standards for commercial buildings.[45] And there have been some measurable successes, such as the carbon reductions following its 1993 climate change policy, the first such policy in the United States. Whereas in 2008 the rest of the cities in the United States saw a 15% rise in per capita greenhouse gas emissions in relation to their 1990 levels, Portland, despite a thriving local economy, held steady.[46]

Policy makers have used a number of initiatives to support mission-driven companies. As noted, standards raise the bar of performance by demanding higher minimums for building efficiency, local content, and carbon neutrality, among other expressions of civic values. Purchasing behavior can elicit improved social and environmental standards. For example, when bids for cleaning products that will be used in schools explicitly allow for the evaluation system to go beyond price to recognize social and environmental elements of bidders, that helps to support those firms. Coastwide Laboratories, from the Portland suburb of Wilsonville, was able to improve prospects for winning bids when local school districts began allocating bid points for green products.[47]

Judging by Portland's experience, having a central body to organize, publicize, and implement policies can be a significant help. Environmentally oriented programs from waste handling to energy conservation to utility regulation were brought together to create Portland's Office of Sustainable Development (OSD) in 2000. Since then the OSD has taken on its own momentum in contributing to the city. The OSD has been led since its inception by Susan Anderson, who combines a thorough knowledge of how the city government operates with meaningful private-sector business experience. Casual and good-natured, but with a keen focus on harmonizing a vision with practical results, Anderson has developed an organization that provides a surprising element of service to companies that seek to reduce their environmental footprints. Using the language of private enterprise is important to Anderson. A program that worked with apartment owners to take the results of energy audits through to the implementation stage was known informally as the concierge service, complete with account executives assigned to work with building owners on moving forward with projects.[48] It all creates a culture that promotes best practices rather than regulatory intrusion.

It is also valuable to publicly cite companies and individuals for stellar performance. Since 1993, the City of Portland and the OSD have given out the BEST Awards for outstanding achievements by green companies

(BEST stands for Businesses for an Environmentally Sustainable Tomorrow). In 2008, the OSD recognized eight businesses, including Mint Dental Works, which became the country's first LEED-certified dental office but which also promoted innovative sustainable practices at its office.[49] No mercury fillings at this office, to be sure. A separate raft of awards also came from *Sustainable Industries*, whose 2008 list of twenty leading green executives gave four of eight awards for "Entrepreneurs" and "Midsize Movers" to Portlanders.[50]

Yet, with all it has been doing, Portland and cities elsewhere have not targeted agglomeration per se. They are simply putting in place practices and policies that facilitate the growth of companies that understand how to grow in the context they create. Governmental policies are just one institutional force that contribute to one point on the diamond discussed here. Important as the policy domain is, the magnitude of its impact depends on the other diamond points. For example, without the requisite trove of skilled talent, incentives for green building may have little effect.

BROAD SKILL-BUILDING INFRASTRUCTURE   The third institutional infrastructure element is organizations that provide education, training, and other ways to improve human capital and apply them to social and environmental goals. Better education facilitates career changes and helps limit shortages of skilled individuals. But often traditional modes of education don't suffice. For example, traditional business school training at top schools is bound by disciplinary fiefdoms and publication norms that restrict interdisciplinary inquiry.

Nontraditional MBA programs are beginning to address this, and their location is no surprise. The Bainbridge Graduate Institute is on Bainbridge Island, a ferry ride away from Seattle, and the Presidio School of Management is in San Francisco. Both are located in areas packed with mission-driven companies but also with larger companies that use the schools to appreciate the growing movement toward responsible business. With such courses as Finance, Accounting, and the Triple Bottom Line (Bainbridge) and teachers such as Natural Capitalism Inc. president Hunter Lovins (Presidio), the schools offer the requisite rigor but are not subject to the strictures that can hamstring traditional programs.

Portland has its own skill-building star, the Natural Step Network, which is the brainchild of Dr. Karl-Henrik Robèrt, a Swedish oncologist. Robèrt used a panel of scientific experts and a consensus process to identify four system conditions that can be used to guide economic activity toward sustainability.[51] Launched in 1989 under the leadership of environmentalist, entrepreneur, and author Paul Hawken, the Natural Step Network established an office in San Francisco. That office closed, leaving the Oregon affiliate office in Portland as the company's U.S. presence. But far from hanging on, the Portland office is bustling and dropped an original reference to Oregon in its title to reflect the nationwide mission it now envisions. Led by the energetic drive of Regina Hauser, who walked away from a law firm partnership to take its helm, the Natural Step Network has delivered training to hundreds of forward-thinking companies. It has expanded to provide a half-dozen open training sessions per year, but it also offers in-house training that can cater to a company's particular issues. Natural Step also hosts executive briefings for member organizations to work through their goals.[52]

When it comes to traditional education, almost every urban area has universities or colleges, and many have programs to provide individuals with training that blends business and sustainability. A growing source of direct training that develops the talent necessary to contribute to companies comes from experiential learning. Under these programs, students work closely with companies on projects of direct interest to the companies. In the San Francisco Bay Area, the Haas School of Business at the University of California at Berkeley worked with sixty companies on 120 consulting projects that connect corporate social responsibility to strategy.[53] The projects go beyond the classroom to place students in real-world situations where they gain experience with managing triple bottom line issues.

The Center for Sustainable Business Practices at the University of Oregon has sponsored a number of projects that have built MBA students' skill sets while serving businesses in Portland. In both a nine-credit dedicated consulting project and within several topical classes, students work closely with companies. One pair of projects addressed an issue faced by Portland's KEEN Footwear, which as of 2007 thought that its sustainability marketing message was outpacing its documentation of activities.[54] Students at the University of Oregon's Lundquist College of Business attacked the problem. First, the team benchmarked best practices in sustainability reporting for companies in KEEN's industry and for companies of its size. A follow-up report then identified content for the report. In 2009, KEEN finalized and unveiled its report. Clearly, having a resource like the Lundquist College was helpful to KEEN, but not to be overlooked were the skills and knowledge acquired by students that worked with KEEN.[55]

One aspect of degree-granting formal university programs is also important. These programs offer an opportunity to enlarge the talent pool when individuals use them to relocate from other areas and leverage the existing relationships between the universities and the surrounding business community.

Collectively, the skill-building infrastructure available to people in a geographic area must deliver to its citizens in several different formats. For example, in addition to the learning modes in Portland that I've mentioned here, there are many other opportunities, running from a series of one-day training seminars to more formal certification programs. All deepen the talent pool and provide human resources to power new mission-driven businesses.

Intercompany Relationships: Networking, Collaboration, and Cross-Purchasing

Many formal models of business relationships found in textbooks suppress social interactions or insist on translating them into dollar terms. All businesspeople know this is nonsense, and worse, it's no fun. Social networks have always been critical to clusters of businesses. AnnaLee Saxenian's classic, *Regional Advantage: Culture and Competition in Silicon Valley and Route 128*, rejected the idea that groups of companies materialize simply because it is cheaper to be closer.[56] Rather, in an elegant, well-researched comparison of two industrial regions moving in opposite directions, Saxenian identified social and cultural patterns that revealed why the electronics industry in Silicon Valley continued to grow while its counterpart around Route 128 withered. In Silicon Valley, dense social networks and a famously footloose workforce created a culture in which competition and collaboration were balanced and informal relationships and flat reporting structures created fluid communications. Route 128, by contrast, was dominated by closed hierarchical structures and norms of secrecy and loyalty.

Networking matters, and there is one important, additional advantage for clusters that are not bound by industries: The delicate balancing act between intense competition and cooperation and exchange of information found by Saxenian in Silicon Valley has no analogue in values clusters. Because mission-driven clusters agglomerate through their identity as mission-driven enterprises, these clusters cut across industries by their nature. When the green grocer exchanges ideas with the importer of fair trade toys, there's no danger of information leaking out that could have competitive implications. For this reason alone, informal business relationships have much greater potential power in cross-industry clusters of mission-driven companies.

NETWORKING EVENTS   Networking events are essential opportunities to learn from leaders in the field and to cement relationships with like-minded individuals. As in any field, the action is often not in the plenary sessions but in the hallways. Although national events, such as Social Venture Network's biannual conference series or the newer Social Capital Markets Conference, take place regularly, local events are more important to developing a network of businesses. In Portland, attending these events can amount to a part-time job, given their frequency. One sold-out event was Go Green '08, which attracted many of the individuals mentioned here and hundreds of parties involved in sustainability-oriented businesses. Annual conferences in Portland held by the University of Oregon and Portland State University also assemble local and regional business leaders.

A number of other regular events provide opportunities to meet, greet, and learn about best practices, for example, breakfasts and brown bag luncheons held by the Natural Step Network. Two other organizations that hold events signify the broadening of this movement in Portland. Seeing an opportunity to facilitate discussion and serve as a "hub in this wheel of commerce," Craig Wessel, publisher of the *Portland Business Journal*, launched a series of quarterly "sustainability luncheons" in 2008. By late that year, the event was drawing 650 people.[57] Speakers included nationally known figures but also local leaders who discussed trends and opportunities for business. Also in 2008, the Portland Business Alliance, the city's chamber of commerce equivalent, kicked off its quarterly "Green Hours" series, which featured representatives of local companies who discussed their programs for a more traditional audience.

CROSS-INDUSTRY ASSOCIATIONS   Collaboration that allows groups of smaller companies to speak with one voice can help cement relationships and elevate legitimacy for small companies in areas that may be seen as lying on the commercial fringe. One approach used by individuals in several places is to piggyback on a national organization that supports local businesses.

Founded in 1987, the Social Venture Network brought together socially conscious entrepreneurs. They found the ability to exchange ideas and form a mutually supportive network invaluable. Through the years, the network has grown to nearly 500 members, including many nonprofits. The Social Venture Network hosts two conferences per year, and recent topics have included company-topical sessions on greening the supply chain, using storytelling as a communications tool, and attracting capital during a recession. The sessions also touch on broader issues, such as how businesses can contribute to urban renewal and new policies under the Obama administration. These conferences not only provide networking opportunities but also allow entrepreneurs to appreciate the trajectory of social and environmental innovation being taken by their peers.

BALLE, the Business Alliance for Local Living Economies, was founded by Judy Wicks, owner of the White Dog Café in Philadelphia, and Laury Hammel, the owner of Longfellow health clubs in Massachusetts. The two conceived BALLE soon after September 11, 2001, as a way "to build community wealth by catalyzing, connecting, and strengthening local business networks dedicated to building Living Economies."[58] BALLE is a decentralized network of chapters in localities where individuals recruit like-minded entrepreneurs to promote local buying and raise collective consciousness.

Other local business organizations arise independently. In Washington, D.C., the Sustainable Business Network of Washington (or SB NOW), has grown impressively since its formation in 2004. As of early 2009, it had 322 members and was growing at a rate of more than a dozen new businesses per month.[59] SB NOW offers members a number of benefits, from bimonthly business tours to a speaker series and networking events. Emerging from this network are cross-purchasing relationships and also familiarity with people who have complementary skills. That's a network Anca Novacovici has relied on to grow her D.C. consulting company Eco-Coach.[60] Based on their skills and the job at hand, Novacovici's network of consultants work with her to solve a client's problems.

Not every geographic area has the interest and commercial activity to support even one business organization such as these. Dallas–Ft. Worth, a city of 6 million inhabitants, has had difficulty supporting even one organization. Sustainable Dallas,[61] an organization for green business that was funded by a local angel, is now "in hibernation" after a difficult period where it couldn't find traction.[62] Although pockets of sustainability can still be found in Dallas, the minimum of energy and funding necessary to run such an organization has yet to materialize.

Portland has not one but several organizations for mission-driven companies. The Natural Step Network operates as one forum, but so does the Sustainable Business Network of Portland, a BALLE network affiliate. Interestingly, a group of firms that includes mission-driven companies actually created a statewide organization to offer an alternative to the powerful lobbying organization Associated Oregon Industries. That association, which is known for representing traditional industries in the state, has had a difficult time shedding its reputation as an opponent of green policy initiatives. In 1998 it opposed a bill in the Oregon legislature to study green taxes, an idea supported by a number of Republican members in favor of taxing "bads" instead of "goods," such as profits. According to Tom Kelly, that episode led to the creation of an alternative statewide body, the Oregon Business Association.[63] The new association was formed as an alternative bipartisan body, which moved from its initial focus on the environment to embrace a number of other issues, from public education to transportation. Although the Oregon Business Association started with smaller companies that weren't terribly well connected, it now has attracted a number of members from the state's business elite, including such companies as Intel, Wells Fargo, and Portland General Electric. So successful has the organization been in attracting support and members that Kelly worries a bit that the presence of larger companies may dilute its strong message.[64]

Nationally, so lively has been the movement to affiliate that the Social Venture Network formed the Social Impact Leadership Coalition as a way to share resources and ideas among the mission-driven community.[65] The coalition, a network of networks, has brought together more than a dozen associations for mission-driven business, including several mentioned here. At first a platform for exchanging best practices, the Social Impact Leadership Coalition has morphed into a vehicle by which these associations can obtain funds from the Kellogg Foundation for a three-year effort to reach out to a more demographically diverse group of social entrepreneurs.[66]

CROSS-PURCHASING   Cross-purchasing, the maintenance of purchasing and sales relationships among mission-driven companies, is an intercompany element and the easiest to appreciate. Agglomeration by mission-driven companies creates a virtuous cycle, because as numbers increase, so do opportunities to purchase locally and from a company that shares social and environmental goals. It is the norm for mission-driven companies to support each other in this way. When Wisteria Loeffler, the director of Zenger Farm, wanted to renovate a century-old house on the farm's property, she hired Carrington Barrs and his Barrs & Genauer Construction company. Barrs & Genauer, which specializes in green construction, rebuilt the home to maximize reclaimed material, minimize use of toxic finishes, and employ innovative water treatment features. The company continued the chain by partnering with Portland Youth Builders to offer job training to at-risk teenagers. And of course, it sourced from Environmental Building Supplies (now part of Seattle-based Ecohaus), which exclusively stocks ecofriendly materials.[67]

When working with other companies that share core values, mission-driven companies also reduce worries that a trading partner will embarrass them or not fully appreciate their core values. Revolution Foods, the provider of healthy school lunches, saw an opportunity when it was approached by Whole Foods Market, which was seeking a branded line of organic children's meals. But founders Kirsten Tobey and Kristin Richmond worried about being distracted from their central focus on schools. So they decided to have the meals produced and delivered independently, leveraging their brand and culinary expertise. They chose Sheryl O'Laughlin, Clif Bar's former CEO, who had created a mission-driven food distributor, Nest Collective, in nearby Emeryville. O'Laughlin didn't need to bone up on Revolution Foods' mission. She knew the importance of their core values and blended in her retailing experience to make the venture a success.[68]

Evidence of the mutual support systems that can be based on cross-purchasing appears on many Web sites of mission-driven companies, which encourage viewers to visit sites of other like-minded companies. Seattle's Blue Sky Bridal will be happy to sell you a new or previously owned wedding gown, and their site will lead you to green options for flowers, invitations, and a gift registry as well as a place to buy responsibly sourced rings. Local options for almost every category are provided.[69]

. . .

Networking, collaboration, and cross-purchasing form the glue that binds together a group of companies and creates a cluster from an assortment of independent operations. They are essential elements that spin a web of interrelationships that moves information, people, and money around. Without such relationships, it would be difficult for companies to cohere to the point where a cluster can form. With them, companies can improve sales, speak with one voice in policy debates, and collectively identify trends and opportunities for further growth.

PLACE MATTERS: THOUGHTS FOR ENTREPRENEURS
Now let's turn the situation around. I've devoted this chapter to developing a framework to explain why mission-driven companies congregate in particular geographic regions. What does this mean for an entrepreneur looking to locate a new business?

Place matters—but not as it does in models of industry-based clustering. In those models, a premium is put on being where the leaders in *your* industry locate. But for values clusters, the location is more about the *indigenous values* of a place and whether or not they resonate with a business owner. Put another way, gDiapers didn't look for a geographic area filled with other diaper makers. It moved to Portland, a city filled with individuals and other businesses that shared its commitment to sustainability and social responsibility.

This dovetails with the work of urban economist Richard Florida, who argues that the choice of where to live and work is the most critical decision anyone makes.[70] Cities that are desirable places to live can provide great foundations on which to grow. As Josh Hinerfeld of Organically Grown says about Portland, "It's a destination place, not a stepping stone, a place where people invest in community and relationships. It's not all about the next rung on the ladder." Because companies and consumers in desirable towns tend to be places where mission-driven companies congregate (see Table 8.1), this removes one element of risk for companies.

One takeaway is to locate where the action is, in cities with thriving communities of mission-driven companies. On the other hand, if you want to take the biblical advice to "Grow where you are planted," you will have to overcome some handicaps. Sometimes there may be local demand for just one business in a given area, as, for example, when a geographic area can support a single natural foods market. But most of the types of businesses that I've discussed will need greater local demand to succeed. Lack of enlightened consumers locally might be offset if a company can sell in cyberspace. But that business model will have a larger carbon footprint and will lack some of the means of creating customer loyalty that geographic proximity offers.

Choosing where to locate a business can be a difficult process involving many irreversible commitments. It's one of the many unique challenges that face mission-driven companies. Challenge of a different type is the theme of the next chapter, in which we'll explore some of the contentious issues that now face the movement of mission-driven companies.

GROWING PAINS

Asking Difficult Questions

Bottle of beer with your pizza?

If you enjoy a cold one with your slice of pepperoni—even from a mission-driven enterprise such as New Belgium Brewing Company—you are patronizing a company that would be screened out of a number of "ethical" mutual funds. One such fund is the United Kingdom's Friends Provident, a financial services group with roots in the Quaker faith.[1] Since 1984, the group has offered investments in mutual funds that screen out companies engaged in, among other things, alcohol production, gambling, and nuclear energy. Like a number of other investment firms, its definition of socially responsible business excludes some activities that many consider benign, if not salutary, for society.

Globally, hundreds of funds engage in socially responsible investments, with several trillion dollars under management.[2] On the one hand, different approaches to what is socially responsible reflect the same differences in the public. In this case, beer is not terribly controversial. Many would consider alcohol to be relatively benign: One investor may avoid alcohol for societal or religious reasons, whereas another might be perfectly at ease with investments in companies that manufacture and sell spirited beverages. But what about nuclear power? One investor may view it as a prohibitively expensive technology that carries enormous environmental risks.

Another may see nuclear power as a clean source of base load power, free of greenhouse gas emissions. For this second investor, wouldn't nuclear power represent a socially responsible investment?[3]

Issues such as these present perplexing challenges for mission-driven companies and spotlight important debates with which the movement struggles. Like business as a whole, the community of mission-driven companies isn't monolithic. For every one of its captains of responsible industry, there are many shopkeepers trying to meet payroll. But as the movement of businesses with multiple goals has expanded, it has begun to face a number of provocative questions. We look at four of them in this chapter: (1) groupthink, (2) confusion over means and ends, (3) buyouts by conventional companies, and (4) public ownership and the social mission.

GROUPTHINK

Although it can be traced to the popular press, the idea of groupthink was more fully developed by psychologist Irving L. Janis.[4] He defined it as "a mode of thinking that people engage in when they are deeply involved in a cohesive in-group, when the members' strivings for unanimity override their motivation to realistically appraise alternative courses of action."[5] Groupthink has often been identified with public policy decisions, particularly poor ones.[6] Among its characteristics are a tendency to discredit and stereotype dissenters, an illusion of moral superiority, and pressure for conformity within the group.[7] Disloyalty is met with disdain.

On occasion, mission-driven companies and even groups of those companies have fallen into these tendencies. This is sometimes manifested in difficulty with criticism, which was discussed in Chapter 6. For example, groupthink may have retarded efforts within the community of mission-driven companies to be self-critical when confronted with evidence that some companies were saying one thing and doing another. But groupthink is also manifested in how the movement chooses to identify, celebrate, and reward some of its heroes.

The Moskowitz Prize for Socially Responsible Investing was established in 1996 to recognize quantitative academic research on socially responsible investing. During its first several years, the studies that won the award demonstrated positive associations between responsible practices and financial performance. But in 1999, the award went to three finance scholars who demonstrated that legislative and shareholder pressure for voluntary disinvestments in South Africa during the apartheid years had little effect on banks and corporations doing business there.[8] Although the winners heard no criticism when they received the award, behind the scenes a number of practitioners were angered by the choice. For them, the study challenged "beliefs that were central to their identities," according to Lloyd Kurtz, one of the leading figures in the social investment movement and the longtime administrator of the award.[9] Apparently, there are still some lingering misgivings about some of the award winners for this research. The Web site of investment advisers Invested Interests lists all the Moskowitz Prize winners along with links to each paper. All the winners appear—except for the 1999 winner, which is conspicuously missing.[10]

Although the Moskowitz Prize–winning papers since 1999 have supported a positive connection between socially responsible practices and profitability and a number of associated links, no study that has challenged this link has won the prize since then.[11] On the other hand, a couple of studies that received honorable mention awards but did not conform to the socially responsible investment community's prevailing ideology have received receptions that were considerably less cordial, according to Kurtz. A 2003 paper in this competition, by a team from the Wharton School of Business, challenged the notion that socially responsible investments outperformed their conventional counterparts.[12] When the paper won an honorable mention, Kurtz recalled the selection committee being "almost harassed."[13]

The movement seems to have some distance to go in terms of confronting contradictory evidence. But for Kurtz, it must do so if the Moskowitz Prize is to "have any meaning." The award must not be subject to a litmus test, even though many socially responsible investment professionals still fiercely resist the appearance of analysis that contradicts their collective rationality.

These episodes are symptomatic of a greater issue with which mission-driven companies must grapple: the organizational issues that emerge when companies and their founders encode strong values into the company's DNA. As noted, these values are the raison d'être for the company and a key route to differentiating its products. But care must be taken to ensure that they don't create a myopic management style that resists contrary evidence and muzzles constructive debate. Occasionally, a company is reminded that its values-based pronouncements may not resonate with all its employees. The Body Shop's management issued a statement against the first Gulf War, only to anger employees with loved ones serving in the conflict.[14] The experience showed that although its sentiments with respect to animal testing, environmental protection, and other causes were widely shared, it did not guarantee that all of management's values were shared.

Groupthink also can erect a barrier between company culture and the meeting of necessary economic objectives. Smith and Hawken, an outdoor furniture and implements catalogue retailer, found that out in the early 1990s. So taken with the social mission were its employees that "you had a bunch of people walking around with this nonprofit mentality, acting like they were working for Greenpeace instead of a direct-mail business," according to its former editorial director, Meredith Moran.[15] The episode recounted in Chapter 5, when Patagonia employees began to exhibit disdain for upscale customers drawn to its performance clothing and gear, is another example of cultural dysfunction that can result from groupthink.[16]

Groupthink blocks therapeutic dialogue that pushes mission-driven companies to question their assumptions in ways that are necessary and healthy. Short of mass layoffs, to confront the pernicious effects of groupthink, managers can institute a number of policies, some of them counterintuitive and risky.

Managers can hire people with whom they agree about values but sometimes disagree when it comes to social and environmental decision making. According to Stanford's Robert I. Sutton, these hiring practices actually enhance creativity.[17] Having people who genuinely feel differently about prevalent notions can dislodge the status quo in ways that promote new thinking. For example, in today's food marketplace some companies are adamant about organic ingredients. Yet, if the only source for those ingredients is distant, it could be helpful to have an internal voice arguing for the value of local sourcing. This type of voice can at least generate some creative tension that will permit self-examination, which is essential to preventing groupthink. Naturally, it's hard to guarantee that these interactions will happen in a context as free of anger and recrimination as possible. But, if done skillfully, these dialogues can provide a platform for introducing positive modes of disagreement and stimulating active listening.

The problem for mission-driven companies, however, is not just that their values are so deeply tied into their culture but that these values are a key part of the selling proposition in the marketplace. Asking difficult questions that unsettle these values can be seen as an attack on the basis of their own authenticity. Therefore, mission-driven companies are uniquely challenged in trying to confront groupthink and encourage—even honor—dissent. As the movement continues to develop, an open question is how they will do so.

It is important to take a historical perspective when considering some of these thorny issues. For example, when it comes to groupthink, the emergence of dissent within the community of mission-driven companies may simply be a sign of maturity.[18] Although socially and environmentally oriented companies are commercial enterprises, their shared values tie them to a bona fide social movement. And most social movements at some point experience self-examination, dissent, and reorientation. The idea that outsiders have questioned the motives of some of these companies might be expected, but when insiders challenge other insiders, this can break down groupthink. This is surely a healthy sign and can promote dialogue that can open up the mission-driven community to new ideas and further reassessment of long-held beliefs. It will also puncture the myth that the mission-driven community is a monolith that demands conformity.

CONFUSION OVER MEANS AND ENDS
(OR DENG XIAOPING, MEET T. J. RODGERS)

In 1962, during a congress of the Communist Youth League, Deng Xiaoping delivered a line that has become a mantra: "Whether white or black, a cat is a good cat so long as it catches the rat."[19] The idea behind repeating this Sichuan proverb was to urge delegates to focus on the goal of economic development for China as a route to jobs and wealth creation rather than on the choice of political pathways to that end. Reviewing Deng's oft-repeated statement suggests a second provocative issue for mission-driven firms: If the movement's true north is to reduce social and environmental impacts of business, why not be enthusiastic about a business that contributes to social and environmental advancement, even if that isn't mission driven?

Cypress Semiconductor CEO T. J. Rodgers certainly would qualify as a black hat to many in the mission-driven movement. No friend of environmentalists and others who confine his libertarian reflexes, Rodgers is as outspoken as he is blunt. For example, Rodgers was seated between representatives from Environmental Defense and the Competitive Enterprise Institute at a 2008 panel discussion on climate change. Likening their remarks to "two loudspeakers screaming political slogans," he said in his typical manner that he "almost would rather have been waterboarded."[20]

In 1996, Rodgers first gained a degree of notoriety with the socially and environmentally oriented community when he replied to a letter from Sister Doris Gormley of the Sisters of St. Francis of Philadelphia. Sister Doris expressed disappointment in the makeup of Cypress's board of directors, which included no women or minority members. "Get down from your high horse," Rodgers urged in his blistering 2,800-word letter of refutation, labeling Sister Doris's requirements "immoral."[21] He argued that he'd be happy to add a woman or minority to his board—so long as they brought the requisite talent for the job. Lost in the biting tone of the letter were the great many positives at Cypress identified by Rodgers, from premium salaries to excellent benefits to an award-winning charity program. The letter was quickly publicized, leading to charges that Rodgers had stooped to "nun-bashing"[22]

Given the ill will that this episode left behind, it is ironic that Rodgers's SunPower, a company largely owned by Cypress Semiconductor until its spin-off in 2008, is now busy manufacturing solar cells that reduce carbon emissions and support energy independence. In the days of cheap oil, SunPower was down to its last watt when Rodgers met with its founder, Dick Swanson, a former classmate at Stanford. Rodgers's initial personal investment, combined with later support from Cypress, sustained the company through thin years to the point where SunPower's improving solar cell performance met rapidly growing demand for its product. SunPower's 2008 revenues of $1.4 billion make it one of the largest solar energy players in a market bustling with high flyers. Although it depends on what electricity sources the company's cells displace, it's safe to say that the reduction in carbon emissions from SunPower's cells has been considerable.

So, should we celebrate T. J. Rodgers's solar energy success story or second-guess his business methods?

How people answer this question, based on an issue that is certainly not limited to Mr. Rodgers, reveals fault lines within the mission-driven community.[23] On the one hand, if Rodgers is steeped in the no-holds-barred technological meritocracy of Silicon Valley, why not convert that impulse to meeting the world's need for clean power? If his workers share these values and pursue a single bottom line approach to business, why should observers quarrel? One response is to argue that the ends do not justify the means, that how a business conducts itself is as important as the products it produces. In fact, for most authors who write on the topic of mission-driven firms, important outputs of firms include not only physical products but also positive social and environmental impacts that occur along the way.[24] This, of course, has been an underlying theme of this book. For these individuals, the pure pursuit of profits to the exclusion of other goals is "hollow," "inadequate," and "fundamentally misguided."[25] Viewed in these terms, a company like SunPower, which is driven solely to maximize profits, cannot in the long run be a very responsible citizen because the company cannot be counted on to serve society in any other way.

An alternative approach to companies like SunPower is to both celebrate and second-guess, using engagement to push social and environmental goals. But even this can be difficult. Portfolio 21 is a $300 million fund that invests in companies that are "integrating intelligent and forward-thinking environmental strategies into their overall business planning."[26] One of its holdings is SunPower, which has an impressive record of overall returns for shareholders. Nonetheless, Portfolio 21's managers write that

regrettably, SunPower does not discuss global warming, or the environmental benefits its products offer. Other concerns include the company's manufacturing operations in the Philippines where environmental regulations are less stringent than in other parts of the world, and its lack of environmental reporting. As SunPower continues to grow we strongly encourage the company to develop comprehensive environmental reporting and an Environmental Management System certified to ISO 14001 standards.[27]

Sadly, the results of the engagement have been disappointing, according to Portfolio 21's Indigo Teiwes.[28] Despite owning a healthy chunk of SunPower stock, the company did not respond to the fund's inquiries.[29] To Teiwes, this is typical of many technology-based companies that often have yet to integrate environmental stewardship into their operations. This lack of understanding of real ecological limits will in time hamper SunPower's ability to grow in the long term and therefore will place a drag on its economic potential. For now, Portfolio 21 is retaining its position in SunPower, but the frustration in Teiwes's voice when she describes the company's intransigence suggests that that may not be for long.

For companies like SunPower, change will come only when enough of its owners (like Portfolio 21) refuse to own its stock, when its customers reject its products, or even when it finds that its social and environmental record makes hiring difficult. In all these cases, the result is one that Milton Friedman would appreciate, because it is social change by means of the working of markets, in this case for stock, solar panels, and human assets, respectively. Change could also come through public policies that, for example, mandate the type of environmental management systems that Portfolio 21 wanted SunPower to implement. Those in the mission-driven movement will have to decide whether attempts at direct engagement have a prospect for success or whether their best efforts should focus on indirectly influencing market outcomes. This could be done by asking colleagues in the social investment field to reexamine SunPower, expanding the number of LOHAS consumers by broadening education efforts, or working toward mandating progressive policies by influencing legislation. In any case, they will have to admit, however grudgingly, that somewhere Milton Friedman will be smiling.

THE OWNERSHIP PUZZLE:
YOU CAN'T BUY LOVE — OR CAN YOU?

Time for a pop quiz: In Table 9.1, match the natural products companies with their corporate parents. The answers illustrate a prominent trend in recent years, as larger companies increasingly are using acquisition as a means to enter the market space created by mission-driven firms.[30] There may be no more provocative issue for mission-driven companies than buyouts, because they spotlight the most fundamental of issues: Who owns and runs the company?

To provide a glimpse into the many issues that could arise from a buyout, consider Ben & Jerry's Homemade Ice Cream, purchased for $326 million in 2000 by Dutch giant Unilever.[31] Started in an old gas station in Burlington, Vermont, by Ben Cohen and Jerry Greenfield, the company grew with social policies that were as legendary as its fanciful flavors. Unilever emerged from a number of suitors, and its bid was ultimately accepted by Ben & Jerry's board over many objections and numerous unusual efforts to keep the company independent.[32] Ben & Jerry's had gone public by selling stock to Vermont residents in an innovative direct sale in 1984.[33] But over time, these shares changed hands such that the

TABLE 9.1
Pop quiz: Match the natural product
with the correct corporate parent

Natural product	Possible corporate parent
Aveda	Coca-Cola
Boca Foods	Clorox
The Body Shop	Colgate-Palmolive
Burt's Bees	Estée Lauder
Cascadian Farm	General Mills
Kashi	Group Danone
Odwalla	Kraft
Seeds of Change	Kellogg
Stonyfield Farm	L'Oréal
Tom's of Maine	Mars

ownership structure looked increasingly like that of a typical company, with shareholders laser-focused on stock price growth. And as a publicly traded company, Ben & Jerry's had fiduciary responsibilities to its shareholders when offers started rolling in.

Unilever provided its target with a number of assurances that would protect the company's social mission.[34] Some, like retaining the Ben & Jerry's brand, simply made strategic sense. Others, like creating an external board to advise the CEO of Ben & Jerry's, represented significant, even innovative, concessions. Unilever's pledge to keep all employees on for two years was honored, but in 2002, a major round of layoffs took place, in the name of greater efficiency. In 2002, of 635 employees, 121 were laid off from two factory closures, net of job increases at an expanded plant.[35]

Job losses were only one of many actions that severely stressed the corporate culture for which Ben & Jerry's was known and on which it relied. Unilever's focus on numbers, the unique corporate jargon its managers brought to Ben & Jerry's, and the appointment of a new top manager whom Cohen and Greenfield publicly opposed all took a toll on morale. The company's 2004 social assessment offered a set of sobering statistics:[36]

- 35% of employees reported "seriously considering leaving Unilever," up from 6% in 2002.
- 61% agreed that "the social mission is important to our success as a business," down from 75% in 2002.
- 43% found Ben & Jerry's "a quirky, offbeat, and fun place to work," down from 53% in 2002.

A couple of clear differences between the case of Ben & Jerry's and most other buyouts can be identified. First—and this is relatively unique among mission-driven companies—Ben & Jerry's was a publicly traded company. Being a public company, as opposed to a privately held firm, drastically reduced Ben & Jerry's latitude with respect to whom it could sell the company to.[37] Second, and related to the first, is that if not a shotgun marriage, Ben & Jerry's founders didn't exactly see Unilever's purchase as a blessed event. By contrast, virtually all the other takeovers that have occurred in this space have been friendly purchases of privately owned companies.

Yet, among the broader set of mission-driven companies that have been purchased, we can identify some more frequently observed detrimental impacts. The issues arise in two related modes: brand impact and integration.

Brand Impact

The simple fact of a purchase of a mission-driven company by a large parent creates fallout. In 2001, the year following its takeover, Ben & Jerry's fell from fifth to thirtieth place in the *Wall Street Journal*'s index of socially responsible companies.[38] According to international research firm YouGov, The Body Shop's Brand Index rating took a hit following its takeover. The brand's "buzz rating" dropped 10 points, from +6 to −4, and customer satisfaction suffered a "massive" drop, from 25 to 14 points.[39]

There are two principal sources of higher postacquisition brand impacts. Although there is no study to prove it, it is likely that brand impacts are related to owners who are outspoken about their social and environmental actions. Ben Cohen and Anita Roddick are household names among the socially responsible business community and among many LOHAS consumers. On the other hand, how many consumers know who the principal owners of Aveda, Boca Foods, or Kashi are—or Burt's last name for that matter?[40] An outspoken founder or CEO has the advantage of personalizing the brand and giving it a human face, but unfortunately that person can also broadcast high-minded rhetoric that contrasts with the realities of a sale.

The second factor that can drag down the brand is the reputation of the purchasing company. Clorox's purchase of Burt's Bees raised eyebrows, given Clorox's fundamental association with deadly chemicals.[41] And when the corporate parent is boycotted for its sins, the sting can be felt by its new addition, as Odwalla found out after campus boycotts of all Coke products.[42] Detractors also were quick to point out that Nestlé owned 24.6% of L'Oréal when it purchased The Body Shop.[43] Nestlé has been the target of activists for decades, beginning with its aggressive marketing of baby formula in the 1970s. The boycott continues to this day—but now includes The Body Shop.[44]

The authenticity that so influences the reputation of companies is already at risk with a sale, but when consumers view the purchaser as being a social or environmental laggard, this effect is magnified. Corporate parents cannot control the brand impacts created by their purchases of mission-driven companies. Hope for a successful purchase rests with skillful integration of the acquired firm. Unfortunately, this process can be a minefield as well.

Integration

Related to the first point and potentially a more powerful underlying problem is integrating the acquired company into its new parent. Researchers Philippe Haspeslagh and David Jemison explored the issue of integration.[45] They found that acquisitions can be placed into one of four categories, based on the need of the acquired firm for organizational autonomy and the extent to which the target firm and the acquiring firm are strategically interdependent. In Figure 9.1, combinations of these two dimensions are shown, with descriptions for the type of integration needed. When both dimensions are low, a simple holding relationship applies, in which the two units operate separately but with close control exercised by the parent. When autonomy is low and interdependence is high, then we have absorption; the acquired company is rapidly assimilated into its new parent. In the case of high autonomy and low interdependence, we have the case of preservation. Here, an arm's-length relationship is adopted, and little cross-fertilization between the companies is expected. Finally, when both dimensions are high, we get the case of symbiosis, where "the two

| | | Need for strategic interdependence | |
		Low	High
Need for organizational autonomy	High	Preservation	Symbiosis
	Low	Holding	Absorption

FIGURE 9.1
Types of acquisition integration.

SOURCE: Philippe C. Haspelagh and David B. Jemison, *Managing Acquisitions: Creating Value Through Corporate Renewal* (New York: Free Press, 1991). Reproduced with permission of the authors.

organizations at first coexist and then become increasingly interdependent."[46] It is necessary to preserve the capabilities and assets possessed by the target firm while trying to take advantage of the value offered by leveraging interdependencies. Symbiotic modes of integration, not surprisingly, are the most complex.

Symbiosis is the mode necessary to make an acquisition of a mission-driven company work. First, the autonomy of mission-driven companies must be preserved for many reasons. Consider the human side of the equation, where important issues such as values and beliefs, leadership and management, and productivity arise.[47] Forcing a new set of values on a company that owes much of its success to its indigenous values is asking for trouble. Even new reward systems designed to improve productivity can engender bad feelings and threaten the web of interpersonal relationships that may be the foundation for organizational efficiencies within the acquired firm.

Yet strategic interdependence between buyer and seller in virtually all these acquisitions is high. It wasn't Toyota that bought Tom's of Maine or Samsung that bought Seeds of Change. For any acquisition to work, the two companies must do more together than apart. Thus the essential problem is how to create value while respecting autonomy. The approach taken by General Mills when it purchased Small Planet Foods, seller of Cascadian Farm and Muir Glen organic brands, represents one way to try to blend autonomy and strategic interdependence.[48] Rather than push change on Small Planet, General Mills provided founder Gene Kahn "a lot of leeway to explore the synergies on [his] own rather than be rushed into them." General Mills's patience has been rewarded by continued 15% growth and the appointment of Kahn to the position of Vice President of Sustainable Development at General Mills, showing how the integrated firm worked to capitalize on interdependencies.

To capture the benefits of symbiosis, parent companies must be patient.[49] General Mills's 31% market share and 36% gross margins in 2008 indicate its strong market position, removing intense, immediate pressure to generate synergies.[50] Instead, it has the luxury of "reaching out rather than reaching in," as Haspeslagh and Jemison put it, allowing those synergies to materialize respectfully and over time.[51] Patience must be matched with understanding to avoid an all too familiar pitfall in acquisitions: companies not respecting the culture of the company they are purchasing.[52]

Thus acquirers walk a tightrope when they buy a mission-driven company. On the one hand, they can assist their new affiliate with infusions of capital and technical skills that can broaden the reach of the brand and improve efficiency. And of course, the financial viability of the acquisition often rests on realizing these gains. The problem comes in implementing change in a way that is respectful of the mission-driven nature of the acquiree. Pushing too hard in the name of meeting postacquisition market or financial goals can destroy the very values that underlie the brand it is trying to promote.[53]

THE OWNERSHIP PUZZLE: IS PUBLIC OWNERSHIP HEALTHY FOR MISSION-DRIVEN COMPANIES?

A final question closely related to the last one spotlights a foundational issue surrounding governance: whether ownership either as a public company or by a public company in some way militates against a strong social and environmental mission. Not surprisingly, given the rest of the discussion in this chapter, many observers and proponents of mission-driven companies believe that it does. I have not been able to find careful studies that could shed light on this topic, because private companies are required to report so little information to the public.

For our purposes, two key legal differences for public and private firms are important. First, in the United States and to an extent in other countries, the management of publicly owned companies carries what's known as a fiduciary responsibility to shareholders. That essentially means that the company must be run in such a way that financial returns to shareholders are maximized. Private companies, where ownership is not openly traded, do not labor under such constraints. The second key difference regards disclosure. Only publicly owned companies must submit a raft of financial and other documents throughout the year.[54]

Which is better for promoting social and environmental missions? It can be argued that if you could put on one dimension (from extreme sinner to extreme saint) the extent to which social and environmental values drive a company, public companies on average would not be any more or any less virtuous than private companies. For every relatively better performer there would be a relatively poorer performer in each case.

But one distinction between the two organizational forms is more important. Given the type of governance mechanisms operating on publicly held companies, the *spread* of the allowable "mission-drivenness" is lower for those organizations. This may be simply due to the fact that publicly owned firms represent most of the largest firms in many economies, and with size comes a degree of standardization of practices. Further, reporting requirements facilitate examination of peers and movement toward similar profiles on activities in the social and environmental domains.

Figure 9.2 illustrates the point here. What the figure shows is that for privately held firms, free of the fiduciary and reporting constraints, the distribution of companies, although having the same rough average, is spread much wider. For private companies, owners are free to totally

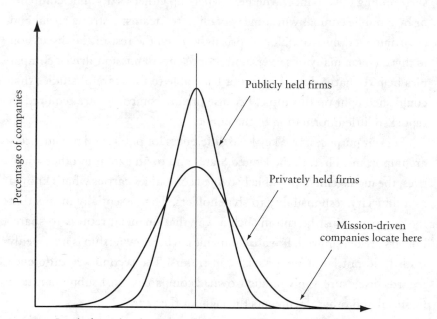

FIGURE 9.2
Social and environmental responsibility performance for privately held firms and publicly held firms.

ignore any social and environmental pursuits beyond legal compliance—or they can make them a centerpiece of their strategies. This explains the long tails and the presence of mission-driven companies on the far right-hand side of the figure. For publicly traded companies, the spread is narrower. One upshot is that privately held companies are freer to pursue the type of business model described in this book. A second takeaway, however, is that it will be difficult to integrate the values inherent in a private company once it is acquired by a public firm, because its level of social and environmental activities will be seen as out of step with corporate norms. It also suggests that, like Ben & Jerry's, once a company goes public, shareholders eventually may enforce their fiduciary prerogatives and try to limit social and environmental activities that they think do not promote profitability.

Governance in Perspective

With time, conventional companies have come to understand that, like many delicate species that thrive only in their ecological niches, many mission-driven companies will not survive removal from these native habitats. Yet founders at some point seek to retire. Original investors seek to cash out. The idea that all acquisitions are misguided or doomed to failure seems wrongheaded. The many acquisitions that have performed reasonably well (and thus for the most part have avoided media scrutiny) suggest that over time, some larger companies have learned the art of assimilating some mission-related values along with their business operations. Indeed, few things are worse for a merger than the failure to recognize, value, and capitalize on a source of true value in the target firm.

It is entirely possible that the problems of governance are not about being owned per se but rather whether or not a mission-driven company is owned by a publicly traded parent. In public companies, the fiduciary responsibilities that lock management into profits as a unitary goal foil many social and environmental programs. Despite promises made, many agreements contain language that commits the mission-driven company, after its purchase, to meet profitability standards in order to maintain a degree of independence. Gary Hirshberg was effusive about his relationship with his new corporate parent after 85% of Stonyfield Farm was bought by Groupe Danone.[55] But if Stonyfield does not maintain double-digit growth, he can be removed.[56] And Group Danone put a limit on how long it will support Hirshberg's generous corporate philanthropy program.[57] The point is not that these constraints cannot be put in place by a privately owned parent—they can. The point is that publicly owned companies *must* put them in place or risk violating their fiduciary responsibilities to shareholders.

And the pitfalls of publicly traded firms extend to mission-driven companies themselves going public. Years ago, a prevalent sentiment on shareholder dissent was the Wall Street rule, under which shareholders were admonished to sell shares in companies when they disagreed with their management. But now, with shareholder suits commonplace, public ownership will continue to be a minefield for mission-driven companies. It's no wonder that the ownership puzzle for mission-driven companies continues to frustrate many in the community. There are signs, however, that point to new methods for securing funding without losing sight of a company's mission.

Avoiding the Trapdoor: Bringing in Investors (and Maybe Even Going Public) While Keeping the Mission Alive

The creeping homogenization that has sanitized commercial zones everywhere meets its match in San Francisco's Mission District. Here, art and capitalism merge in a mélange of loud colors, hand-painted bilingual signs, and the occasional splash of neon. As if to defy this visual frenzy, a tallish, drab office building rises on the southeast corner of 22nd and Mission. On the fourth floor, down a hallway stripped of all ornamentation, are the offices of Good Capital. The company's vision has more in common with the street scene than its office space, for it aims to strike out on a very different path of financing companies. Good Capital is a venture capital firm whose mission is to support nonprofit and for-profit social enterprises. The company has organized its Social Enterprise Expansion Fund to support organizations and companies that are well managed and have good economic fundamentals in addition to "measurable and profound social impact."[58] The fund's first two investments were in Better World Books, an Indiana for-profit company that collects and sells books online to fund its literacy initiatives across the world, and Adina for Life Inc., which uses a variety of globally sourced recipes to create organic, sustainably sourced beverages.

Virtually all investors who are not kin of the founder of a company (and even many who are) at some point seek to cash out their investments. This so-called liquidity event can be a trapdoor for mission-driven companies, which can then be forced into an initial public offering (IPO) that can lead to their ownership by investors seeking solely economic returns. Wes Welke of Good Capital admits this is a serious wrinkle even for his company.[59] But Good Capital has tried to structure deals to provide what he calls a put-call approach to investment. Under these arrangements, at a preestablished date after funding, investors can take the company public in an IPO. But the company and its managers have the option to instead pay off investors if they can raise the funds internally or through debt and keep the company private. There's no guarantee here, but at least there's a possibility to avoid the type of pressures that can come from public ownership.

In the long run, a "social stock exchange" may be developed that works to direct funding to mission-driven companies without introducing the type of disruption that can follow. Armed with a $500,000 grant from the Rockefeller Foundation to research the idea, Mark Campanale and Pradeep Jethi are exploring such a fund for United Kingdom companies.[60] But for now, in terms of preserving social and environmental values, the taking of outside money remains fraught with risk.[61]

Another promising development is the movement to create B corporations, which create a legal governance framework that specifically gives voice—and rights—to stakeholders other than owners. The B corporation approach (B stands for societal benefits) is to legally redefine the purpose of the company to permit owners to adopt a triple bottom line without fear of shareholder litigation. This is done by giving "legal permission and protection" to company directors and officers to consider interests of stakeholders other than shareholders, endowing shareholders with rights to hold directors and officers accountable to the interests of these other stakeholders, and limiting this second set of rights to shareholders and not stakeholders.[62] These changes, of course, have to be approved by existing boards of directors and shareholders because they involve amending articles of incorporation and other governing documents. Although it is difficult or impossible for a large publicly traded firm to become a B corporation for this reason (imagine the difficulty of getting most institutional investors to agree to this change), a number of small companies—including many profiled in this book—have made these changes. Being a B corporation has the potential to help owners, especially founders, maintain the missions of their companies across generations.[63]

One doesn't just declare oneself a B corporation, though. A certification team from B Lab must conclude that a candidate's social and environmental programs and policies are consistent with best practices. Follow-up audits are intended to combat backsliding in future years. B corporations are off to an impressive start. In November 2009, there were 220 B corporations, totaling nearly $1.1 billion in sales.[64] The founders of the B Lab program seek to certify companies responsible for 5–7% of the U.S. GDP in a generation.[65] That sounds audacious, but then again, think about how many Fortune 500 companies didn't exist thirty or forty years ago.

One surprising aspect of mission-driven companies is that, to date, they have not used two relatively straightforward methods for raising funds while retaining a good degree of management control. Both involve going public. The first is to issue preferred stock instead of common stock. Preferred stock is so named because its holders are given preference in terms of their claims on the company's assets. For example, those with preferred shares are first in line for dividends. And if the company is liquidated, those with preferred stock usually are paid off before those with common stock.[66] But in return, holders of preferred shares do not have voting rights and therefore have only indirect leverage on managers.

The second method is to issue two types of stock, A shares and B shares, which have different voting rights. Let's say that A shares are sold to the general public and that B shares are retained by management. Holders of A shares could each have 1 vote, whereas holders of B shares could each have 10 or 100 votes or whatever is necessary to ensure that those with B shares control the company. This was the approach used by Google; managers possessed enough B shares (at 10 votes each) to control the company.[67] It is true that selling shares without voting rights will reduce the amount of funds raised in an IPO. In the case of Google, because the shares held by management have not traded, we cannot directly estimate this discount. But New York University finance expert Kenneth Froewiss estimated it at "a couple of percentage points."[68] Surely, that's a small price to pay in return for maintaining control of the economic, social, and environmental missions of a company.

. . .

The mission-driven movement is in its adolescence, and skeptics detect the arrogance of youth among its companies. They see adolescents that can't grasp the reality of adulthood, with its predilection for conformity and appreciation of nuance. For skeptics, far from challenging dilemmas, the issues raised in this chapter represent fundamental contradictions that these companies can never resolve. Mission-driven companies will remain a poor fit with the capitalist system, destined to remain quaint idiosyncrasies.

Admirers of the mission-driven movement see an adolescent less as an individual with much to learn than as a person struggling with difficult rites of passage yet laden with emerging potential. Heightened expectations will arrive with maturity, but so will the confidence borne of resolving contentions and the excitement of new challenges on the horizon. Admirers appreciate that capitalism is not static but an evolving creature of its own sociocultural and political context. For them, there is little question that this evolution favors a far-reaching role for mission-driven companies.

BRINGING IT ALL TOGETHER
Taking Stock, Looking Ahead

I began this book by asserting that successful mission-driven companies pursue strategy in ways that replicate best practices—but with a twist. The mission-driven movement is not a whole new way to do business, but neither does it reflect unimportant or uninteresting variations on strategic truisms. This movement is notable and well worth studying by a wide audience that includes entrepreneurs, managers of large companies, and curious academics. As we conclude, it is worth taking a step back to wrap up what we've learned and ponder what the future has in store for these companies.

A TWIST ON STRATEGY

The models of strategy in popularized academic models simply don't do justice to the principles put into practice by mission-driven companies. In several pivotal areas, we've learned that mission-driven companies present a provocative challenge to mainstream methods of doing business.

Taking the Triple Bottom Line Seriously

Mission-driven companies found myriad ways to tie social and environmental initiatives to their products and services. In the successful companies, the elements of the triple bottom line are self-reinforcing and create positive feedback. Enhanced profits support philanthropy, job opportunities for the less privileged, microlending, and other socially desirable activities; social achievements support the brand by creating tangible social benefits of purchases.

Yet to truly practice a triple bottom line approach, managers need to go beyond looking for win-win situations to actually wrestle with situations in which they must forgo financial gains to advance their social and environmental agendas. Without this type of reflection, companies find themselves back in the world of the single bottom line. Often, the situation is not simply one of pursuing goals but of respecting moral imperatives.

Put it this way: The world of economics, from which most strategic management theory and practice emerges, is one of trade-offs. A company should exercise every legal option to maximize profits. In the pure economic view, the company allocates resources, such as money, people, and physical assets, across possible uses in order to realize this goal. Its social and environmental investments become one more element of this exercise in optimization. The rule is to continue to increase the company's performance in these areas (i.e., more contributions, cleanups, and campaigns) so long as the economic return (including reputation, brand, and recruiting benefits) from those activities outweighs the possible (risk-adjusted) return from other potential uses of those resources.

The world of mission-driven companies violates this basic norm of strategy because it introduces the idea of *moral imperatives* that are not subject to an economic test. Ideas such as setting maximum pay ratios between top and bottom echelons, banning the use of particular (legal) substances, and paying above-market rates for commodities from developing countries all represent a core principle of mission-driven companies: that it can't all be about money.

Yes, many of these actions can improve organizational performance, promote a company and its brand, and generate profits. I've argued that here. But it is a mistake to see all social and environmental initiatives in strictly financial terms because this strips away their moral content and treats them like some other factor of production. In large measure, the key is that mission-driven companies do not take these actions solely for economic reasons. The mission zone, developed in Chapter 1, graphically illustrates a class of activities that mission-driven companies undertake that will not yield economic gains but will advance social and environmental welfare. But that zone is only a slice. When Jamtown's founder, John Hayden, finds poor-quality skins on the decorative talking drums he sources from Ghana under fair trade certification, he must take action and sometimes even change suppliers. It pains him to do so, but the former Hewlett-Packard computer salesman knows there is a point where he must shield his financial viability.[1]

Nonetheless, many observers continue to complain about the triple bottom line. The sentiments expressed in a survey on corporate social responsibility (CSR) published by *The Economist* are typical.

One problem with the triple bottom line is quickly apparent. Measuring profits is fairly straightforward; measuring environmental protection and social justice is not. The difficulty is partly that there is no single yardstick for measuring progress in those areas. How is any given success for environmental action to be weighed against any given advance in social justice—or, for that matter, against any given change in profits? And how are the three to be traded off against each other? (CSR advocates who emphasize sustainable development implicitly insist that there must be such a trade-off, at least when it comes to weighing profit against either of the other two.) Measuring profits—the good old single bottom line—offers a pretty clear test of business success. The triple bottom line does not.[2]

The survey focuses primarily on mainstream businesses, but it does capture some of the reasons that critics look askance at mission-driven companies. The writer of the article insists that the difficulty of measurement relegates social and environmental activities to the domain of dangerous diversions. The implicit message of the passage is that to truly matter, a method for placing social and environmental impacts in dollar terms is necessary.

But imperfect metrics have not stopped thousands of companies from trying to meet goals that go beyond economic ones. (It is also important to recognize that economic measures of performance, even after many years of refinement, still suffer from their own bundle of problems, running from their exclusion of externalities to the ability of companies to manipulate seemingly objective measures.) In any case, collectively, across the variety of sectors and specialties that we've studied, many companies *have* made a triple bottom line approach work. Throughout this book, I have stressed how the managerial challenge of the triple bottom line can be profound. But if anything, even in difficult economic times, this movement is not melting away.

Speaking of metrics, another complaint lodged by critics is that so few of these companies have grown into billion dollar players. It is true that for a number of reasons, mission-driven companies are smaller and take long stretches of time to grow. One reason is their relative youth. But another is the difficulty they've experienced growing without compromising their values through changes in ownership that dilute their commitments or that (especially in the case of rapid growth) divert attention from that commitment. And some just prefer to stay small. Here again, for those who keep score on only a single financial dimension of growth, these firms disappoint. For those willing to broaden their indexes of evaluation to encompass social and environmental performance, however, there is much to appreciate.

The Governance Puzzle

Another twist: the serious implications that managing a mission-driven company has for governance. Repeatedly we have seen that when founders and like-minded individuals no longer maintain a controlling interest in a company, problems materialize. For a single bottom line company, strategic theory would suggest that going public or selling to another company might well bring change, but it would not challenge the primacy of financial goals. In the case of mission-driven companies, however, the instances of postpurchase dilutions of social and environmental commitments are frequent enough to suggest that ownership transitions in mission-driven companies demand close scrutiny.

For entrepreneurs, the message is that discerning the optimal path of growth is even more important than for their counterparts who run mainstream companies. Most mission-driven companies seek to grow at a pace that allows them to reach more customers, bring down costs, and expand their social and environmental reach. But if growth is too rapid, the problems will extend beyond growth-related issues faced by many traditional entrepreneurs, because they may include challenges to those social and

environmental programs. In particular, the cash infusions typically necessary to support that growth must be examined carefully for evidence that
the new structure of control will not threaten the company's triple bottom
line commitment. As I've noted here, changed governance can undermine
the very basis for the mission-driven company. At the least, new investors
and owners must appreciate the situations where social and environmental
programs *do* contribute to the bottom line, however circuitously. Without
that intuition, future trouble is guaranteed.

George Herbert said, "Living well is the best revenge." Perhaps something similar is true of mission-driven companies for whom staying small
(and independent) is the best revenge against societal and business norms
that sanctify growth and generate social pressure on entrepreneurs to
stretch to their limits.

Creating Community

Finally, place is important for mission-driven companies, but for reasons
other than those advanced in economic models of clustering. Clustering
based on values is another takeaway from this study that conflicts with
norms of strategic thinking. Economics-based models of clustering, such as
Porter's diamond schema, don't place enough emphasis on the gravitational
pull of a values-based segment of commercial enterprise. Entrepreneurs
should look to settle down where many like-minded companies reside.

In essence, the failure of many elements of conventional models of strategic management to apply to mission-driven companies is the failure of
those models to appreciate the more human side of management and the
embeddedness of companies within their social contexts.[3] Mission-driven
companies are in a unique position to benefit from values-based ties that
bind them to other companies following the same path. Those companies
can form an economic and personal support structure in difficult times as
well as be a continual source of inspiration and new ideas.

ENTREPRENEURS TAKE NOTE:
TIMELESS, INESCAPABLE TRUTHS
This book was written with entrepreneurs in mind. And I've tried to offer
a raft of practical suggestions for their businesses. Many of these recom-

mendations are based on the unique nature of mission-driven enterprises. But it is important to stress one more time a fundamental reality that mission-driven companies share with their mainstream counterparts: Success is defined by *skillful management*. Let's review a few of the managerial truths that emerged from the variety of topics I have covered in this book. Each offers a cornerstone for entrepreneurs seeking to carve out competitive advantages.

First, *experience is invaluable*. Many if not most of the companies have managers with substantial work experience. In case after case, the top management of a company came from the mainstream segment of its industry. In some instances, such as advertising, it's easy to see why a more responsible company was attractive: disenfranchisement with the prevailing values of the profession. Big Think Studios in San Francisco, which does advocacy advertising for nonprofits, is fully populated with first-class professionals who could no longer accept mainstream values in advertising.[4] For other companies, it's not about mainstream values but about missed opportunities. Several owners with long-standing relationships in mature industries created new mission-driven businesses to capitalize on the inertia that kept their old companies from recognizing and responding to opportunities in that market space. A case in point is Excellent Packaging and Supply, the food service supplies company we met in Chapter 6. Its top management team left mainstream companies that just couldn't appreciate the opportunities in biopackaging.[5] In both cases, founders brought the full value of their industry-specific experience and talent base to their new companies.

Second, *the business plan must be compelling*. Founders and managers in successful mission-driven companies intuitively understand the markets and customers that they'll serve. They see gaps in products and services as opportunities. They have a strategy for expansion in mind and can visualize it unfolding. They aren't controlled by numbers, but they have worked through financial projections to appreciate their limits and key contingencies. Most important, however, they understand how to infuse the product or service with social and environmental values. They appreciate how their offering will be positioned in the marketplace to maximize its differentiation by being authentic and by maintaining a transparent supply chain.

Third, *the product is paramount*. Skilled managers know how to re-cruit a winning team and create a product that maximizes prospects in the marketplace. They know that it's not just about bringing a social or environmental element to the product but rather about squeezing out the most meaning from the social and environmental attributes of the company in a product that is outstanding to begin with. Seth Goldman, founder of Honest Tea, makes it his top tip: "You need to have a great product—the consumer comes first. It must taste great, look great, have good packaging—you have to be competitive along every dimension of the product line."[6] Alysa Rose of Rejuvenation Hardware puts it in irreducible terms: "The product is kick-ass."[7] Add to a great product a company with authentic social and environmental commitments and first-class supply chain, and you've got the ingredients for a marketplace winner.

These are just three managerial truths. There are others, such as the importance of hiring outstanding employees and attention to detail in ex-ecution. Entrepreneurs are well advised to appreciate the power of strong management. Although many of the dicta of strategy do not apply equally to mission-driven companies, some rules simply cannot be ignored. Through it all, economic viability must be preserved. As Brian Rohter, one of the founders of New Seasons Market, puts it, "No margin, no mission."[8]

LOOKING AHEAD

There certainly are challenges for mission-driven companies. Along with all businesses, they have to weather economic downturns. In such situ-ations, loyal customers may stay loyal, but those on the fringe may not. Convulsive economic waters will bring significant pressure to keep busi-ness operations afloat. Many conventional companies will retreat from social and environmental initiatives or at least focus on areas such as resource efficiency, where there need be no conflict between economic and environmental goals. But for mission-driven companies that can squeeze through tough times with their social and environmental ini-tiatives intact, the payoff will be galvanized commitment to the triple bottom line and the glow that comes from holding true to their values through thick and thin. They might even be able to grow if the gap be-tween their social and environmental performance and the performance in the mainstream grows. Imagine the benefits to an organization's culture of running those rapids.

Another challenge will be for the leaders of the mission-driven movement to broaden inclusion on several dimensions. One of their networking associations, the Social Venture Network, has had some success in working to promote greater diversity in a movement that, as recounted by its executive director, Deborah Nelson, was dominated by "white, wealthy males."[9] She began working to reach out to underrepresented groups through peer contacts. It took years, but the group was able to recruit new leaders into its fold, and its board eventually was headed by an African American entrepreneur, Melissa Bradley. Bradley helped the Social Venture Network broaden its mission and step up efforts to address economic justice.[10] If these initiatives bear fruit by creating economic opportunities for lower income citizens, pleas for "eco-equity," most recently by activist Van Jones, will not be in vain.[11]

Another, even more daunting fortress to conquer: inclusion of individuals representing a broad range of political persuasions. Says Nelson, "When it comes to race, age, gender, sexual orientation, we've made so much progress along those lines, but when it comes to political ideology . . . Whew! We're not even to (a point of) tolerance. And we've got to get beyond that. It's not serving us in any way."[12] Such an imbalance sustains the type of groupthink noted in Chapter 9, and it prevents mission-driven companies (or at least one of their major peak organizations) from being seen as a less partial business group. There cannot be a perceived political litmus test for prospective members if associations of mission-driven companies are to evolve in a way that maximizes their relevance and impact in the business and public policy arenas.

Overcoming these last two challenges will democratize the mission-driven movement. As Bianca Alexander of Conscious Planet Media puts it, "It's the challenging conversations that get us moving" toward a more inclusive business campaign for social equity and environmental stewardship.[13]

Finally, many institutional barriers impede the mission-driven approach to business. Public policy has not had a leading role in the story arc of this movement, although its presence in a supporting role from time to time should be acknowledged. For example, the transparency movement has marched forward with little impetus from government. Yet, for some story lines, policy makers must take leading roles. Most critical are issues concerning company governance. The issue of fiduciary responsibility takes us into legal terrain that is complex and provocative.[14] But let's assume that legislation permits a type of publicly owned corporation that tempers the primacy of economic return with respect for other social and environmental goals. Further, the organization maintains the advantages of publicly traded firms to issue debt and raise capital and uses a board to represent shareholder interests. By creating a second type of publicly held corporation where executives do not toil under the yoke of profit maximization, mission-driven companies could secure capital to facilitate growth. Naturally, many issues will arise from these organizations, including the need to clearly delineate performance goals for managers. At some level, trust will need to supplement rigorous evaluation in determining the overall effectiveness of the company.

IN PRAISE OF COMPANIES ON A MISSION

Yes, many a mission-driven company has had to suffer through missteps and detours in its journey to meet the challenge of the triple bottom line. Entrepreneurs have learned from these episodes, and in its adolescence the movement has developed norms that guide behavior. Compared to so many mainstream companies that consistently duck social and environmental leadership, isn't it preferable to have mission-driven companies that seek to be leaders, even if they are inconsistent at times? An old adage states, "It's better to be approximately right than precisely wrong." A more fair (if less pithy) statement comparing mission-driven companies to their mainstream counterparts might be, "It's better to be approximately right than stubbornly mediocre."

And the movement of mission-driven companies *is* much more frequently right than wrong. These companies have shown that it's possible to create viable business models that in some sense defy economics and finance textbooks. They have repeatedly anticipated and reacted to social and environmental demands ahead of policy makers and mainstream companies. They have proven that openness and transparency reduce, not increase, business risk and that consumers not only don't want to live and work by different sets of morals but that they don't want to purchase by another set of morals either.

In the final analysis, global citizens owe much to the original leaders of the mission-driven movement. Those entrepreneurs thought that just maybe the time was right for business to be a transformational force for progressive social and environmental values—to lead on social and environmental issues instead of being dragged along by a cumbersome policy process that has always been three exits behind on the road leading to positive change. Together, these pioneers have launched a modern commercial movement whose social and environmental return on their innovative impulses goes beyond anything an income statement could capture.

And isn't that the point?

Reference Matter

ACKNOWLEDGMENTS

I emerge from this project with a great many debts of gratitude. And understanding that some debts will continue to accrue interest because I've forgotten a few obligations, I would like to acknowledge a number of individuals who have helped to bring this book into being.

The intellectual roots of this project lie in two places. The first was at Stanford University, where I had the great fortune to work with Gil Masters. He was the first to reveal to me the world of opportunity in using science and enterprise for the common good. The second source of inspiration was seminars taken as a Ph.D. student at the Haas School of Business at the University of California, Berkeley. Learning from scholars whose fields spanned law (Edwin Epstein), political science (David Vogel), economics (David Teece), and organization science (Paul Lawrence) confirmed the value of interdisciplinary training that promotes seeing issues from multiple viewpoints. This training applies seamlessly to the study of companies that manage to a triple bottom line, in which differing objectives must be evaluated and balanced. The type of critical thinking that was stressed in all the Berkeley classes also pushed me to regard the status quo with a healthy dose of skepticism and to appreciate the social nature of enterprise while giving equal time to the hard realities of running a business.

This book also owes much to the Lundquist College of Business and its outstanding faculty and support staff, starting with former dean James Bean, who saw the value of this project and found a way to allow me the requisite time that the project demanded. I am indebted to my colleagues in the Management Department: Jennifer Howard-Grenville, Alan Meyer, Peter Mills, Rick Mowday, Andrew Nelson, Anne Parmigiani, Taryn Stanko, Bill Starbuck, Rick Steers, and Jim Terborg. Their enthusiasm for the project never waned, even as my obsession for the topic area inflated to somewhat dysfunctional dimensions. Special thanks also go to faculty members who shared their expertise and perspectives with me, including Larry Dann, Bob Madrigal, and Don Upson. I am also grateful for the contributions of several graduate students who pursued research leads and provided support for analyses. I am indebted to Andrew Earle, Elizabeth Hannah, Jennifer Irwin, Travis Nanchy, and Suzanne Tilleman. Thanks to the Lundquist College's information technology gurus, a week's worth of writing was recovered from a damaged disk. Einar Ingebretson, Michele Reniff, and Tony Saxman worked together to convert a potential tragedy into a humorous sidebar.

An extraordinary and especially well-deserved debt is owed to students who have taken my "Sustainable Business Development" class since 1994. By pushing me to refine my ideas and suggesting alternative ways to approach problems, they made the decade-long genesis of this book a process of improvement and not simply delay. Colleagues associated with the Center for Sustainable Business Practices, notably Beth Hjelm, Nagesh Murthy, and Tom Osdoba, supported this project steadily, as did members of the Center's Business Advisory Committee. A final acknowledgment is reserved for Tom Stewart, whose support through the Thomas C. Stewart Distinguished Professorship allowed me to throw myself into the preparation of the manuscript.

I must call out the interviewees in this book for special praise. As a group, they were amazingly responsive to setting up meeting times and very open in their discussions with me—only on one or two occasions was I asked to keep information confidential. Interviewees, despite the multiple draws on their time and occasional crises and life events, were uniformly generous in offering their time to explain their personal philosophies, business models, and assessments of the movement of mission-driven companies. The book is far richer for their participation, and for a researcher more used to analysis of statistical data, it was a revelation to connect with so many entrepreneurs. If nothing else, this project confirmed my conviction that business school academics need to shut off their computers now and then and engage with the professionals who confront business issues on a daily basis.

Thanks also go to a number of individuals who assisted me with arranging for interviews. Marc Gunther (*Fortune*), Sang Myung Lee (Hanyang University), Jost Hamschmidt (oikos Foundation), Johanna Mair and Joan Ricart (IESE Business School), Deborah Nelson (Social Venture Network), and Pamela Skarda (Sustainable Business Network of Washington) all provided introductions and recommendations for people to interview as well as other sources of information about mission-driven companies.

An assortment of others must be thanked, as well. Wendy Beck performed the initial editing, with good cheer and tolerance for my uneasy relationship with the English language. I thank Cynthia Twohy of Oregon State University for patiently explaining the science of cloud formation to me, confirming what I had seen while in the mountains. Students at the Presidio School of Management received an initial version of Chapter 8, and their suggestions throughout a lecture there in 2009 were helpful in refining my ideas about values clusters. I thank Presidio's dynamic leader, Seyed Amiry, for this invitation. I also thank Jon Entine for sharing several of his files with me.

I am deeply appreciative of the reviews of David Vogel and Andrew Winston. Both wrote detailed and frank appraisals of the draft of this book, and the finished product is much better for their input. Let me add, of course, that any errors in the book are solely my responsibility.

Stanford University Press was a pleasure to work with on this project. Geoffrey Burn, its managing director, was an early and enthusiastic supporter of the project. My editor, Margo Crouppen, was skilled and supportive, and a great traveling companion on the long and winding road to publication. She offered nothing but positive support for the book and was especially attentive to improving its style and organization. If a sign of a great editor is the ability to guide a project forward while reserving the full measure of autonomy and intellectual freedom for the author, then Margo qualifies for the distinction. At Stanford, Carolyn Brown expertly and expeditiously led the production process and retained Mimi Braverman, whose incisive editing greatly enhanced the final manuscript.

My final expression of thanks is for my family, who encouraged me to explore my passionate interest in mission-driven companies, although they may not have realized it would mean enduring a collective two months away while I was conducting interviews. My love and utmost gratitude go to my wife, Wendy, whose generous spirit and unfailing support for the project helped sustain its momentum. Thank you, Wendy, for tolerating my absences, indulging my quirks, and being a sounding board for my nascent ideas. Finally, I must thank my sons, Andy and David, who provided much welcome diversion from the working world. I hope Wendy and I have taught you to appreciate nature, to be responsible citizens, and to take the beauty and opportunity that you've enjoyed and find ways to share them with those in need.

A NOTE ON THE LITERATURE
AND RESEARCH APPROACH

Research for this book began with a thorough review of publications that could be placed in the following typology of books and other published studies (see figure). In this typology, two distinctions are important: whether the work focuses on small and medium-size enterprises or on larger companies, and whether the work is more descriptive or more analytical in nature. Descriptive contributions tend to be less rigorous and carefully researched but often are more closely tied to practice.

A considerable amount of literature fits in the bottom two cells of the figure, including a number of relatively recent books. For example, Lynn Sharp Paine's *Value Shift*, David Vogel's *The Market for Virtue*, and Simon

Focus on small and medium-size enterprises		
Large company focus		
	Descriptive	Analytical

Typology of previous research on socially and environmentally responsible business.

Zadek's *The Civil Corporation* are well-known contributions that focus on corporate social responsibility and ethics challenges faced by larger, more established firms. More recently, Kellie McElhaney's *Just Good Business* adds a more strategic spin to corporate social responsibility, and Daniel Esty and Andrew Winston's *Green to Gold* focuses more on sustainability. These contributions are more analytical. Examples of books with a more descriptive approach are *The Triple Bottom Line*, by Andrew Savitz and Karl Weber, and *Strategies for a Green Economy*, by Joel Makower.

In the top half of the diagram, a number of books can be placed on the left-hand side. These include books by founders of mission-driven companies, such as *What Matters Most*, by Jeffrey Hollender and Stephen Fenichell, and *Revolution in a Bottle*, by Tom Szaky. Also on this side are a series of books associated with the Social Venture Network, including *Mission, Inc.*, by Kevin Lynch and Julius Walls Jr., and *Growing Local Value*, by Laury Hammel and Gun Denhart. For a number of reasons, including imperfect knowledge about the many mission-driven companies that exist and a lack of public data to support formal analysis, there was little work to place in the upper right-hand side of the diagram. This book aims to populate this cell.

The lack of data on mission-driven companies is not absolute, and I was able to marshal some data from Green America on companies that met its criteria for inclusion. And in several other places, I was able to locate facts and figures to contribute to the analysis. The rest of the basis for the study and its conclusion was reliance on published academic and professional literature and a great many interactions with mission-driven companies and their founders and managers. The most formal of these interactions were interviews, mostly semistructured, with the companies listed in what follows. The interviews generally ran roughly an hour in length.

INTERVIEWS

All interviews were conducted in person unless noted with an asterisk.
Artemis Foods, Portland, Oregon, Grace Pae, September 9, 2008
Associated Oregon Industries, Salem, Oregon, Jay Clemens*,
    January 14, 2009

B Corp., Berwyn, Pennsylvania, Bart Houlahan*, April 17, 2009

Big Think Studios, San Francisco, California, Peter Bridgeman, February 12, 2009

Calvert-Jones Company Inc., Arlington, Virginia, Stan Peregoy and Gerry Rodino, October 24, 2008

Coastwide Laboratories, Wilsonville, Oregon, John Martilla and Grant Watkinson, February 18, 2009

Community IT Innovators, Washington, D.C., David Deal, October 24, 2008

Conscious Planet Media, Chicago, Illinois, Bianca Alexander*, July 15, 2009

DKV Seguros, Barcelona, Spain, Josep Santacreu, Daniela Toro, and Carlos Martinez, July 1, 2009

Dolphin Blue, Dallas, Texas, Tom Kemper, September 22, 2008

Eco-Coach, Washington, D.C., Anca Novacovici, October 24, 2008

Ecohaus, Seattle, Washington, Tim Taylor, January 23, 2009

Ecotrust, Portland, Oregon, Spencer Beebe, November 21, 2008

Egg, Seattle, Washington, Hilary Bromberg and Marty McDonald, January 23, 2009

Excellent Packaging and Supply, Richmond, California, Allen King, February 12, 2009

Freitag, Zurich, Switzerland, Filippo Castagna and Daniel Freitag, August 22, 2008

gDiapers Company, Portland, Oregon, Jason Graham-Nye, October 8, 2008

Gerding-Edlen Development Company, Portland, Oregon, Mark Edlen, January 5, 2009

Give Something Back Business Products, Oakland, California, Mike Hannigan, November 10, 2008

Golden Temple Foods, Eugene, Oregon, Guru Hari Khalsa, April 20, 2009

Good Capital, San Francisco, California, Wes Welke,
    November 11, 2008

GreenBiz.com, Oakland, California, Joel Makower, February 11, 2009

GreenWorks Realty, Seattle, Washington, Ben Kaufman,
    January 22, 2009

iCoop, Seoul, South Korea, Oh Hang Sik, October 20, 2008

Jamtown, Seattle, Washington, John Hayden, January 22, 2009

KEEN Footwear, Portland, Oregon, Kate Lee and Kirk Richardson,
    October 8, 2008

MBL Group, Portland, Oregon, Jim Morris, October 8, 2009

Michelle Kaufmann Designs, Oakland, California, Michelle Kaufmann
    and Tracy Melia-Teevan, February 11, 2009

Natural Step Network, Portland, Oregon, Regina Hauser,
    November 21, 2008

Natural Value, Sacramento, California, Beki Cohen*,
    September 25, 2008

Neil Kelly Company, Portland, Oregon, Tom Kelly,
    November 20, 2008

Nelson Capital Management, Palo Alto, California, Lloyd Kurtz*,
    July 22, 2008

New Seasons Market, Portland, Oregon, Lisa Sedlar, January 29, 2008

Office of Sustainable Development, Portland, Oregon, Susan Anderson,
    November 21, 2008

Oregon Business Association, Tigard, Oregon, Jef Green*, January 14,
    2009

Organically Grown Company, Clackamas, Oregon, Josh Hinerfeld,
    November 20, 2008

Organically Happy, Wheaton, Maryland, Vincent Ben Avram,
    October 24, 2008

Portfolio 21 Investments, Portland, Oregon, Carsten Henningsen,
    October 8, 2008; and Indigo Teiwes*, October 1, 2008

Portland Business Journal, Portland, Oregon, Craig Wessel,
    January 5, 2009

Rejuvenation Hardware, Portland, Oregon, Alysa Rose,
    January 5, 2009

Revolution Foods, Alameda, California, Kristin Richmond and Kirsten
    Tobey, November 10, 2008, and February 11, 2008

Seventh Generation, Burlington, Vermont, Gregor Barnum*,
    November 14, 2008

ShoreBank, Chicago, Illinois, Jean Pogge*, July 29, 2009

ShoreBank Pacific, Portland, Oregon, Dave Williams,
    September 16, 2008

Social Venture Network, San Francisco, California, Deborah Nelson,
    February 13, 2009

Staples, Framingham, Massachusetts, Mark Buckley*, July 13, 2009

Stumptown Coffee Roasters, Portland, Oregon, Matt Lounsbury,
    January 5, 2009

Sustainable Asset Management, Zurich, Switzerland, Pierin Menzli and
    Reto Ringger, August 29, 2008

Sustainable Industries, San Francisco, California, Brian Back,
    February 13, 2009

Sustenta Soluciones, Mexico City, Mexico, Santiago Lobeira*,
    October 31, 2008

World of Good, Emeryville, California, Priya Haji, February 11, 2009

FOREWORD

1. Hunter Lovins is one of the creators of the concept of natural capitalism. President of Natural Capitalism Solutions, she cofounded the Rocky Mountain Institute and was a founding professor of the Presidio Graduate School. Hunter was named Time Magazine Hero for the Planet in 2000, and in 2008 she received the Sustainability Pioneer Award given to the creators of the Dow Jones Sustainability Index. She was called a "green business icon" by *Newsweek*.

2. For a list of these studies, see http://www.natcapsolutions.org.

3. From the article "Sustainable Executives," http://www.natcapsolutions .org/resources.htm#ART. Corporate managers are increasingly realizing that value returned to the owners, the real metric of success, derives from more than just attention to next quarter's profits—indeed the Financial Accounting Standards Board (FASB) has recently announced that it will revise its definition of profit away from this short-term fixation.

CHAPTER 1

1. See Haas School of Business, "Feature Story: Your Haas Network," *CalBusiness* (summer), 14–17 (2007).

2. The Haas School routinely is ranked at or near the top of surveys on social and environmental content and opportunity in MBA programs. The Aspen Institute's 2007–2008 survey placed it fourth overall and first in "course content" for dedicated courses offered in these areas. See Aspen Institute, "Beyond Grey Pinstripes" (2008), http://www.beyondgreypinstripes.org/index.cfm, accessed March 2, 2009.

3. Ron Haskins, "The School Lunch Lobby," *Education Next* 5(3) (summer

2005), http://www.hoover.org/publications/ednext/3219311.html, accessed February 24, 2009.

4. Interview with Kirsten Tobey, Revolution Foods, Alameda, California, November 10, 2008.

5. Interview with Kirsten Tobey, November 10, 2008.

6. Interview with Kristin Richmond, Revolution Foods, Alameda, California, February 11, 2009.

7. Interview with Kristin Richmond, February 11, 2009.

8. Telephone interview with Kirsten Tobey, Revolution Foods, Alameda, California, March 19, 2009. Sales figure is from Nicole Perlroth, "Entrepreneurs: Revolution Foods Wants Schoolkids to Trade French Fries for Roasted Potatoes. Can It Make Good Food—and Money, Too?" *Forbes*, February 2, 2009, 42.

9. Interview with Kristin Richmond, February 11, 2009.

10. See Lynn Sharp Paine, *Value Shift: Why Companies Must Merge Social and Financial Imperatives to Achieve Superior Performance* (New York: McGraw-Hill, 2004).

11. In theory, values can compose a much greater set of principles that would make a range of companies mission driven, from tobacco sellers (personal freedom) to computer makers (technological advancement). However, as generally used, *mission-driven* refers to companies with socially and environmentally oriented values.

12. Jeanette Borzo, "From Land's End to Fair Trade," *Fortune*, February 5, 2006, B3.

13. Social Investment Forum, *2007 Report on Socially Responsible Trends in the United States* (Washington, DC: Social Investment Forum, 2007).

14. See SRI-Asia, "The Size of the Socially Responsible Investing Market" (2009), http://www.sri-asia.com/background/sri-market-size.html, accessed July 29, 2009.

15. SRI-Asia, "Size."

16. See Organic Trade Association, "U.S. Organic Sales Grow by a Whopping 17.1 Percent in 2008" (2009), http://www.organicnewsroom.com/2009/05/us_organic_sales_grow_by_a_who.html, accessed July 12, 2009. See also Rick Callahan, "Going 'All Natural' Gets Old: Organics Faltering—Farmers Worry as Once-Booming Organic Industry Expects 1st Sales Drop in Years; Some Want Out" (2009), http://www.abcnews.go.com/Business/WireStory?id=7935580&page=1, accessed July 12, 2009.

17. CNN Money, "Organic Food Sales Growth Slows" (January 28, 2009), http://money.cnn.com/2009/01/28/news/economy/organic_food.reut/, accessed March 19, 2009.

18. Natural Marketing Institute, "NMI's 2009 Consumer Segmentation Model" (2009), http://www.nmisolutions.com/lohasd_segment.html, accessed November 7, 2009.

19. Natural Marketing Institute, "New LOHAS Market-Size Data Released: A $209 Billion Opportunity," press release (January 31, 2007), http://www.prlog

.org/10006954-new-lohas-market-size-data-released-209-billion-opportunity.html, accessed July 12, 2009.

20. Keith Hammonds, "Now the Good News," *Fast Company*, December 2008, 110–118.

21. See Responsible Shopper, http://www.coopamerica.org/programs/rs/; and Good Guide, http://www.goodguide.com/. Both accessed July 29, 2009.

22. See, for example, Philip Kotler and Kevin L. Keller, *A Framework for Marketing Management*, 3rd ed. (Upper Saddle River, NJ: Prentice-Hall, 2007).

23. See New Seasons Market, "Sustainability Awards and Recognition" (2009), http://www.newseasonsmarket.com/dynamicContent.aspx?loc=1298& subloc=1&menuId=1430, accessed July 13, 2009.

24. See, for example, Paine, *Value Shift*, 61; and Andrew W. Savitz and Karl Weber, *The Triple Bottom Line* (San Francisco: Jossey-Bass, 2006), 23. For expository convenience, I also combine social and environmental domains.

25. I stress that this conceptualization of overlapping circles reflects the improvement impacts of actions rather than the domains of the actions themselves. This latter conceptualization has been justifiably and perceptively criticized by Simon Zadek because it suggests that some economic activities lie outside the natural environment, which is inconsistent with reality. See Simon Zadek, *The Civil Corporation: The New Economy of Corporate Citizenship* (London: Earthscan, 2001), 109–113.

26. Note that to some degree the mission zone is also dependent on the industry and country context. Society recognizes many moral imperatives and has codified them into law, placing them in the win-win zone for both types of companies. But remaining moral imperatives that are perceived by mission-driven companies (in the United States, one is typically the provision of health care benefits to workers) will vary across countries and cultures.

27. Interview with Lisa Sedlar, New Seasons Markets, Portland, Oregon, September 29, 2008.

28. Anne Murphy, "The Seven (Almost) Deadly Sins of High-Minded Entrepreneurs," *Inc.*, July 1994, 47–49.

29. The seminal work in the area is Michael E. Porter, *The Competitive Advantage of Nations* (New York: Free Press, 1990). This book focused on clusters within countries, but a number of follow-up studies looked at regional clusters.

30. For an analysis of the Ben & Jerry's situation and other pertinent cases, see Jeffrey Hollender and Stephen Fenichell, *What Matters Most: How a Small Group of Pioneers Is Teaching Social Responsibility to Big Business, and Why Big Business Is Listening* (New York: Basic Books, 2004).

31. M. Friedman, "The Social Responsibility of Business Is to Increase Its Profits," *New York Times Magazine*, September 13, 1970, 32–33, 122, and 126.

32. For a review of many studies in the area, see Joshua D. Margolis and James P. Walsh, "Misery Loves Companies: Rethinking Social Initiatives by Business," *Administrative Science Quarterly* 48: 268–305 (2003).

33. Forest L. Reinhardt, "Environmental Product Differentiation: Implications for Corporate Strategy," *California Management Review* 40(4): 43–73 (1998).

34. See, for example, Thomas Donaldson, *The Ethics of International Business* (New York: Oxford University Press, 1989); R. Edward Freeman, *Strategic Management: A Stakeholder Approach* (Boston: Pittman, 1984); David Vogel, *The Market for Virtue* (Washington, DC: Brookings Institution, 2005); and Paine, *Value Shift*.

35. Michael V. Russo and Paul A. Fouts, "A Resource-Based Perspective on Corporate Environmental Performance and Profitability," *Academy of Management Journal* 40(3): 534–559 (1997).

36. Paul Hawken has recently written eloquently about the movement of nonprofit "organizations working toward ecological sustainability and social justice," which he believes numbers more than a million globally. See Paul Hawken, *Blessed Unrest: How the Largest Movement in History Is Restoring Grace, Justice, and Beauty to the World* (New York: Penguin, 2007).

37. Daniel Bornstein, *How to Change the World: Social Entrepreneurs and the Power of New Ideas* (Oxford, U.K.: Oxford University Press, 2007).

38. See Greg Dees, *Social Enterprise: Private Initiatives for the Common Good*, Harvard Business Case 9-395-116 (Boston, MA: Harvard Business Press, 1994); Jed Emerson and Sheia Bonini, "The Blended Value Map: Tracking the Intersects and Opportunities of Economic, Social, and Environmental Value Creation" (2004), http://www.blendedvalue.org/publications/, accessed November 4, 2009. More recent contributions that focus primarily on the nonprofit sector but do profile and discuss some for-profit companies are Jane Wei-Skillern, James E. Austin, Herman Leonard, and Howard Stevenson, *Entrepreneurship in the Social Sector* (Thousand Oaks, CA: Sage, 2007); and John Elkington and Pamela Hartigan, *The Power of Unreasonable People: How Social Entrepreneurs Create Markets That Change the World* (Boston: Harvard Business Press, 2008).

39. The $1,500 figure comes from an early contribution in this area: C. K. Prahalad and Stuart L. Hart, "The Fortune at the Bottom of the Pyramid," *strategy + business* 26: 1–14 (2002). For more comprehensive discussion of the possibilities, see C. K. Prahalad, *The Fortune at the Bottom of the Pyramid: Eradicating Poverty Through Profits* (Philadelphia: Wharton School Publishing, 2004). For a personal account of the origins of microlending, see Mohammad Yunus, *Banker to the Poor: Micro-Lending and the Battle Against World Poverty* (New York: Public Affairs, 1999).

CHAPTER 2

1. Remarks by Lee Scott, October 10, 2007.

2. Gary McWilliams, "Wal-Mart Era Wanes amid Big Shifts in Retail; Rivals Find Strategies to Defeat Low Prices; World Has Changed," *Wall Street Journal*, October 3, 2007, A1.

3. Reportedly, a McKinsey & Company study found that up to 8% of shoppers

avoid Wal-Mart because of its reputation. See Marc Gunther, "Wal-Mart Saves the Planet," *Fortune*, August 7, 2006, 48.

4. For a well-researched source on Wal-Mart and its impacts, see Charles Fishman, *The Wal-Mart Effect: How the World's Most Powerful Company Really Works—and How It's Transforming the American Economy* (New York: Penguin Press, 2006).

5. See Joel Makower, "The Many Shades of the Eco-LOHAS-Sustainable-Green Consumer," Greenbiz.com (2007), http://makower.typepad.com/joel_makower/2007/05/the_many_shades.html, accessed December 17, 2007.

6. Interestingly, of the four studies for which Makower ("Many Shades") provides segment percentages, three report that 16–19% of consumers are in the most socially and environmentally conscious categories. A separate assessment identified "Cultural Creatives," who display "serious ecological and planetary perspectives, emphasis on relationships and women's point of view, commitment to spirituality and psychological development, disaffection with the large institutions of modern life, including both left and right in politics, and rejection of materialism and status display. Surveys set their number at 26% of adult Americans. See Paul H. Ray and Sherry R. Anderson, *The Cultural Creatives: How 50 Million People Are Changing the World* (New York: Three Rivers Press, 2000).

7. See the Web site of the Natural Marketing Institute, www.nmisolutions.com.

8. Natural Marketing Institute, *Understanding the LOHAS Market Report* (Hershey, PA: Natural Marketing Institute, 2006).

9. These figures are taken from Natural Marketing Institute, *Understanding the LOHAS Consumer Report: A Focus on Consumer Packaged Goods* (Hershey, PA: Natural Marketing Institute, 2004).

10. The study, the 2009 Cone Consumer Environmental Survey, is available through Cone's Web site: "Cone Releases 2009 Consumer Environmental Survey," http://www.coneinc.com/content2032, accessed March 12, 2009.

11. See Enviromedia Social Marketing, "82 Percent of Consumers Buying Green Despite Battered Economy," press release (2009), http://www.enviromedia.com/news-item.php?id=685, accessed March 12, 2009.

12. Joel Makower, "Green Consumers' Irrational Exuberance" (2009), http://www.greenbiz.com/blog/2002/02/23/green-consumers-irrational-exuberance, accessed March 12, 2009.

13. This question was taken from the 2009 Cone Consumer Environmental Survey.

14. See, for example, Robert J. Fisher, "Social Desirability Bias and the Validity of Indirect Questioning," *Journal of Consumer Research* 20: 303–315 (1993).

15. Interestingly, the two ORC studies mentioned asked similar questions but used different means: One was a telephone survey, the other an online survey. The lower number for lessened green purchases that emerged from the telephone

study might be due to a certain embarrassment in reporting this to a person. The survey approach may not have created this effect when the questions focused on increased purchases.

16. On the general topic of conjoint analysis, see P. E. Green and V. Srinivasan, "Conjoint Analysis in Marketing: New Developments with Implications for Research and Practice," *Journal of Marketing* 54(4): 3–19 (1990).

17. For a recent article that discusses this body of research, see P. N. Bloom, S. Hoeffler, K. Keller, and C. E. Basurto Meza, "How Social-Cause Marketing Affects Consumer Perceptions," *Sloan Management Review* 47(2): 49–55 (2006).

18. For one of the first of these studies, see T. B. Bjorner, L. G. Hansen, and C. S. Russell, "Environmental Labeling and Consumers' Choice: An Empirical Analysis of the Effect of the Nordic Swan," *Journal of Environmental Economics and Management* 47: 411–434 (2004).

19. Matt Benson, "LOHAS: An Interview About Natural Marketing with Gwynne Rogers," CleanTechies.com (2009), http://blog.cleantechies.com/2009/02/26 /lohas-gwynne-rogers-natural-marketing-institute/, accessed July 12, 2009.

20. See Commission for Environmental Cooperation, "Taking Stock: 2004 North American Pollutants and Transfers" (2007), http://www.cec.org/takingstock /takingstock.cfm?activityId=90&varlan=english, accessed December 18, 2007.

21. See, for example, the Web sites of the Worker Rights Consortium (www .workersrights.org), the Fair Labor Association (www.fairlabor.org), and Social Accountability International (www.saasaccreditation.org).

22. A. Chatterji and D. Levine, "Breaking Down the Wall of Codes: Evaluating Non-Financial Performance Measurement," *California Management Review* 48(2): 29–51 (2006).

23. See Co-op America, "Responsible Shopper" (2007), http://www.coopamerica. org/programs/rs/, accessed December 18, 2007.

24. www.goodguide.com.

25. Bryan Walsh, "#10 Ecological Intelligence," from "10 Ideas That Are Changing the World," *Time*, March 23, 2009, 66.

26. Daniel Goleman, *Ecological Intelligence: How Knowing the Hidden Impacts of What We Buy Can Change Everything* (New York: Broadway Books, 2009).

27. This is the correct quote, although it is less snappy than the frequently seen "Sunshine is the best disinfectant." See Louis D. Brandeis, "What Publicity Can Do, in Other People's Money and How the Bankers Use It," *Harper's Weekly*, December 20, 1913, 379.

28. Don Tapscott and David Ticoll, *The Naked Corporation: How the Age of Transparency Will Revolutionize Business* (New York: Free Press, 2003).

29. See Richard Edelman, *2009 Edelman Trust Barometer Executive Summary* (2009), http://www.edelman.com/trust/2009/, accessed July 29, 2009.

30. See Francesco Perrini, "The Practitioner's Perspective on Non-Financial Reporting," *California Management Review*, 48(2): 73–103 (2006).

31. See Global Reporting Initiative, "GRI Annual Review of Activities,"

available for various years at http://www.globalreporting.org/AboutGRI/WhatWeDo/, accessed December 19, 2007.

32. Perrini, ("Practitioner's Perspective") provides data for ninety companies that had nonfinancial reports in 2002 and 2003, of which forty-one used the GRI format, by far the most popular. Based on this ratio, the number of reporting companies would be roughly 2,100. The actual number may be lower, however, because the GRI format is emerging as a standard. One reason is pressure from socially responsible investment firms that companies adopt the GRI standards. See CMA Management, "Socially Responsible Investment Firms Ask for GRI Standard Reports," *CMA Management*, December/January 2005, 12.

33. Tapscott and Ticoll, *Naked Corporation*.

34. Bill Turque, "Rail Project for Dulles Raises Concerns," *Washington Post*, March 23, 2007.

35. Amy Feldman, R. Paul Herman, and Sara Olsen, "Sensible Investing: Oil," *Fast Company*, February 2008, 90–96.

36. Worldwatch Institute, *State of the World 2004: A Worldwatch Institute Report of Progress Toward a Sustainable Society* (New York: Norton, 2004).

37. Belinda Goldsmith, "Most Women Own 19 Pairs of Shoes—Some Secretly," Reuters (September 10, 2007), http://www.reuters.com/articlePrint?articleId=USN0632859720070910, accessed December 28, 2007.

38. Clive Hamilton, Richard Denniss, and David Baker, *Wasteful Consumption in Australia*, Discussion Paper 77 (Manuka: Australia Institute, 2005).

39. National Association of Home Builders, "Housing Facts, Figures, and Trends" (May 2007), http://www.nahb.org/fileUpload_details.aspx?contentTypeID=7&contentID=2028, accessed December 20, 2007. The 2007 figure was reported in Robert Frank, "Post-Consumer Prosperity: Finding New Opportunities amid the Economic Wreckage," *American Prospect*, April 2009, 12–15.

40. See Centers for Disease Control and Prevention, "U.S. Obesity Trends, 1985–2006," http://www.cdc.gov/nccdphp/dnpa/obesity/trend/maps/, accessed December 18, 2006.

41. Jess Blumber, Katy June-Friesen, and David Zax, "Livin' Large," *Smithsonian*, September 2007, 128.

42. Blumber et al., "Livin' Large," 128.

43. The trend line for the longitudinal data is actually slightly on the decline. See Gary Gardner and Erik Assadourian, "Rethinking the Good Life," in Worldwatch Institute, *State of the World 2004: A Worldwatch Institute Report of Progress Toward a Sustainable Society* (New York: Norton, 2004), 164–180. Gardner and Assadourian updated data from David G. Myers, *American Paradox: Spiritual Hunger in the Age of Plenty* (New Haven, CT: Yale University Press, 2000).

44. See Inge Ropke, "Work-Related Consumption Drivers and Consumption at Work," in Lucia A. Reisch and Inge Ropke, eds., *The Ecological Economics of Consumption* (Cheltenham, U.K.: Edward Elgar, 2004), 60–75.

45. The now classic source on the movement is Joe Dominguez and Vicki

Robin, *Your Money or Your Life: Transforming Your Relationship with Money and Achieving Financial Independence* (New York: Penguin, 1992).

46. Kevin J. Lansing, "Spendthrift Nation," *FRBSF Economic Letter*, November 2005, 1–3. For a contrarian perspective, see Charles Steindel, "How Worrisome Is a Negative Saving Rate?" *Current Issues in Economics and Finance* 13(4): 1–7 (2007).

47. Federal Reserve Board, "Household Debt Service and Financial Obligations Ratios" (December 12, 2007), http://www.federalreserve.gov/releases/housedebt, accessed December 12, 2007.

48. See, for example, Jeffrey Ballinger, "The New Free Trade Heel: Nike's Profits Jump on the Back of Asian Workers," *Harper's Magazine*, August 1992, 46–47; or Sydney H. Schanberg, "Six Cents an Hour," *Life Magazine*, June 1996, 37–46.

49. See, for example, Debora L. Spar, "The Spotlight and the Bottom Line: How Multinationals Export Human Rights," *Foreign Affairs* 77(2): 7–12 (1998).

50. Rebecca Clarren, "Paradise Lost: Greed, Sex Slavery, Forced Abortions and Right-Wing Moralists," *Ms. Magazine*, spring 2006, 35–41.

51. Clarren, "Paradise Lost."

52. Clarren, "Paradise Lost."

53. These frustrations, combined with widespread outrage over financial improprieties, have eroded trust in mainstream business and its ability to act responsibly. See polling data in Joel. M. Podolny, "The Buck Stops (and Starts) at Business School," Harvard Business Review, 87(6): 62–67 (2009); and Richard Stengel, "The Responsibility Revolution," *Time*, September 29, 2009, 38–42.

54. See Environmental Protection Agency, "Municipal Waste: Basic Facts" (2007), http://www.epa.gov/msw/facts.htm, accessed February 27, 2008. In 2006, the figure was roughly 1,700 pounds of waste per capita.

55. "Matters of Scale," *WorldWatch Magazine*, January–February 2008, 32.

56. Union of Concerned Scientists, "What's Your Carbon Footprint?" (2007), http://www.ucsusa.org/publications/greentips/whats-your-carb.html, accessed February 27, 2008.

57. The number is calculated by dividing total toxic releases of 4.34 billion pounds in 2005 by the United States population of 298 million. For an overview of release data, see Environmental Protection Agency, "2005 TRI Public Data Release Brochure" (2007), http://www.epa.gov/tri/tridata/tri05/brochure/brochure.htm, accessed December 31, 2007.

58. Chris Carroll, "High Tech Trash," *National Geographic*, January–February 2008, 64–87.

59. Media Distribution Services, "Top Circulation Magazines" (2007), http://www.prplace.com/topcirculation.html, accessed February 27, 2008.

60. See National Public Radio, "In Tough Times, Savings Rate on the Rise" (2009), http://www.npr.org/news/graphics/2009/mar/saving-rate/index.html, accessed March 12, 2009.

61. Robert Frank, *Falling Behind: How Rising Inequality Harms the Middle Class* (Berkeley: University of California Press, 2007).

62. See Jagdish Bhagwati, *In Defense of Globalization* (New York: Oxford University Press, 2004).

63. James H. Gilmore and B. Joseph Pine II, *Authenticity: What Consumers Want* (Boston: Harvard Business School Press, 2007).

64. This term was used previously by R. E. Freeman, J. Harrison, and A. C. Wicks, *Managing for Stakeholders*, Working Paper (Charlottesville: Darden School of Business, University of Virginia, 2006).

CHAPTER 3

1. Interview with Tim Taylor, Ecohaus, Seattle, Washington, January 23, 2009.

2. Ecohaus, "How We Select Our Products," http://www.ecohaus.com/about /product-selection.html, accessed March 5, 2009.

3. Interview with Tim Taylor, January 23, 2009.

4. Interview with Tim Taylor, January 23, 2009.

5. "Ecohaus Builds on Success," *Sustainable Industries*, May 2008, 11.

6. Michael E. Porter, *Competitive Advantage: Creating and Sustaining Superior Performance* (New York: Free Press, 1985), 14.

7. See Philip Kotler and Kevin L. Keller, *A Framework for Marketing Management*, 3rd ed. (Upper Saddle River, NJ: Prentice-Hall, 2007).

8. Here, a differentiation strategy can be contrasted with a low-cost strategy (see Porter, *Competitive Advantage*). Although it is possible to pursue both strategies simultaneously, this is rarely achievable because it generally means a completely different business model, although some companies that have disrupted industries with new business models are discussed in Chapter 4.

9. The terms *conventional company* and *mainstream company* are used equivalently in this book.

10. Patagonia Environmental Grants Program, http://www.patagonia.com /web/us/patagonia.go?assetid=2927, accessed January 22, 2008.

11. Patagonia's Mission Statement, http://www.patagonia.com/web/us /patagonia.go?assetid=23429, accessed January 22, 2008.

12. Interview with Mike Hannigan, Give Something Back Business Products, Oakland, California, November 10, 2008.

13. See "Awards & Kudos," http://www.givesomethingback.com/documents /GSBawardsandkudos.pdf, accessed July 14, 2009.

14. Elizabeth Kolbert, "Mr. Green," *New Yorker*, January 22, 2007, 34–40.

15. Rachel Lianna, "Wal-Mart Seeks Help from Environmental Consultant," *Benton County Daily Record*, June 2, 2006, http://www.nwanews.com/bcdr /News/35568/, accessed February 25, 2008.

16. William McDonough and Michael Braungart, *Cradle to Cradle: Remaking the Way We Make Things* (New York: North Point Press, 2002).

17. Laurie Gorton, "LEEDing the Way," *Baking & Snack*, November 2007, 38–43.

18. Jim Green, Kettle Foods Ambassador, email message to author, January 28, 2008.

19. See B Corporation, "About B Corp.," http://www.bcorporation.net/about, accessed July 14, 2009.

20. Interview with Bart Houlahan, B Corporation, April 17, 2009.

21. See Y. Chouinard, *Let My People Go Surfing: The Education of a Reluctant Businessman* (New York: Penguin, 2005).

22. Susan Casey, "Patagonia: Blueprint for Green Business," *Fortune*, May 29, 2007, 62–70.

23. Presentation by Sheryl O'Laughlin, CEO of Clif Bar, at the Sustainable Advantage Conference, University of Oregon, Eugene, April 2006.

24. Green Seal, "Green Seal Environmental Standard for Recycled-Content Latex Paint" (2006), http://www.greenseal.org/newsroom/GS-43_Recycled_Content_Latex_Paint.pdf, accessed February 23, 2008.

25. Aaron Chatterji and David Levine, "Breaking Down the Wall of Codes: Evaluating Non-Financial Performance Measurement," *California Management Review* 48(2): 29–51 (2006).

26. FLO-CERT GmbH, http://www.flo-cert.net/flo-cert/index.php, accessed January 29, 2008.

27. California Integrated Waste Management Board, "Recycled Content Products Directory Home Page," http://www.ciwmb.ca.gov/RCP/, accessed February 23, 2008.

28. John Cloud, "My Search for the Perfect Apple," *Time*, March 2, 2007, 42–50.

29. Business Alliance for Local Living Economies, http://www.livingeconomies.org, accessed February 27, 2008.

30. Keith Seiz, "Greyston Bakery Builds for the Future," *Baking Management*, May 1, 2004, http://baking-management.com/successful_plants/bm_imp_6190/, accessed July 9, 2009.

31. The founder of Greyston Bakery, Julius Walls Jr., is a co-author of a fine book on mission-driven companies. See Kevin Lynch and Julius Walls Jr., *Mission, Inc.: The Practitioners Guide to Social Enterprise* (San Francisco: Berrett-Koehler, 2009).

32. Interview with Carlos Martinez Gantes, DKV Seguros, Barcelona, Spain, July 1, 2009.

33. Interview with Josep Santacreu, DKV Seguros, Barcelona, Spain, July 1, 2009.

34. See Philip White, Steve Belletire, and Louise St. Pierre, *Okala Ecological Design Course Guide* (Great Falls, VA: Industrial Designers Society of America, 2004).

35. See Hartmann & Forbes Inc., "Press Releases," http://www.hfshades.com/in_the_media/index.html, accessed July 29, 2009.

36. For more detail on certification requirements, see the Web site of the Forest Stewardship Council (http://www.fsc.org).

37. Letter to author from Jon Anderson, editor of *Random Lengths*, November 12, 2007.

38. In a test of whether or not consumers would pay a 2% premium for certified wood products when certified wood and its conventional counterpart were placed side by side in Home Depot outlets, researchers from Oregon State University found that 37% of consumers were willing to pay the premium. This study suggests that only a small premium is viable for significant segments of the marketplace. See Roy Anderson and Eric Hansen, "Determining Consumer Preferences for Ecolabeled Forest Products: An Experimental Approach," *Journal of Forestry* 102(4): 28–32 (2004).

39. For an excellent discussion of the connection between private benefits and price premiums, see Forest L. Reinhardt, "Environmental Product Differentiation: Implications for Corporate Strategy," *California Management Review* 40(4): 43–73 (1998).

40. Barry Estabrook, "Clean 'n' Green," *On Earth* 26(4): 34–38 (2004).

41. Barry Janoff, "Supermarkets Go Au Naturel," *Progressive Grocer* 78(3): 75–79 (1999).

42. S. Dembkowski and S. Hanmer-Lloyd, "The Environmental Value-Attitude-System Model: A Framework to Guide the Understanding of Environmentally Conscious Consumer Behavior," *Journal of Marketing Management* 10(7): 593–603 (1994).

43. See Daniel R. Goldstein and Michael V. Russo, "Seventh Generation: Balancing Customer Expectations with Supply Chain Realities," in Michael V. Russo, ed., *Environmental Management Readings and Cases*, 2nd ed. (Thousand Oaks, CA: Sage, 2008), 504–520.

44. Interview with Guru Hari Khalsa, Golden Temple, Eugene, Oregon, April 20, 2009.

45. I faced some trade-offs in collecting these data. For some products, I could not locate national retail prices, so I used wholesale prices. Data for most products reflect prices from 2006, 2007, and 2008. I believed that the need to span different types of private benefit situations was more important than collecting data from precisely the same years.

46. See U.S. Department of Agriculture, "Organic Farmgate and Wholesale Prices," Agricultural Marketing Service (2007), http://www.ers.usda.gov/data/organicprices/, accessed February 21, 2008.

47. The source for carrots and eggs is U.S. Department of Agriculture, "Organic Farmgate and Wholesale Prices." For milk, see Carolyn Dimitri and Kathryn M. Venezia, *Retail and Consumer Aspects of the Organic Milk Market*, Report LDP-M-155-01 (Washington, DC: Economic Research Service, U.S. Department of Agriculture, May 2007).

48. http://www.hardwarestore.com, accessed February 20, 2008.

49. http://www.drugstore.com, accessed February 20, 2008.

50. For the green power premiums, see Lori Bird, Leila Dagher, and Blair Swezey, *Green Power Marketing in the United States: A Status Report*, 10th ed., Technical Report TP-670-42502 (Golden, CO: National Renewable Energy Laboratories, December 2007). For average residential prices, see Energy Information Administration, *Electric Power Annual 2006*, Report DOE/EIA-0348 (Washington, DC: U.S. Department of Energy, 2007).

51. See Brian Nattrass and Mary Altomare, *The Natural Step for Business: Wealth, Ecology, and the Evolutionary Corporation* (Gabriola Island, CA: New Society, 1999), esp. ch. 7 ("Collins Pine Company: Journey to Sustainability").

52. The prices were provided on a confidential basis, so I can provide only the percentage premium. Also, they are prices at the mill and do not include additional margins. Other sources in the industry confirmed that the price premium for ultimate customers remains as low as these figures suggest. The price premium for Ponderosa Pine, also sold by Collins, was similar to that of White Fir.

53. We also found that the effect strengthened in states where deregulation had taken place and consumers for the first time were able to specify their choice of generation options. See Magali Delmas, Michael V. Russo, and Maria Montes-Sancho, "Deregulation and Environmental Differentiation in the Electric Utility Industry," *Strategic Management Journal* 28: 189–209 (2007).

54. Jill Bamburg, *Getting to Scale: Growing Your Business Without Selling Out* (San Francisco: Barrett-Koehler, 2006), xv.

55. An interesting issue is that a number of researchers have argued that larger companies can reduce their cost structures by using first-class environmental management. See, for example, Stuart E. Hart, "A Natural Resource Based View of the Firm," *Academy of Management Review* 20(4): 986–1014 (1995); and Michael V. Russo and Paul A. Fouts, "A Resource-Based Perspective on Corporate Environmental Performance and Profitability," *Academy of Management Journal* 40(3): 534–559 (1997). Some of these cost reductions are available to mission-driven firms. But for the companies that form the focus of this work, these advantages are overwhelmed by the cost-inflating impact of small scale.

CHAPTER 4

1. Much of this account was taken from an interview with Daniel Freitag and Filippo Castagna, Freitag's head of the Commercial Department, Zurich, Switzerland, August 22, 2008.

2. Celeste Neill, "Bags of Style," *Easy Jet Magazine*, December 2007, http://www.easyjetinflight.com/features/2007/12/bags-of-style, accessed July 14, 2009.

3. See Paul Hardy and Stuart L. Hart, *Deja Shoe (A): Creating the Environmental Footwear Company*, Teaching Case (Ann Arbor: Corporate Environmental Management Program, University of Michigan, 1996).

4. This number was obtained by multiplying Freitag's unit sales of 150,000

by its average product price (reported in an interview with the company) of 142 euros, or roughly $200.

5. See Paul Hardy and Stuart L. Hart, *Deja Shoe (B): Product Launch*, Teaching Case (Ann Arbor: Corporate Environmental Management Program, University of Michigan, 1996).

6. For Freitag, the trend continues. Freitag's 2007 press review contains forty-three separate press stories in nine countries ranging from Sweden to the United Arab Emirates to Japan.

7. For a classic work on the topic, see John O'Shaughnessy, *Why People Buy* (Oxford, U.K.: Oxford University Press, 1987).

8. J.-P. Felenbok and E. Schwalm, "Winning with the 'Big-Box' Retailers," *European Business Forum*, winter 2005, 84–85.

9. See Derek O. Reiber and Michael V. Russo, "Coastwide Laboratories: Clean and Green," in Michael V. Russo, ed., *Environmental Management: Readings and Cases*, 2nd ed. (Thousand Oaks, CA: Sage, 2009), 537–556.

10. Reiber and Russo, "Coastwide Laboratories."

11. "Wine Goes Green," *Wine Spectator*, June 30, 2007, 56–88.

12. The issue of which option is in fact greener has received attention. Conventional cotton, used in most cloth diapers, is grown using pesticides. Furthermore, in some dry states, avoiding the water used to wash cloth diapers may tip the balance in favor of disposables. For a brief introduction to the debate see "Diapers," http://en.wikipedia.org/wiki/Diaper, accessed July 14, 2009.

13. "Eco-Sanity and Diapers: A Messy Dilemma," Eco-Mama.org (1995), http://www.realmama.org/archives-fall-2005/diapers.php, accessed September 15, 2008.

14. Jason Graham-Nye, remarks at Lundquist College of Business, April 23, 2009.

15. Telephone interview with Beki Cohen, Natural Value, September 25, 2008.

16. Interview with Michelle Kaufmann and Kelly Melia-Teevan, Michelle Kaufmann Studios, Oakland, California, February 11, 2009.

17. National Building Museum, "A Green House" (2008), http://www.nbm.org/exhibitions-collections/exhibitions/the-green-house/in-the-green-house.html, accessed March 19, 2009.

18. Chicago Museum of Science and Industry, "Smart Home: Green and Wired '08" (2008), http://www.msichicago.org/whats-here/exhibits/smart-home/, accessed March 19, 2009.

19. See Michelle Kaufmann and Kelly Melia-Teevan, *Redefining Cost: A Beacon of Hope Shines Through Housing Market Gloom* (Oakland, CA: Michelle Kaufmann Companies, 2008).

20. See TerraChoice, "The Six Sins of Greenwashing" (2008), http://www.terrachoice.com/Home/Six%20Sins%20of%20Greenwashing, accessed September 15, 2008.

21. See C. Goodyear, "S.F. First City to Ban Plastic Shopping Bags," *San Francisco Chronicle*, March 28, 2007, http://www.sfgate.com/cgi-bin/article.cgi?f=/c/a/2007/03/28/MNGDROT5QN1.DTL&type=printable, accessed September 18, 2008.

22. Andrew Martin, "Whole Foods Chain to Stop Use of Plastic Bags," *New York Times*, January 23, 2008, http://www.nytimes.com/2008/01/23/business/23bags.html?n=Top/Reference/Times%20Topics/People/M/Martin,%20Andrew, accessed September 18, 2008.

23. C. Carr, "String Theory," *Time*, July 28, 2008, Global 10.

24. Carr, "String Theory."

25. Interview with Joel Makower, GreenBiz.com, Oakland, California, February 11, 2009.

26. Interview, Mark Buckley, Staples, July 13, 2009.

27. The company is profiled in Richard Seireeni, *The Gort Cloud: The Invisible Force Powering Today's Most Visible Green Brands* (White River Junction, VT: Chelsea Green, 2009).

28. See Tom Szaky, *Revolution in a Bottle: How TerraCycle Is Redefining Green Business* (New York: Portfolio, 2009).

29. For a survey of the groundwork in this area, see J. B. Cohen and C. S. Areni, "Affect and Consumer Behavior," in T. S. Robertson and H. H. Kassarjian, eds., *Handbook of Social Cognition* (Englewood Cliffs, NJ: Prentice-Hall, 1991), 188–240.

30. Michel Tuan, J. B. Pracejus, J. W. Hughes, and G. David, "Affect Monitoring and the Primacy of Feelings in Judgment," *Journal of Consumer Research* 28(2): 167–188 (2001).

31. R. D. Straughan and J. A. Roberts, "Environmental Segmentation Alternatives: A Look at Green Consumer Behavior in the New Millennium," *Journal of Consumer Marketing* 16(6): 558–575 (1999). See also J. A. Roberts, "Green Consumers in the 1990s: Profile and Implications for Advertising," *Journal of Business Research* 36(3): 217–231 (1996).

32. S. Sen and C. B. Bhattacharya, "Does Doing Good Always Lead to Doing Better? Consumer Reactions to Corporate Social Responsibility," *Journal of Marketing Research* 38(2): 225–243 (2001).

33. Sen and Bhattacharya, "Doing Good."

34. C. Conley and E. Friedenwald-Fishman, *Marketing That Matters: 10 Practices to Profit Your Business and Change the World* (San Francisco: Berrett-Koehler, 2006), 111.

35. Interview with Vincent Ben Avram, Washington, D.C., October 24, 2008.

36. Interview with Marty McDonald and Hilary Bromberg, Egg, Seattle, Washington, January 23, 2009.

37. Telephone interview with Hilary Bromberg, Egg, July 15, 2009.

38. Newman's Own, "$250 Million for the Common Good" (2008), http://www.newmansown.com/commongood.cfm, accessed September 24, 2008.

39. Nadia Mustafa, "A Shoe That Fits So Many Souls," *Time*, February 5, 2007, C2.

40. Blake Mycoskie, remarks made in 2007 while accepting Cooper-Hewitt People's Choice Award. A video of the award announcement can be found at http://peoplesdesignaward.cooperhewitt.org/2007/winner.

41. TOMS Shoes, "Our Cause" (2008), http://www.tomsshoes.com/ourcause.aspx, accessed October 27, 2008.

42. The company's excellent Web site, with a complete side-by-side English translation, is at http://www.sustenta.com.

43. Telephone interview with Santiago Lobeira, October 31, 2008. I had a business relationship with Sustenta Soluciones in 2005 and 2006.

44. Peter K. Mills, *Managing Service Industries: Organizational Practices in a Postindustrial Economy* (Cambridge, MA: Ballinger, 1986).

45. C. K. Prahalad and Venkat Ramaswamy, *The Future of Competition: Co-Creating Unique Value with Customers* (Boston: Harvard Business School Press, 2004).

46. See Philip Evans and Thomas S. Wurster, *Blown to Bits: How the New Economics of Information Transforms Strategy* (Boston: Harvard Business School Press, 2000).

47. Although it was not the source of my ideas, the idea of cocreation also appears in Kevin Lynch and Julius Walls Jr., *Mission, Inc: The Practitioner's Guide to Social Enterprise* (San Francisco: Berrett-Koehler, 2009).

48. Postacquisition, Nau donates 2% of its sales to charities selected by customers.

49. "Our Carbon Offset Projects," CarbonFund.org (2008), http://www.carbonfund.org/site/pages/our_projects/, accessed October 27, 2008.

50. See Daniel Goleman, *Emotional Intelligence: How Knowing the Hidden Impacts of What We Buy Can Change Everything* (New York: Broadway Books, 2009).

51. See D. Atkin, "Commitment Is a Two-Way Street," in his *Culting of Brands: When Customers Become True Believers* (New York: Portfolio, 2004), 121–134.

52. Interview with Tom Kemper, Dolphin Blue, Dallas, Texas, September 22, 2008.

53. Interview with Filippo Castagna, Freitag, Zurich, Switzerland, August 22, 2008.

54. Hardy and Hart, *Deja Shoe (A)*.

55. University of Michigan Corporate Environmental Management Program, *Deja, Inc.: An Interactive Case Study*, videotape (Ann Arbor: Corporate Environmental Management Program, University of Michigan, 1996).

56. *Deja, Inc.* videotape.

57. Neill, "Bags of Style."

58. "Innocent: Little Tasty Drinks," Innocent (2008), http://www.innocentdrinks.co.uk/, accessed October 28, 2008.

59. TOMS Shoes, press articles (2008), http://www.tomsshoes.com/articles.aspx, accessed October 29, 2008.

60. Isaac Mizrahi, remarks during presentation of Cooper-Hewitt People's Choice Award. Video available at http://peoplesdesignaward.cooperhewitt.org/2007/winner, accessed October 29, 2008.

61. For another source on the advantages of blogs, see Jeremy Wright, *Blog Marketing: The Revolutionary New Way to Increase Sales, Build Your Brand, and Get Exceptional Sales Results* (New York: McGraw-Hill, 2006).

62. gDiapers Facebook site (2008), http://www.facebook.com/pages/gDiapers/27546807545, accessed November 4, 2008.

63. Joel Makower, "'Climate Counts' Reveals Which Companies Are Walking the Walk," Two Steps Forward Blog, GreenBiz.com (June 19, 2007), http://makower.typepad.com/joel_makower/2007/06/climate_counts_.html, accessed November 4, 2008.

64. The account appears in D. Kirkpatrick, "Why There's No Escaping the Blog," *Fortune*, January 10, 2005, 44–50.

65. J. Hollender, "Strange Bedfellows? Why Seventh Generation Is Doing Business with Wal-Mart's Marketside Stores" (October 6, 2008), http://www.seventhgeneration.com/learn/inspiredprotagonist/strange-bedfellows-why-seventh-generation-doing-business-wal-mart-s-market, accessed November 3, 2008.

66. Hollender, "Strange Bedfellows."

67. Hollender, "Strange Bedfellows."

68. Kirkpatrick, "No Escaping."

69. See Wright, *Blog Marketing*. Another exchange at least reflects Hollender's acknowledgment that he has lost a long-time customer. The blog entry reads:

"I appreciate your candor . . . but based on your article I have purchased my last Seventh Generation Product. I have purchased Seventh Generation products for about 16 years, ever since I found a mail order catalog in high school. You've searched your soul, I've searched mine. I don't want anything more to do with you, please remove me from your e-mailing lists."

Hollender's response:

"I'm so sorry you feel compelled to part ways with Seventh Generation after so many years—16 years is a long time. We will take your name off our mailing list."

70. Richard Seireeni, *The Gort Cloud: The Invisible Force Powering Today's Most Visible Green Brands* (White River Junction, VT: Chelsea Green, 2009).

71. Environmental Leader, "LOHAS Consumers Most Likely to Use Online Social Networks" (2009) (a description of research conducted by the Natural Marketing Institute), http://www.environmentalleader.com/2009/04/17/lohas-consumers-most-likely-to-use-online-social-networks/, accessed July 29, 2009.

CHAPTER 5

1. Interview with David Deal, Community IT Innovators, Washington, D.C., October 24, 2008.

2. See Greater U Street Historic District, City of Washington, D.C., http://www.planning.dc.gov/PLANNING/frames.asp?doc=/planning/lib/planning/preservation/brochures/u_st._brochure.pdf, accessed November 13, 2008.

3. David Deal, email message to author, March 6, 2009.

4. This quote appears in D. W. Bakke, *Joy at Work: A Revolutionary Approach to Fun on the Job* (Seattle: PVG, 2005). It is from L. S. Paine, *Value Shift: Why Companies Must Merge Social and Financial Imperatives to Achieve Superior Performance* (New York: McGraw-Hill, 2003), 193.

5. Recently, Nikos Mourkogiannis, in his book *Purpose: The Starting Point of Great Companies*, has argued that these great companies have a purpose that goes well beyond a set of corporate values. This is because Mourkogiannis believes that most corporate values are "often not moral" and "simply ways of regulating behavior." For him, it is the greater purpose of the company that attracts great employees. In this way, Mourkogiannis's ideas of purpose and the ideas of developing values that we discuss here have much in common. See N. Mourkogiannis, *Purpose: The Starting Point of Great Companies* (New York: Palgrave Macmillan, 2006), esp. 53–54.

6. ShoreBank Corporation, "Our Story" (2008), http://www.shorebankcorp.com/bins/site/templates/child.asp?area_4=pages/nav/story/right_side.dat&area_7=pages/titles/shore_story_title.dat&area_2=pages/about/shore_story.dat, accessed December 15, 2008.

7. Green Mountain Coffee Roasters, "Purpose and Principles" (2008), http://www.greenmountaincoffee.com/ContentPage.aspx?Name=VisionAndValues&DeptName=careers-at-gmcr, accessed December 15, 2008.

8. Interview with David Deal, October 24, 2008.

9. Green Mountain Coffee Roasters, "Corporate Responsibility Report, Executive Summary" (2006), http://www.greenmountaincoffee.com/ContentPage.aspx?Name=Corporate-Social-Responsibility-Report&DeptName=SocialResponsibility, accessed December 15, 2008.

10. J. P. Kotter and J. L. Hesketh, *Corporate Culture and Performance* (New York: Free Press, 1992).

11. J. B. Sorensen, "The Strength of Corporate Culture and the Reliability of Firm Performance," *Administrative Science Quarterly* 47: 70–91 (2002).

12. Y. Chouinard, *Let My People Go Surfing: The Education of a Reluctant Businessman* (New York: Penguin, 2005), 85–116

13. The issue was dated January 30, 1989.

14. See K. L. Holland and J. C. Collins, *Lost Arrow Corporation/Patagonia (A)*, teaching case (Stanford, CA: Stanford Graduate School of Business, 1990).

15. Holland and J. C. Collins, *Lost Arrow Corporation*, 12.

16. M. Albion, *Making a Life, Making a Living: Reclaiming Your Purpose and Passion in Business and in Life* (New York: Warner Books, 2000).

17. C. Williams, *Management*, 5th ed. (Mason, OH: Southwestern Cengage Learning, 2009), 478.

18. Williams, *Management*.

19. D. B. Turban and D. W. Greening, "Corporate Social Performance and Organizational Attractiveness to Prospective Employees," *Academy of Management Journal* 40(3): 658–672 (1997).

20. D. W Greening and D. B. Turban, "Corporate Social Performance as a Competitive Advantage in Attracting a Quality Workforce," *Business & Society* 39(3): 254–280 (2000).

21. S. Sen, C. B. Bhattacharya, and D. Korschun, "The Role of Corporate Social Responsibility in Strengthening Multiple Stakeholder Relationships: A Field Experiment," *Journal of the Academy of Marketing Science* 34(2): 158–166 (2006).

22. Respondents also reported higher propensities to purchase the product and to invest in the stock of the company if they were aware of its gift.

23. See the Sustainable Asset Management website at http://www.sam-group .com/htmle/main.cfm.

24. Interview with Reto Ringger, Sustainable Asset Management, Zurich, Switzerland, August 29, 2008.

25. Interview with David Williams, ShoreBank Pacific, Portland, Oregon, September 16, 2008.

26. Interview with Kate Lee and Kirk Richardson, KEEN Footwear, Portland, Oregon, October 8, 2008.

27. Hybrid Life, KEEN Footwear, "Hybrid Life," http://www.keenfootwear .com/hybrid_life.aspx, accessed on March 6, 2009.

28. Interview with Kate Lee and Kirk Richardson, October 8, 2008.

29. Provided by David Deal to author.

30. See J. G. Dees, "Enterprising Nonprofits," *Harvard Business Review* 76(1): 54–67 (1998); or J. G. Dees, *Social Enterprise: Private Initiatives for the Common Good*, Harvard Business School Case 9-395-116 (Cambridge, MA: Harvard Business School Press, 1994). The two sources use somewhat different boundaries for which organizations are categorized as social enterprises, but in the years since these sources were published, the social enterprise category generally has grown to include for-profit, mission-driven companies.

31. Interview with Daniel Freitag, Freitag, Zurich, Switzerland, August 22, 2008.

32. The one-year figure comes from Plante & Moran, an accounting firm. See S. E. Jackson, R. S. Schuler, and S. Werner, *Managing Human Resources*, 10th ed. (Mason, OH: Southwestern Cengage Learning, 2009), 219.

33. Interview with Grace Pae, Artemis Foods, Portland, Oregon, September 29, 2008.

34. Artemis Foods, "Sample Menus," http://www.artemisfoods.com/Menus.html, accessed November 24, 2008.

35. See G. M. Spreitzer, "Psychological Empowerment in the Workplace: Dimensions, Measurement, and Validation," *Academy of Management Journal* 38: 1442–1465 (1995). Spreitzer built on a four-element framework that was originally advanced in K. W. Thomas and B. A. Velthouse, "Cognitive Elements of Empowerment," *Academy of Management Review* 15: 666–681 (1990).

36. Several studies have shown a positive relationship between employee commitment and the company's level of corporate citizenship and social responsibility. See Dane K. Peterson, "The Relationship Between Perceptions of Corporate Citizenship and Organizational Commitment," *Business & Society* 27(4): 537–543 (2004); or Stephen Brammer, Andrew Millington, and Bruce Rayton, "The Contribution of Corporate Social Responsibility to Organizational Commitment," *International Journal of Human Resource Management* 18(10): 1701–1719 (2007).

37. J. Abrams, *The Company We Keep: Reinventing Small Business for People, Community, and Place* (White River Junction, VT: Chelsea Green, 2005), 8–9.

38. Abrams, *The Company We Keep*, 28–40. For an appraisal of the Mondragón Cooperative, see F. J. Forcadell, "Democracy, Cooperation, and Business Success: The Case of Mondragón Corporación Cooperativa," *Journal of Business Ethics* 56: 255–275 (2005).

39. Abrams, *The Company We Keep*, 39.

40. See Ben Cohen and Mal Warwick, *Values-Driven Business: How to Change the World, Make Money, and Have Fun* (San Francisco: Berrett-Koehler, 2006), 40–42.

41. Interview with Hang Sik Oh, iCOOP Association of Consumers' Cooperatives, Seoul, South Korea, October 20, 2008.

42. Kim T. Gordon, "Cheer Leaders," *Entrepreneur*, September 2006, 95–96.

43. J. Combs, Y. Liu, A. Hall, and D. Ketchen, "How Much Do High-Performance Work Practices Matter? A Meta-Analysis of Their Effects on Organizational Performance," *Personnel Psychology* 59: 501–528 (2006). For an example of one of the studies included in this analysis, see M. A. Huselid, "The Impact of Human Resource Management Practices on Turnover, Productivity, and Corporate Financial Performance," *Academy of Management Journal* 38: 635–672 (1995). For more accessible treatments of this topic, see P. Pfeffer, *Competitive Advantage Through People: Unleashing the Power of the Work Force* (Boston: Harvard Business School Press, 1994); and P. Pfeffer, *The Human Equation: Building Profits by Putting People First* (Boston: Harvard Business School Press, 1998).

44. One study of Belgian companies explored the impact of internal stakeholders, including employees, and whether the effects were associated with environmental leadership. The investigators found a strong positive effect. See K. Buysse and A. Verbeke, "Proactive Environmental Strategies: A Stakeholder Management Perspective," *Strategic Management Journal* 24: 453–470 (2003).

45. P. Bansal, "From Issues to Actions: The Importance of Individual Concerns and Organizational Values in Responding to Natural Environmental Issues," *Organization Science* 14: 510–527 (2003).

46. Interview with Kate Lee and Kirk Richardson, October 8, 2008.

47. Interview with Kate Lee and Kirk Richardson, October 8, 2008.

48. Remarks by Jeffrey Hollender, Lundquist College of Business, University of Oregon, Eugene, February 26, 2004.

49. Remarks by Jeffrey Hollender, February 26, 2004.

50. Telephone interview with Gregor Barnum, director of Corporate Consciousness, Seventh Generation, November 14, 2008.

51. R. S. Dooley and G. E. Fryxell, "Attaining Decision Quality and Commitment from Dissent: The Moderating Effects of Loyalty and Competence in Strategic Decision-Making Teams," *Academy of Management Journal* 42: 389–402 (1999).

52. Interview with Jason Graham-Nye, gDiapers, Portland, Oregon, October 8, 2008.

53. J. P. Kotter, *Leading Change* (Boston: Harvard Business School Press, 1996), 90.

54. Kotter, *Leading Change*, 97.

55. Interview with Josh Hinerfeld, Organically Grown, Gresham, Oregon, November 20, 2008.

56. G. Erickson and L. Lorentzen, *Raising the Bar: Integrity and Passion in Life and Business* (San Francisco: Jossey-Bass, 2004).

57. Erickson and Lorentzen, *Raising the Bar*, 96–98.

58. See Jon Entine, "Shattered Image: Is the Body Shop Too Good to Be True?" *Business Ethics*, September–October 1994, 23–28.

59. See A. Wolff, "The Other Basketball," *Sports Illustrated*, June 13, 2005, 66–77. I first saw this story in M. Albion, *True to Yourself: Leading a Values-Based Business* (San Francisco: Berrett-Koehler, 2006), 80–82.

60. Albion, *True to Yourself*, 80–82.

61. The quote comes from Albion, *True to Yourself*, 31.

62. Albion, *True to Yourself*, 31.

63. Interview with Alysa Rose, Rejuvenation Hardware, Portland, Oregon, January 5, 2009.

64. "Rejuvenation Cuts Staff," *Portland Business Journal*, February 27, 2009, http://www.bizjournals.com/portland/stories/2009/02/23/daily59.html, accessed March 8, 2009.

65. Interview with Jason Graham-Nye, October 8, 2008.

66. See Paul Tracey and Owen Jarvis, "An Enterprising Failure: Why a Promising Social Franchise Collapsed," *Stanford Social Innovation Review*, spring, 66–70 (2006).

67. See J. Bamburg, *Getting to Scale: Growing Your Business Without Selling Out* (San Francisco: Berrett-Koehler, 2006).

CHAPTER 6

1. For the autobiography, see Anita Roddick, *Body and Soul: Profits with Principles—The Amazing Success Story of Anita Roddick and The Body Shop* (New York: Crown Trade Paperbacks, 1991).

2. The Body Shop, *The Body Shop Social Statement: 95* (Watersmead, U.K.: The Body Shop, 1996).

3. See Jon Entine, "Shattered Image: Is the Body Shop Too Good to Be True?" *Business Ethics*, September–October 1994, 23–28.

4. The story about Hill & Knowlton was found in London Greenpeace, "What's Wrong with the Body Shop," posted at the Beyond McDonald's Web site, http://www.mcspotlight.org/beyond/companies/bs_ref.html, accessed July 8, 2008.

5. London Greenpeace, "What's Wrong."

6. Kirk O. Hanson, *Social Evaluation: The Body Shop International 1995* (Watersmead, U.K.: The Body Shop, 1995).

7. Hanson, *Social Evaluation*, 25.

8. Joan Bavaria, Eric Becker, and Simon Billenness, "Body Shop Scrutinized: Faces Allegations on Social Performance," *Franklin Research's Insight*, September 15, 1994.

9. See Scott Simon, "Roddick's Body Shop: An Empire Built on a Ruse?" (2007), http://www.npr.org/templates/story/story.php?storyId=14442261, accessed July 15, 2008.

10. See Daniel R. Goldstein and Michael V. Russo, "Seventh Generation: Balancing Customer Expectations with Supply Chain Realities," in Michael V. Russo, ed., *Environmental Management: Readings and Cases*, 2nd ed. (Thousand Oaks, CA: Sage, 2009), 504–520.

11. See Seventh Generation, *Widening the Lens: 2004 Corporate Responsibility Report* (Burlington VT: Seventh Generation, 2005).

12. See S. Bikhchandant, D. Hirshleifer, and I. Welsh, "A Theory of Fads, Fashion, Custom, and Cultural Exchange as Information Cascades," *Journal of Political Economy* 100: 992–1026 (1992); and J. P. Bonardi and G. D. Keim, "Corporate Political Strategies for Widely Salient Issues," *Academy of Management Review* 30(3): 555–576 (2005).

13. *Webster's College Dictionary* (McGraw-Hill ed.) provides several definitions of both authenticity and credibility, but for our purposes, we contrast two of them. *Authenticity* is defined as "not false or copied; genuine; real," whereas *credibility* is defined as "capable of being believed; trustworthy." Thus credibility has a more external focus—it depends not just on factlike properties but also on perceptions.

14. Nike Inc., "Company Overview" (2008), http://www.nikebiz.com/company_overview/, accessed July 9, 2008.

15. See D. L. Spar, *Hitting the Wall: Nike and International Labor Practices*, Harvard Business School Case 5-701-020 (Boston: Harvard Business School Press, 2000).

16. See "Creative Destruction," *Business Week*, July 4, 2005.

17. See D. Raths, "100 Best Corporate Citizens, 2006," *Business Ethics Magazine* 20(1): 20–28 (2006).

18. J. Manning, "Nike Battles Back, but the Activists Hold the High Ground," *The Oregonian*, November 10, 1997, A7.

19. See Kinder, Lydenberg, and Domini, "KLD Indexes Announces Change to KLD's Domini 400 Social Index," press release, December 19, 2005.

20. Kinder, Lydenberg, and Domini, "KLD Indexes Announces Change."

21. See Ben & Jerry's, "Company Timeline," http://www.benjerry.com/our_company/about_us/our_history/timeline/index.cfm, accessed July 16, 2008.

22. Jeff Glasser, "Dark Cloud: Ben & Jerry's Inaccurate in Rainforest Nut Pitch," *Boston Globe*, July 30, 1995.

23. Interview with Allen King, Excellent Packaging and Supply, Berkeley, California, February 12, 2009.

24. I served as an adviser during the development of KEEN's report.

25. T. Stuart, H. Huang, and R. Hybels, "Interorganizational Endorsements and the Performance of Entrepreneurial Ventures," *Administrative Science Quarterly* 44: 325–349 (1999).

26. For the seminal and still relevant treatment of stakeholder management, see R. Edward Friedman, *Strategic Management: A Stakeholder Approach* (Boston: Pittman, 1984).

27. See G. R. Carroll, "Long-Term Evolutionary Change in Organizational Populations: Theory, Models, and Empirical Findings from Industrial Demography," *Industrial and Corporate Change* 6: 119–145 (1997).

28. See U. Steger, A. Nick, O. Salzmann, and A. Ionescu-Somers, *Transforming the Global Fishing Industry: The Marine Stewardship Council at Full Sail?* Case IMD-2-0083 (Lausanne, Switzerland: International Institute for Management Development, 2006).

29. Marine Stewardship Council, *Annual Report 2008/09* (London: MSC, 2009).

30. See George Radler and Ulrich Steger, *The Marine Stewardship Council (A): Is Joint Venture Possible Between Suits and Sandals?* Case IMD-008 (Lausanne, Switzerland: International Institute for Management Development, 2000).

31. See "How Much Does Carbon Offsetting Cost? Price Survey!" http://www.ecobusinesslinks.com/carbon_offset_wind_credits_carbon_reduction.htm, accessed November 6, 2009; and Matthew J. Kotchen, "Offsetting Green Guilt," *Stanford Social Innovation Review* 7(2): 26–31 (2009).

32. http://www.ewea.org, accessed July 14, 2008.

33. http://www.ewea.org, accessed July 14, 2008.

34. See Derek O. Reiber and Michael V. Russo, "Coastwide Laboratories: Clean and Green," in Michael V. Russo, ed., *Environmental Management: Readings and Cases*, 2nd ed. (Thousand Oaks, CA: Sage, 2009), 537–556.

35. Organic Federation of Australia, "Strategic Plan for the Australian Organic

Industry, July" (2001), http://www.ofa.org.au/about/strategicplan.htm, accessed July 14, 2008.

CHAPTER 7

1. Interview with Priya Haji, World of Good, Emeryville, California, February 11, 2009.

2. The Swedish International Development Cooperation Agency provides one definition: "The informal economy is the unregulated non-formal portion of the market economy that produces goods and services for sale or for other forms of remuneration." The agency's report goes on to characterize the informal economy as characterized by "low entry requirements in terms of capital and professional qualifications, a small scale of operations, skills often acquired outside of formal education, and labour-intensive methods of production and adapted technology." See Swedish International Development Cooperation Agency, *The Informal Economy* (Stockholm: SIDA, 2004), 13.

3. "East Palo Alto Regarded as Drug Haven," *Stanford Daily*, January 30, 2002.

4. Anya Kamenetz, "Trade Goods," *Fast Company*, October 2008, 88–90.

5. Leslie Berger, "She's Crafty: World of Good Brings Female Artisans' Wares to Global Markets," *Stanford Social Innovation Review*, summer, 71–72 (2008).

6. http://worldofgood.ebay.com/.

7. See James S. Kunen, "Enron's Vision (and Values) Thing," *New York Times*, January 19, 2002, http://www.nytimes.com/2002/01/19/opinion/enron-s-vision-and-values-thing.html, accessed July 15, 2009.

8. See N. Mourkogiannis, *Purpose: The Starting Point of Great Companies* (New York: Palgrave Macmillan, 2006).

9. Tom Chappell, *Managing Upside Down: The Seven Intentions Of Values-Centered Leadership* (New York: William Morrow, 1999). Cited in Mourkogiannis, *Purpose*, 48.

10. For financial reports, see Circuit City, "Download Library," http://investor.circuitcity.com/downloads.cfm, accessed January 28, 2009.

11. Jennifer Reingold, "Walking the Walk," *Fast Company*, November 2005, 80–85.

12. Dennis Bakke, founder of AES Corporation, argues that they are worthless unless they are "(1) shared by the majority of the people in the organization, (2) lived with some consistency by leaders, (3) considered at least equal to economic criteria in all major decisions by leaders, (4) taught to employees by senior leaders at every opportunity, and (5) constantly communicated to people and stakeholders outside the organization, including shareholders." See Dennis W. Bakke, *Joy at Work: A Revolutionary Approach to Fun on the Job* (Seattle: PVG, 2005), 163.

13. Michael Barbaro, "At Wal-Mart, Lessons in Self-Help," *New York Times*, April 5, 2007, http://www.nytimes.com/2007/04/05/business/05improve.html, accessed January 29, 2009.

14. Adam Werbach recounted this story at Wal-Mart's "Live Better Sustainability Summit" on October 10, 2007. Werbach's Act Now consulting company was hired by Wal-Mart to create and run the program.

15. Chip Conley, *Peak: How Great Companies Get Their Mojo from Maslow* (San Francisco: Jossey-Bass, 2007).

16. W. C. Willett and A. Ascherio, "Trans Fatty Acids: Are the Effects Only Marginal?" *American Journal of Public Health* 85(3): 411–412 (1995).

17. U.S. Food and Drug Administration, "Trans Fat Now Listed with Saturated Fat and Cholesterol on the Nutrition Facts Label," http://www.cfsan.fda.gov/~dms /transfat.html, accessed January 30, 2009.

18. Reka Balu, "Companies' Use of Trans Fat in Foods Begins to Draw Focus of FDA, Buyers," *Wall Street Journal*, June 8, 1998.

19. See S. H. Swan, K. M. Main, F. Liu et al. "Decrease in Anogenital Distance Among Male Infants with Prenatal Phthalate Exposure," *Environmental Health Perspectives* 113(8): 1056–1061 (2005).

20. Nicholas Casey and Melanie Trottman, "Toys Containing Banned Plastics Still on Market; Restrictions on Phthalates Don't Take Effect Until '09; Fears of Reproductive Defects," *Wall Street Journal*, October 23, 2008, http://online .wsj.com/article/SB122472242723860917.html?mod=googlenews_wsj, accessed February 3, 2009.

21. See, for example, Seventh Generation, "The Dirty Dozen," http://www.pg beautyscience.com/phthalates-safety-in-cosmetics.html, accessed February 2, 2009.

22. See Procter & Gamble, "Phthalates Safety in Cosmetics," http://www.pg beautyscience.com/phthalates-safety-in-cosmetics.html, accessed February 2, 2009.

23. See Colgate-Palmolive, "Recognizing Customer Concerns," http://www .colgate.com/app/Colgate/US/Corp/LivingOurValues/Sustainability/RespectFor People/RespectForConsumers/RecognizingConsumerConcerns.cvsp, accessed February 2, 2009.

24. See "Does Method Contain Phthalates?" http://methodhome.custhelp .com/cgi-bin/methodhome.cfg/php/enduser/std_adp.php?p_faqid=2 53&p_created=1182208684&p_sid=wSi7Rcrj&p_accessibility=0&p_redirect=&p_ lva=&p_sp=cF9zcmNoPSZwX3NvcnRfYnk9JnBfZ3JpZHNvcnQ9JnBfcm93 X2NudDo5Miw5MiZwX3Byb2RzPSZwX2NhdHM9JnBfcHY9JnBfY3Y9 JnBfc2VhcmNoX3R5cGU9YW5zd2Vycy5zZWFyY2hfbmwwmcF9wYWdlPTE* &p_li=&p_topview=1, accessed February 22, 2009.

25. See a Web site maintained by Smart Balance, a buttery spread: "The Truth About Trans Fat Labeling," http://www.thetruthabouttransfat.com, accessed March 17, 2009. The Web site lists trans fats per serving of its competitors, running from 0.47 gram down to Smart Balance's 0.07 gram. All can claim to have "0 grams trans fats."

26. A total ban is unlikely, as minute amounts of trans fats occur naturally. See American Heart Association, "Trans Fats," http://www.americanheart.org/ presenter.jhtml?identifier=3045792, accessed March 17, 2009.

27. See Nike Inc., "Nike Contract Factory Disclosure List: Current as of April 28, 2008," http://nikeresponsibility.com/#workers-factories/active_factories, accessed February 2, 2009.

28. Gregor Barnum, director of Corporate Consciousness, Seventh Generation, telephone conversation with author, February 1, 2009.

29. Responsible Shopper, "Procter & Gamble," http://www.coopamerica.org/programs/responsibleshopper/company.cfm?id=279, accessed February 2, 2009.

30. Interview with Priya Haji, February 11, 2009.

31. Fair Wage Guide, http://www.fairtradecalculator.com/, accessed March 19, 2009.

32. Also, the Web site will request whether the good was produced in a rural or an urban setting and whether or not the artisan paid for the materials.

33. See for example Wikipedia's entry "Proof of Concept," http://en.wikipedia.org/wiki/Proof_of_concept, accessed July 18, 2009.

34. Vancity, "2006–07 Accountability Report," https://www.vancity.com/MyMoney/AboutUs/WhoWeAre/CorporateReports/AccountabilityReport/0607AccountabilityReport/, accessed February 4, 2009.

35. Interview with Mark Buckley, Staples, July 13, 2009.

36. The multiple layers are needed to serve different purposes, such as to keep out air, light, and water, but also to provide a printable surface on the outside.

37. Coeli Carr, "Clean Goes Green," *Time*, March 24, 2008, Global 10.

38. See, for example, Yves L. Doz and Gary Hamel, *Alliance Advantage: The Art of Creating Value through Partnering* (Boston: Harvard Business School Press, 1998).

39. Interview with Reto Ringger, Sustainable Asset Management, Zurich, Switzerland, August 29, 2008.

40. Interview with Stan Peregoy and Gerry Rodino, Calvert-Jones Company, Alexandria, Virginia, October 24, 2008.

41. Interview with Stan Peregoy and Gerry Rodino, October 24, 2008.

42. Interview with John Martilla and Grant Watkinson, Coastwide Laboratories, Portland, Oregon, February 18, 2009.

43. A stubborn case was that of degreasers, notoriously toxic substances. The green alternative required more time to use, which raised its costs.

44. Interview with John Martilla and Grant Watkinson, February 18, 2009.

45. Thomas Barron, Carol Berg, and Linda Bookman, *How to Select and Use Safe Janitorial Chemicals: Project Completion Report*, report prepared for the U.S. Environmental Protection Agency, Region IX (December 1999), http://www.p2pays.org/ref/21/20377.pdf, accessed November 6, 2009.

46. Interview with Stan Peregoy and Gerry Rodino, October 24, 2008.

47. Partnerships with other members of the organization of mission-driven companies, Sustainable Business Network of Washington, also are helping Calvert-Jones.

48. Interview with Stan Peregoy and Gerry Rodino, October 24, 2008.

49. Interview with Stan Peregoy and Gerry Rodino, October 24, 2008.

50. Ben Cohen and Mal Warwick, *Values-Driven Business: How to Change the World, Make Money, and Have Fun* (San Francisco: Berrett-Koehler, 2006).

51. With respect to performance standards like certifications, the question of "stickiness" arises. When mainstream companies adopt standards originally championed by their mission-driven counterparts, smaller companies will be pressured to find a way to create new points of social and environmental performance that will differentiate them from what has gone from best-in-class to an industry-wide standard. And there may well be pushback from mainstream companies that might have devoted considerable time, effort, and money to meet those initial standards. On the other hand, given the trajectory of societal expectations that was discussed in Chapter 2, it would be wise for mainstream companies to appreciate that, although adoption of shared standards affords breathing room, it is likely that this respite will be temporary.

52. Elkington portrays this ebb and flow as shifting tectonic plates, which create shear zones between the three elements of the triple bottom line. See J. Elkington, *Cannibals with Forks* (Gabriola Island, Canada: New Society, 1998).

CHAPTER 8

1. Interview with Jason Graham-Nye, gDiapers, Portland, Oregon, October 8, 2008.

2. The term social impact banking comes from Albina Community Bank. See "Go Green 2008: Speaker List," http://www.gogreenpdx.com/speakers/, accessed September 8, 2008.

3. M. E. Porter, *The Competitive Advantage of Nations* (New York: Free Press, 1990). A visual representation of the diamond model appears on p. 72 of the book.

4. One report that cites Porter and others and that studied clusters across the world was Ecotec Research and Consulting, "A Practical Guide to Cluster Development: Report to the Department of Trade and Industry and the English RDAs" (2004), http://www.wired-nation.net/file/show/uk-practical-guide-to-cluster-development.pdf, accessed December 23, 2008.

5. M. E. Porter, "The Competitive Advantage of Nations," *Harvard Business Review* 68(2): 73–91 (1990).

6. M. E. Porter, "Clusters and the New Economics of Competition," *Harvard Business Review* 76(6): 77–90 (1998).

7. Co-op America, "National Green Pages" (2008), http://www.coopamerica.org/pubs/greenpages/, accessed December 23, 2008.

8. Some other sources of companies did not have active screening and so attracted a broad range of companies. For example, in the list attached to its city rankings on Sustain Lane, nine of the forty-five businesses in Dallas were Chipotle Restaurants. See Sustain Lane, "Directory: Dallas, TX" (2008), http://www.sustainlane.com/local/dallas-tx, accessed December 19, 2008.

9. This data set consists of all unique listings in the *National Green Pages*. It was gathered during October and November 2008 by coding company locations from an alphabetical list generated by Co-op America's user interface. Less than 1% of listings did not include location information. Urban areas are defined as "Metropolitan Statistical Areas" at http://www.whitehouse.gov/omb/bulletins/fy2008/b08-01.pdf. The population was taken from U.S. Census Bureau,'s online data service. See U.S. Census Bureau, *Annual Estimates of the Population of Metropolitan and Micropolitan Statistical Areas: April 1, 2000, to July 1, 2007*, at http://www.census.gov/popest/metro/CBSA-est2007-annual.html, accessed November 6, 2009.

10. There is little doubt that these numbers understate the actual population of mission-driven companies in these areas, because many mission-driven companies have not seen a reason to appear in the Green Pages. Nonetheless, if the chance of obtaining (or not obtaining) a listing is relatively stable across the cities, the data will show the relative placement of cities with relative accuracy.

11. It is a mathematical property that the distributions that track the accumulation of many small effects (such as the founding of mission-driven companies) naturally will resemble a bell-shaped curve. Thus it is important to see whether this agglomeration reflects a causal factor, such as the presence of LOHAS consumers or talented workers. For a review of properties of normal distributions, see Wikipedia, "Normal Distribution" (2008), http://en.wikipedia.org/wiki/Normal_distribution, accessed December 16, 2008.

12. Perhaps this absolute focus on economics and economic explanations (along with a marked absence of humor) is one reason *The Economist* described the book as "unbendingly earnest." See "Oh Mr. Porter, What Shall We Do?" *The Economist*, May 19, 1990, 99.

13. Interview with Dave Williams, ShoreBank Pacific, Portland, Oregon, September 16, 2008.

14. G. Hardin, "The Tragedy of the Commons," *Science* 162(3859): 1243–1248 (December 13, 1968).

15. Interview with Thomas Kemper, Dolphin Blue, Dallas, Texas, September 22, 2008.

16. See Amitai Etzioni, *The Moral Dimension: Toward a New Economics* (New York: Free Press, 1988). More recently, Miller has addressed the tendency to overestimate the power of the individual and its impact on the economy. See Matt Miller, *The Tyranny of Dead Ideas: Letting Go of the Old Ways of Thinking to Unleash a New Prosperity* (New York: Times Books, 2009).

17. See C. L. Grossman, "Charting the Unchurched in America," *USA Today*, March 7, 2002, http://www.usatoday.com/life/2002/2002-03-07-no-religion.htm, accessed November 6, 2009. The survey asked about memberships in organized religions only and so may not pick up other forms of spirituality.

18. ShoreBank Corporation, "Our Story: Mission and Values" (2008), http://www.ShoreBankcorp.com/bins/site/templates/child.asp?area_4=pages/nav/story

/right_side.dat&area_7=pages/titles/shore_story_title.dat&area_2=pages/about
/shore_story.dat, accessed December 22, 2008.

19. Telephone interview with Bianca Alexander, Conscious Planet Media, Chicago, Illinois, July 15, 2009.

20. See *The Soul of Green*, http://www.soulofgreen.com/, accessed July 29, 2009.

21. Richard L. Florida, *Cities and the Creative Class* (New York: Routledge, 2005), 98. The talent index, a ranking from 1 to 50, is defined as the percentage of the population holding a bachelor's degree.

22. As noted, apparent clustering can be a statistical artifact. But to the extent that the connection between local talent and clustering reflects a causal relationship—a plausible assumption—this is not so.

23. The top ten cities for concentrations of mission-driven companies and their talent indexes are as follows (there is no talent index for San Jose–Sunnyvale–Santa Clara, so the eleventh city, Chicago, was used).

City	Green Pages listings per 100,000 residents	Talent index
San Francisco–Oakland	4.97	3
Portland	3.08	17
Washington, D.C.	2.69	1
Austin	1.56	4
Seattle-Tacoma	1.54	6
Minneapolis	1.50	8
Boston	0.98	2
Tampa–St. Petersburg	0.84	49
San Diego	0.84	14
Chicago	0.66	13

24. Interview with Jim Morris, MBL Group, Portland, Oregon, October 8, 2008.

25. L. Tobias, "Community Opposes Natural Foods Giant Whole Foods Building New Store in Eugene, Oregon," *The Oregonian*, May 28, 2006.

26. Michael Pollan, *The Omnivore's Dilemma: A Natural History of Four Meals* (New York: Penguin, 2006).

27. See Stacie Stukin, "Taking a Bite Out of 'Organics,'" *Los Angeles Times*, August 1, 2006. The exchange can be accessed on Pollan's Web site, http://www.michaelpollan.com/write.php.

28. Carol Ness, "Whole Foods, Taking Flak, Thinks Local," *San Francisco Chronicle*, July 26, 2006.

29. Interview with Matt Lounsberry, Stumptown Coffee Roasters, Portland, Oregon, January 5, 2009.

30. Interview with Brian Back, *Sustainable Industries*, San Francisco, California, February 13, 2009.

31. Interview with Spencer Beebe, Ecotrust, Portland, Oregon, November 21, 2008.

32. Another candidate for a Portland-based cluster would be organic and natural foods, which has elements that parallel that of green building.

33. Interview with Mark Edlen, Gerding-Edlen Development, Portland, Oregon, January 5, 2009.

34. The ranking is based on the number of LEED-certified buildings, with differential impacts of platinum, gold, and silver levels. See Sustain Lane, "2008 City Rankings: Green Building" (2008), http://www.sustainlane.com/us-city-rankings /categories/green-building, accessed January 6, 2009.

35. Michael R. Morris, "The Dean of Green: Tom Kelly Shrewdly Leads Neil Kelly Co. Through the Downturn," *Professional Remodeler*, November 2008, 20–26.

36. Interview with Tom Kelly, Neil Kelly Cabinet Company, Portland, Oregon, November 20, 2008.

37. For an analysis along these lines, see J. H. Allen and T. Potiowsky, "Portland's Green Building Cluster: Economic Trends and Impacts," *Economic Development Quarterly* 22(4): 303–315 (2008).

38. Becky Brun, "Oracle of Oregon: Equilibrium Capital's David Chen Bets on Northwest Entrepreneurs," *Sustainable Industries*, December 2007, 24–25.

39. Brun, "Oracle of Oregon," 24–25.

40. The effect of civic leadership might not be uniform across cities of comparable size. For example, civic leadership within the mission-driven sector in Chicago is still limited compared with conventional companies, according to Jean Pogge of ShoreBank (interview, July 29, 2009). As of 2007, Illinois boasted of sixty-six companies in the Fortune 500, the vast majority of which were headquartered in and around Chicago. Thus these companies and their interests still strongly influence the civic agenda. See http://money.cnn.com/magazines /fortune/fortune500/2007/states/IL.html.

41. See, for example, T. Bresnahan, A. Gambardella, and A. Saxenian, "'Old Economy' Inputs for 'New Economy' Outcomes: Cluster Formation in the New Silicon Valleys," *Industrial and Corporate Change* 10(1): 835–860, esp. 857 (2001).

42. National Governors Association, *Cluster-Based Strategies for Growing State Economies* (Washington, DC: NGA, 2007), 3.

43. For an excellent biography of McCall that places his accomplishments in historical context, see Brent Walth, *Fire at Eden's Gate: Tom McCall and the Oregon Story* (Portland: Oregon Historical Society Press, 1994).

44. See Hal Balenstrem, "Mt. Hood Freeway: The Road Not Taken," *Southeast Examiner*, December 8, 2008, http://news.mywebpal.com/news_tool_v2.cfm? pnpID=667&NewsID=939294&CategoryID=2148&show=localnews&om=1, accessed December 30, 2008.

45. See Portland Office of Sustainable Development, "City of Portland Proposed High Performance Green Building Policy" (2008), http://www.portlandonline.com /osd/index.cfm?c=45879&, accessed December 30, 2008.

46. Interview with Susan Anderson, Office of Sustainable Development, Portland Oregon, November 21, 2008.

47. See Derek O. Reiber and Michael V. Russo, "Coastwide Laboratories: Clean and Green," in Michael V. Russo, ed., *Environmental Management: Readings and Cases*, 2nd ed. (Thousand Oaks, CA: Sage, 2009), 537–556.

48. Interview with Susan Anderson, November 21, 2008.

49. See Office of Sustainable Development, "City of Portland Recognizes Eight Local Businesses at the 16th Annual BEST Awards" (2008), http://www .portlandonline.com/osd/index.cfm?c=44851&a=193151, accessed January 3, 2009.

50. A. Westervelt, "20 Leading Green Executives," *Sustainable Industries*, June, 15–22 (2008).

51. See Oregon Natural Step Network, "What Is the Natural Step," http:// www.ortns.org/framework.htm, accessed January 8, 2009. For a more complete explanation of the Natural Step framework and case studies of its application, see Brian Nattrass and Mary Altomare, *The Natural Step for Business: Wealth, Ecology, and the Evolutionary Corporation* (Gabriola Island, Canada: New Society, 1999).

52. Interview with Regina Hauser, Oregon Natural Step Network, Portland, Oregon, November 21, 2008.

53. See Center for Responsible Business, Haas School of Business, University of California at Berkeley, "Request for Projects: Spring 2009 MBA Strategic CSR Course" (2009).

54. See Michael V. Russo, "Collaborative Opportunities: The Oregon Experience," presentation to the Retail Industry Leaders Association's Environmental Sustainability and Compliance Conference, Dallas, Texas, September 22, 2008.

55. I served in an advisory role during the final development of the report.

56. AnnaLee Saxenian, *Regional Advantage: Culture and Competition in Silicon Valley and Route 128* (Cambridge, MA: Harvard University Press, 1994).

57. Interview with Craig Wessel, *Portland Business Journal*, January 5, 2009.

58. BALLE, "History" (2009), http://www.livingeconomies.org/aboutus/press, accessed January 12, 2009.

59. Personal communication, Pamela Skarda, executive director, Sustainable Business Network of Washington, Washington, D.C., January 14, 2009.

60. Interview with Anca Novacovici, Eco-Coach, Washington, D.C., October 24, 2008.

61. The organization still exists but references events mostly outside the city. Sustainable Dallas, http://www.sustainabledallas.org/, accessed January 12, 2009.

62. Interview with Thomas Kemper, September 22, 2008.

63. Interview with Tom Kelly, November 20, 2008.

64. Interview with Tom Kelly, November 20, 2008.

65. Social Impact Leadership Coalition, http://www.svn.org/index.cfm ?fuseaction=Page.viewPage&pageId=550, accessed March 20, 2009.

66. Interview with Deborah Nelson, Social Venture Network, San Francisco, California, February 13, 2009.

67. This story is told in the 2005 film Architecture to Zucchini: The People, Companies, and Organizations Pioneering Sustainability, produced and directed by David Decker and Douglas Freeman for Arnold Creek Productions, Lake Oswego, Oregon. The film won one of the Office of Sustainable Development BEST Awards in 2006, showing yet another linkage between members of the Portland community.

68. Interview with Kirsten Tobey, Revolution Foods, Alameda, California, November 10, 2008.

69. Blue Sky Bridal, "Green Wedding Resources" (2009), http://www.blue skybridal.com/resources.html, accessed January 13, 2009.

70. See Richard Florida, *Who's Your City: How the Creative Economy Is Making Where to Live the Most Important Decision of Your Life* (New York: Basic Books, 2008).

CHAPTER 9

1. Friends Provident, "About Us," http://www.friendsprovident.co.uk/about /;jsessionid=BVWHLSVQ1WF50CWCDYYCFGAKYIPDIIWA, accessed August 5, 2008.

2. See SRI Asia, "The Size of the Socially Responsible Investing Market," http:// www.sri-asia.com/background/sri-market-size.html, accessed July 18, 2009.

3. Although it still avoids some sectors altogether, a more positive approach is used by Portfolio 21, as of mid-2009 a quarter billion dollar mutual fund. Carsten Henningsen, one of its two cofounders, explains that rather than excluding laggards, Portfolio 21 uses a "positive screen" to identify and invest in companies that are social and environmental leaders. Thus the Portfolio 21 approach places more emphasis on excellence, by rewarding the "best in class." For information on its holdings, see Portfolio 21, "Holdings," http://www.portfolio21.com/in_depth_hold. php, accessed July 28, 2009. Interview with Carsten Henningsen, Portfolio 21, Portland, Oregon, October 8, 2008.

4. The term *groupthink* apparently was coined by *Fortune* writer William H. Whyte Jr. See William Safire, "The Way We Live Now, 8-8-04: On Language— Groupthink," *New York Times Magazine*, August 8, 2004, http://query.nytimes. com/gst/fullpage.html?res=9C01E2DD173CF93BA3575BC0A9629C8B63&sec= &spon=&pagewanted=print, accessed July 23, 2008.

5. See Irving L. Janis, *Victims of Groupthink* (Boston: Houghton Mifflin, 1972), 9.

6. An extreme and catastrophic example of groupthink is the prewar intelligence

that was used to justify the Iraq war. See United States Senate, Select Committee on Intelligence, *Report on the U.S. Intelligence Community's Prewar Intelligence Assessments on Iraq* (Washington, DC: United States Senate, July 7, 2004). The report identified a "group think dynamic" responsible for the lack of questioning of assumptions during the process. See William Branigan and Dana Priest, "Senate Report Blasts Intelligence Agencies' Flaws," *Washington Post*, July 9, 2004, http://www.washingtonpost.com/ac2/wp-dyn/A38459-2004Jul9?language=printer, accessed July 23, 2008.

7. I. L. Janis and L. Mann, *Decision Making: A Psychological Analysis of Conflict, Choice, and Commitment* (New York: Free Press, 1977). Other characteristics of groupthink are self-censorship (members withhold their dissenting views and counterarguments), illusion of invulnerability (members ignore obvious danger, take extreme risks, and are overly optimistic), illusion of unanimity (members perceive falsely that everyone agrees with the group's decision; silence is seen as consent), and mind guards (some members appoint themselves to the role of protecting the group from adverse information that might threaten group complacency).

8. The study eventually was published in a premier journal. See Siew-Hong Teoh, Ivo Welch, and Paul Wazzan, "The Effect of Socially Activist Investment Policies on the Financial Markets: Evidence from the South African Boycott," *Journal of Business* 72(1): 35–90 (1999).

9. Telephone interview with Lloyd Kurtz, Nelson Capital Management, Palo Alto, California, July 22, 2008.

10. See Invested Interests, "Moskowitz Prize Winners," http://www.investedinterests.com/content/tools-research/moskowitz-prize-winners/, accessed July 28, 2008.

11. For a full list of winners of the award, now associated with the Haas School of Business at the University of California, Berkeley, see Haas School of Business, Center for Responsible Business, "Moskowitz Prize Winners," http://www.haas.berkeley.edu/responsiblebusiness/MoskowitzPrizeWinners.html, accessed July 23, 2008.

12. C. Geczy, R. Stambaugh, and D. Levin, *Investing in Socially Responsible Mutual Funds*, Working Paper (Philadelphia: Wharton School, 2003).

13. Interview with Lloyd Kurtz, July 22, 2008.

14. See Anne Murphy, "The Seven (Almost) Deadly Sins of High-Minded Entrepreneurs," *Inc.*, July 1994, 47–51.

15. Murphy, "Seven (Almost) Deadly Sins," 51.

16. J. L. Dickerson and J. C. Collins, *Lost Arrow Corporation/Patagonia (A)*, Teaching Case (Stanford, CA: Stanford Business School Publishing, 1990).

17. R. I. Sutton, "The Weird Rules of Creativity," *Harvard Business Review* 79(8): 94–103 (2001); and R. I. Sutton, "Weird Ideas That Spark Innovation," *MIT Sloan Management Review* 43(2): 83–87 (2002).

18. Note that here the focus has been on issues with managerial implications, so I have avoided some of the larger philosophical issues. Just to name one, when

it comes to the environment, the best choice may well be to not buy anything—to do without, to stretch existing household and corporate implements and supplies. Is it better to reuse kitchen towels or purchase ecofriendly, disposable paper towels? What are the implications of nonconsumption for companies whose financial viability depends on sales? These philosophical debates, worthy as they are, form a topic for another book.

19. Richard Evans, *Deng Xiaoping and the Making of Modern China* (London: Hamish Hamilton, 1993).

20. See Hoover Institution, "Uncommon Knowledge with Peter Robinson: The Free Market Case for Green with T. J. Rodgers" (April 7, 2008), http://fora .tv/2008/04/07/Uncommon_Knowledge_T_J__Rodgers, accessed July 29, 2008.

21. T. J. Rodgers, Letter to Doris Gormley, OSF, May 23, 1996. Posted at http://www.enterstageright.com/archive/articles/0996rodgers.htm, accessed July 29, 2008.

22. Graef Crystal, "Nun-Bashing Cypress CEO T. J. Rodgers Ain't No Saint," *San Francisco Business Times*, September 2, 1996, http://www.bizjournals.com /sanfrancisco/stories/1996/09/02/newscolumn6.html, accessed July 28, 2008.

23. Another individual that has received significant attention—although for a different reason—is Jim Rogers, CEO of Duke Energy. That company obtains 70% of its power from coal, yet Rogers has been working to support federal legislation on climate change. Is Rogers a hypocrite or an essential advocate? See Clive Thompson, "A Green Coal Baron?" *New York Times Magazine*, June 22, 2008, 26–31; and A. G. Little, "Rogers and Me: An Interview with Duke Energy CEO Jim Rogers," *Grist*, http://www.grist.org/news/maindish/2007/04/04/rogers/, accessed August 5, 2008. Then of course, there is the colorful T. Boone Pickens, who announced plans in 2008 for a 4,000 megawatt wind farm in Texas. See CNN, "Billionaire Oilman Backs Wind Power," http://www.cnn.com/2008/US/05/19 /pickens.qa/index.html, accessed July 18, 2009. Financing and market challenges later caused him to delay the project.

24. See, for example, M. Albion, *True to Yourself: Leading a Values-Based Business* (San Francisco: Berrett-Koehler, 2006); J. Hollender and S. Fenichell, *What Matters Most: How a Small Group of Pioneers Is Teaching Social Responsibility to Big Business, and Why Big Business Is Listening* (New York: Basic Books, 2004); B. Cohen and M. Warwick, *Values-Driven Business: How to Change the World, Make Money, and Have Fun* (San Francisco: Berrett-Koehler, 2006); and T. Chappell, *The Soul of a Business: Managing for Profit and the Common Good* (New York: Bantam, 1993).

25. See Cohen and Warwick, *Values-Driven Business*, xvi; and Hollender and Fenichell, *What Matters Most*, xi.

26. See Portfolio 21, "Philosophy" (2008), http://www.portfolio21.com /fund_snapshot.php, accessed August 4, 2008.

27. See Portfolio 21, "Sun Power" (2008), http://www.portfolio21.com /profiles/sunpower.php, accessed August 4, 2008.

28. Telephone interview with Indigo Teiwes, Portfolio 21, Portland, Oregon, October 1, 2008.

29. Interview with Carsten Henningsen, Portfolio 21, Portland, Oregon, October 8, 2008.

30. As of mid-2009, the answers to this pop quiz were Aveda–Estée Lauder, Boca Foods–Kraft, Body Shop–L'Oréal, Burt's Bees–Clorox, Cascadian Farm–General Mills, Kashi–Kellogg, Odwalla–Coca-Cola, Seeds of Change–Mars, Stonyfield Farm–Groupe Danone, and Tom's of Maine–Colgate-Palmolive.

31. "Unilever Gets Ben & Jerry's for $326 Million," *Dairy Foods*, May 2000, 11.

32. There have been a number of accounts of this tumultuous episode, which would take considerably more space to fully document. A comprehensive account appears in Hollender and Fenichell, *What Matters Most*, ch. 8. See also David Goodman, "Culture Change: Does the Selling of Stonyfield Farm Yogurt Signal the End of Socially Responsible Businesses—or a New Beginning," *Mother Jones*, January–February 2003, 52–57, 78.

33. See Ben & Jerry's Inc., "Our History: Timeline" (2008), http://www.benjerry .com/our_company/about_us/our_history/timeline/, accessed August 8, 2008.

34. See J. Austin and J. Quinn, *Ben & Jerry's: Preserving Mission and Brand Within Unilever*, Case 9-306-037 (Boston: Harvard Business School, 2007).

35. See E. Mariani and V. J. Yu, *Ben & Jerry's and Unilever: The Bohemian and the Behemoth*, Case UV0597 (Charlottesville, VA: Darden School of Business Administration, 2003).

36. Ben & Jerry's Inc., *Social and Environmental Assessment, 2004: One Scoop at a Time* (South Burlington, VT: Ben & Jerry's, 2005). Available at http:// www.benjerry.com/our_company/about_us/social_mission/social_audits/2004 /index.cfm, accessed August 8, 2008.

37. For example, executives of publicly traded companies are bound to seek the highest price when selling, whereas executives (frequently also owners) of privately held firms can sell to whomever their circle of investors deems to be the best suitor. In the latter case, the owners need not make the price of the offer the overriding factor in their decision.

38. Mariani and Yu, *Ben & Jerry's and Unilever*, 6.

39. Suzanne Bidlake, "Body Shop Brand Reputation Is Battered by Sale to L'Oréal," *Brand Republic*, March 6, 2006, http://www.brandrepublic.com /News/549982/, accessed August 10, 2008.

40. The founders are Horst Rechelbacher, Greg Steltenpohl, and Philip and Gayle Tauber, respectively. Burt of Burt's Bees is Burt Shavitz.

41. Louise Story, "Can Burt's Bees Turn Clorox Green?" *New York Times*, January 6, 2008, http://www.nytimes.com/2008/01/06/business/06bees.html, accessed September 2, 2008.

42. The boycott is organized by an organization calling itself KillerCoke, in protest of Coke activities globally, particularly in Colombia. See "Murder: It's the

Real Thing—Student Activism, Killer Coke," http://www.killercoke.org/student.htm, accessed October 1, 2008.

43. Baby Milk Action, "Body Shop to Be Added to Nestlé Boycott List If L'Oréal Takeover Goes Ahead" (March 17, 2006), http://www.babymilkaction.org/press/press17march06.html, accessed September 2, 2008.

44. Baby Milk Action, "Body Shop."

45. See Philippe C. Haspeslagh and David B. Jemison, *Managing Acquisitions: Creating Value Through Corporate Renewal* (New York: Free Press, 1991).

46. Haspeslagh and Jemison, *Managing Acquisitions*, 149.

47. See J. Robert Carleton and Claude S. Lineberry, *Achieving Post-Merger Success: A Stakeholder's Guide to Cultural Due Diligence, Assessment, and Integration* (New York: Pfeiffer, 2004).

48. See Jon Birger, "Mergers Without Tears: Entrepreneurs Inside the Machine," *Fortune*, May 14, 2007, 22.

49. See Haspeslagh and Jemison, *Managing Acquisitions*, 161.

50. These figures were brought together at the General Mills page on the Wikinvest Web site. See "General Mills," http://www.wikinvest.com/stock/General_Mills_(GIS), accessed November 7, 2009.

51. See Haspeslagh and Jemison, *Managing Acquisitions*, 222 and ch. 13.

52. Dennis C. Carey, Dayton Ogden, and Judith A. Roland, *The Human Side of M&A: Leveraging the Most Important Factor in Deal Making* (Oxford, U.K.: Oxford University Press, 2004), x.

53. Problems can also occur when the parent needs cash and squeezes out spending at acquired firms that it may consider peripheral. For example, when the Eugene, Oregon, natural foods company Emerald Valley Kitchens was purchased by Monterey Gourmet Foods, it continued to post strong earnings. But the rest of Monterey's lines were pulling the parent company into the red. So some of Emerald Valley's programs were canceled. See Diane Dietz, "Economic Casualties Piling Up Locally," *Eugene Register-Guard*, December 4, 2008, A1.

54. On the costs and constraints of public companies, see Jeremy Kahn, "The Burden of Being Public," *Fortune*, May 26, 2003, 35–36.

55. See Hollender and Fenichell, *What Matters Most*, 236.

56. Hollender and Fenichell, *What Matters Most*, 235–237.

57. See Goodman, "Culture Change." See also D. Brady, "The Organic Myth," *Business Week*, October 16, 2006, 51–56.

58. See "Our Investments," http://www.goodcap.net/ourfund_ourinvestments.php, accessed December 12, 2008.

59. Interview with Wes Welke, Good Capital, San Francisco, California, November 11, 2008.

60. Third Sector, "Social Stock Exchange to Begin in 2009" (April 4, 2008), http://www.thirdsector.co.uk/News/DailyBulletin/800035/Social-stock-exchange-begin-2009/E802EC256D64A0A9280DCE2DC1DFEBC9/?DCMP=EMC-DailyBulletin, accessed December 12, 2008.

61. Despite the issues facing for-profit entrepreneurs, a nonprofit organization actually went through a traditional IPO in September 2008. Do Something, an organization that promotes teenage volunteerism, offered purchasers of its shares "a significant social return on investment" but "no provision for cash returns at any time." See "Non-Profit Capitalism," *The Economist*, September 13, 2008, 72.

62. B Corporation, "Understand Legal," http://www.bcorporation.net/become /legal, accessed March 20, 2009.

63. Marjorie Kelly, "Not Just for Profit," *strategy + business*, spring 2009, 1–10.

64. B Corporation home page, http://www.bcorporation.net/, accessed November 7, 2009.

65. B Corporation, "Why B Corps Matter," http://www.bcorporation.net/ why, accessed March 20, 2009.

66. See Richard A. Brealey, Stuart C. Myers, and Franklin Allen, *Principles of Corporate Finance*, 8th ed. (New York: McGraw Hill–Irwin, 2005).

67. See Google Inc., "Form S-1 Registration Statement Under the Securities Act of 1933" (April 24, 2004), http://www.sec.gov/Archives/edgar /data/1288776/000119312504073639/ds1.htm, accessed December 13, 2008.

68. See B. Elgin, "Democracy and Control in Google's IPO," *Business Week*, April 30, 2004, http://www.businessweek.com/technology/content/apr2004 /tc20040430_0301_tc024.htm, accessed December 13, 2008.

CHAPTER 10

1. Interview with John Hayden, Jamtown, Seattle, Washington, January 22, 2009.

2. "The World According to CSR," *The Economist*, January 20, 2005.

3. The classic academic reference in this area is Mark Granovetter, "Economic Action and Social Structure: The Problem of Embeddedness," *American Journal of Sociology* 91: 481–510 (1985).

4. Interview with Peter Walbridge, Big Think Studios, San Francisco, California, February 12, 2009.

5. Interview with Allen King, Excellent Packaging and Supply, Berkeley, California, February 12, 2009.

6. April Thompson, "Ten Tips for Socially Responsible Startups," Greenbiz .com (December 3, 2007), http://www.greenbiz.com/feature/2007/12/03/ten-tips -socially-responsible-startups, accessed February 16, 2009.

7. Interview with Alysa Rose, Rejuvenation Hardware, Portland, Oregon, January 5, 2009.

8. See *Architecture to Zucchini: The People, Companies, and Organizations Pioneering Sustainability*," film produced and directed by David Decker and Douglas Freeman for Arnold Creek Productions (2005).

9. Interview with Deborah Nelson, Social Venture Network, San Francisco, California, February 13, 2009.

10. Interview with Deborah Nelson, February 13, 2009.

11. See Van Jones, *The Green Collar Economy: How One Solution Can Fix Our Two Biggest Problems* (New York: Harper One, 2008), esp. ch. 3, where Jones sends out a powerful call for eco-equity.

12. Interview with Deborah Nelson, February 13, 2009.

13. Telephone interview with Bianca Alexander, Conscious Planet Media, Chicago, Illinois, July 15, 2009.

14. See, for example, James P. Hawley and Andrew T. Williams, *The Rise of Fiduciary Capitalism: How Institutional Investors Can Make Corporate America More Democratic* (Philadelphia: University of Pennsylvania Press, 2000).

INDEX

Italicized page numbers indicate tables and figures.